成人高等教育公共课系列教材

综合英语新教程

主　编　孙倚娜　徐　萍
副主编　周明亚　项　莉　沈婉芳
审　阅　Phillip Garrott　Katie Garrott

苏州大学出版社

图书在版编目(CIP)数据

综合英语新教程 / 孙倚娜,徐萍主编. —苏州:苏州大学出版社,2020.1(2025.1重印)
成人高等教育公共课系列教材
ISBN 978-7-5672-3091-0

Ⅰ. ①综… Ⅱ. ①孙… ②徐… Ⅲ. ①英语 – 成人高等教育 – 教材 Ⅳ. ①H319.39

中国版本图书馆 CIP 数据核字(2020)第 006919 号

书　　名	综合英语新教程
主　　编	孙倚娜　徐　萍
责任编辑	汤定军
策划编辑	汤定军
装帧设计	刘　俊
出版发行	苏州大学出版社
	（地址：苏州市十梓街 1 号　215006）
印　　刷	常州市武进第三印刷有限公司
开　　本	787 mm × 1 092 mm　1/16
字　　数	457 千
印　　张	18.75
版　　次	2020 年 1 月第 1 版
	2025 年 1 月第 6 次印刷
书　　号	ISBN 978-7-5672-3091-0
定　　价	55.00 元

苏州大学出版社网址　http://www.sudapress.com

前言
Preface

迈入21世纪的中国,经济和社会事业实现了跨越式发展,因此也迎来了继续教育的美好春天。全球化时代的中国继续教育必然包括英语教育,英语不仅是当前各国科技文件、贸易合同、互联网交流的主要语言工具,而且英语学习正在成为更多中国公民发展个人事业、提高生活质量的直接需求。有鉴于此,作为长期参与我国英语教育的资深高校英语教育者,我们依据《江苏省成人本科教育学士学位英语水平考试大纲》和《全国英语等级考试(第三级)考试大纲》,把脉最新英语学习需求,针对英语学习特点,编写了这部颇具时代特点的继续教育英语教材,其主要特色如下:

一、体现以学生为本的原则

本教材的设计力求为学生们提供传载时代信息和反映当代职场特点的语言素材,由课文至练习,从词汇、句子到语篇层面均呈现真实的英语使用范例,旨在利于学生们在英语学习过程中展现知识、运用知识、交流知识、拓展知识,利于学生们应用英语有效提升交际自信与交际能力,乃至提高职业技能和综合文化素养。

二、遵循二语习得的科学规律

依据当前国内外二语习得和外语教学前沿研究成果,编者尊重外语学习者语言学能、学习动机、认知风格、个性特征的个体差异,从课文话题到练习形式,最大程度地提供多元途径,帮助学生优化英语学习输入、内化、输出过程。教材课文中的对话、短文均配以标准的英语录音,学生们可以通过听、说、读、写等多途径获得感官刺激,以达到促进联想、加强记忆等学习效果。

三、集课堂教学和计算机自主学习为一体的新型模式

鉴于成人学生可支配英语学习时间的多样性,编者以话题为主轴,设计了独立的阅读、听力理解、口头交流、写作、翻译等形式的练习,不仅为成人英语学习者提供了以互联网等现代教育技术为媒介的、个性化的英语学习平台,而且提供了具有灵活性的、适宜于自主学习的学习条件;同时,以话题为主线,具有融合性质的练习又有利于教师在课堂上引导学生综合运用英语进行口头和书面讨论、合作学习,锻炼学生们的批判性思维能力。此外,教材的练习设计还满足了很多学生准备参加各类英语水平考试的需求,力争有效提高学生们的应试技能。

四、教材编写框架

本部教材共有 10 个单元,每单元由读、听、说、写四个部分组成,简介分别如下:

第一部分:阅读(Reading),由 Text A 和 Text B 两部分组成,这两部分的词汇总表附于书后。Text A 由正课文、词表、课文注释和练习四个部分组成。练习部分主要包括:

课文理解(Comprehension of the Text);

语感培养(Language Sense Enhancement),含课文背诵、格言集锦;

词汇练习(Vocabulary);

结构练习(Structure);

完形填空(Cloze);

翻译练习(Translation)。

第二部分:听力理解(Listening),包括简短对话、较长对话和短文理解,录音文字附于书后。

第三部分:口语(Speaking),主要是组织任务型、小组合作口语实践活动。

第四部分:写作(Writing),主要为学生提供贴近现实社会和生活的作文话题以及段落提纲。

编　者
2019 年 8 月

目录 Contents

Unit 1　Dream & Pursuit　/ 001

◎ Part Ⅰ　Reading　/ 001
　　　　　　Text A　You've Got to Find What You Love（Ⅰ）/ 001
　　　　　　Text B　You've Got to Find What You Love（Ⅱ）/ 011
◎ Part Ⅱ　Listening　/ 014
◎ Part Ⅲ　Speaking　/ 016
◎ Part Ⅳ　Writing　/ 017

Unit 2　Maintaining a Healthy Lifestyle　/ 018

◎ Part Ⅰ　Reading　/ 018
　　　　　　Text A　A Low Carbon Lifestyle　/ 018
　　　　　　Text B　Modern Lifestyle Threatens Body and Mind　/ 028
◎ Part Ⅱ　Listening　/ 032
◎ Part Ⅲ　Speaking　/ 034
◎ Part Ⅳ　Writing　/ 035

Unit 3　Leisure & Entertainment　/ 036

◎ Part Ⅰ　Reading　/ 036
　　　　　　Text A　The Sunday Visit　/ 036
　　　　　　Text B　*Precious* Impresses Me　/ 047
◎ Part Ⅱ　Listening　/ 050
◎ Part Ⅲ　Speaking　/ 051
◎ Part Ⅳ　Writing　/ 052

Unit 4 Love / 053

- Part Ⅰ Reading / 053
  - Text A   How Real Is Your Love? / 053
  - Text B   Cyberstepmother / 063
- Part Ⅱ Listening / 066
- Part Ⅲ Speaking / 068
- Part Ⅳ Writing / 069

Unit 5 Fashion / 070

- Part Ⅰ Reading / 070
  - Text A   Lo and Behold / 070
  - Text B   The Life Cycle of a Fashion Trend / 080
- Part Ⅱ Listening / 083
- Part Ⅲ Speaking / 085
- Part Ⅳ Writing / 086

Unit 6 Shopping / 087

- Part Ⅰ Reading / 087
  - Text A   In Praise of Shopping / 087
  - Text B   Shopping Can Be Fun—Honest! / 097
- Part Ⅱ Listening / 101
- Part Ⅲ Speaking / 102
- Part Ⅳ Writing / 103

Unit 7 Job & Occupation / 104

- Part Ⅰ Reading / 104
  - Text A   Nursing / 104
  - Text B   My First Job / 114
- Part Ⅱ Listening / 118
- Part Ⅲ Speaking / 119
- Part Ⅳ Writing / 120

Unit 8   Science & Technology / 121

- Part Ⅰ   Reading / 121
  - Text A   Only Disconnect / 121
  - Text B   How to Live Without a Cell Phone / 131
- Part Ⅱ   Listening / 135
- Part Ⅲ   Speaking / 136
- Part Ⅳ   Writing / 137

Unit 9   Health / 138

- Part Ⅰ   Reading / 138
  - Text A   The Healing Power of Music / 138
  - Text B   100 Candles on Her Next Cake / 149
- Part Ⅱ   Listening / 153
- Part Ⅲ   Speaking / 154
- Part Ⅳ   Writing / 155

Unit 10   Transportation / 156

- Part Ⅰ   Reading / 156
  - Text A   Well, America: Is the Car Culture Working? / 156
  - Text B   Bike Sharing / 166
- Part Ⅱ   Listening / 170
- Part Ⅲ   Speaking / 172
- Part Ⅳ   Writing / 172

单元练习题 / 173

全国英语等级考试第三级历年真题（一） / 219

全国英语等级考试第三级历年真题（二） / 233

Appendix Ⅰ   Transcripts for Listening / 247

Appendix Ⅱ   Glossary / 267

UNIT 1

Dream & Pursuit

Part I Reading

Text A You've Got to Find What You Love (I)[1]

Steve Jobs

1 I am honored to be with you today at your commencement from one of the finest universities in the world. I never graduated from college. Truth be told, this is the closest I've ever gotten to a college graduation. Today I want to tell you three stories from my life. That's it. No big deal. Just three stories.

2 The first story is about connecting the dots[2].

3 I dropped out of Reed College after the first 6 months, but then stayed around as a drop-in for another 18 months or so before I really quit. So why did I drop out?

4 It started before I was born. My biological mother was a young, unwed college graduate student, and she decided to put me up for adoption. She felt very strongly that I should be adopted by college graduates. So everything was all set for me to be adopted at birth by a lawyer and his wife except that when I popped out they decided at the last minute that they really wanted a girl. So my parents, who were on a waiting list, got a call in the middle of the night asking: "We have an unexpected baby boy; do you want him?" They said, "Of course." My biological mother later found out that my mother had never graduated from college and that my father had never graduated from high school. She refused to sign the final adoption papers. She only relented a few months later when my parents promised that I would someday go to college.

5 And 17 years later I did go to college. But I naively chose a college that was almost as

expensive as Stanford[3], and all of my working-class parents' savings were being spent on my college tuition. After 6 months, I couldn't see the value in it. I had no idea what I wanted to do with my life and no idea how college was going to help me figure it out. And here I was spending all of the money my parents had saved their entire life. So I decided to drop out and trust that it would all work out OK. It was pretty scary at the time, but looking back it was one of the best decisions I ever made. The minute I dropped out I could stop taking the required classes that didn't interest me, and begin dropping in on the ones that looked interesting.

6   It wasn't all romantic. I didn't have a dorm room, so I slept on the floor in friends' rooms, I returned coke bottles for the 5¢ deposits to buy food with, and I would walk the 7 miles across town every Sunday night to get one good meal a week at the Hare Krishna temple. I loved it. And much of what I stumbled into by following my curiosity and intuition turned out to be priceless later on. Let me give you one example:

7   Reed College at that time offered perhaps the best calligraphy instruction in the country. Throughout the campus, every poster, every label on every drawer, was beautifully hand-calligraphed. Because I had dropped out and didn't have to take the normal classes, I decided to take a calligraphy class to learn how to do this. I learned about serif and sans serif typefaces[4], about varying the amount of space between different letter combinations, about what makes great typography great. It was beautiful, historical, artistically subtle in a way that science can't capture, and I found it fascinating.

8   None of this had even a hope of any practical application in my life. But 10 years later, when we were designing the first Macintosh computer[5], it all came back to me. And we designed it all into the Mac. It was the first computer with beautiful typography. If I had never dropped in on that single course in college, the Mac would have never had multiple typefaces or proportionally spaced fonts. And since Windows just copied the Mac, it's likely that no personal computer would have them. If I had never dropped out, I would have never dropped in on this calligraphy class, and personal computers might not have the wonderful typography that they do. Of course it was impossible to connect the dots looking forward when I was in college. But it was very, very clear looking backwards 10 years later.

9   Again, you can't connect the dots looking forward; you can only connect them looking backwards. So you have to trust that the dots will somehow connect in your future. You have to trust in something—your gut, destiny, life, karma, whatever. This approach has never let me down, and it has made all the difference in my life.

(792 words)

(To be continued)

New Words

honor /ˈɒnə/ vt. 〈美〉=honour 给……以荣誉；使增光
commencement /kəˈmensmənt/ n. 〈美〉学位授予典礼(日)；毕业典礼(日)
deal /diːl/ n. 〈口〉交易
connect /kəˈnekt/ vt. 连接；连结
dot /dɒt/ n. 点；微小的东西
drop-in /ˈdrɒpɪn/ n. 〈美俚〉旁听生
quit /kwɪt/ (quit 或 quitted; quitting) vi. 离开；放弃
biological /ˌbaɪəˈlɒdʒɪkəl/ a. 生物的；与生命过程有关的
unwed /ˌʌnˈwed/ a. 没有结婚的，未婚的
adoption /əˈdɒpʃn/ n. 收养
adopt /əˈdɒpt/ vt. 收养
birth /bɜːθ/ n. 出生
pop /pɒp/ (popped; popping) vi. 冷不防地出现(或发生)
sign /saɪn/ vt. 签(名)
relent /rɪˈlent/ vi. 变温和；变宽容
naively /naɪˈiːvli/ ad. 天真地；幼稚地
tuition /tjuˈɪʃn/ n. 学费
value /ˈvæljuː/ n. 价值
scary /ˈskeəri/ a. 惊恐的
romantic /rəʊˈmæntɪk/ a. 浪漫的
dorm /dɔːm/ n. 〈美口〉宿舍(dormitory 的缩略)
deposit /dɪˈpɒzɪt/ n. 存款，押金
temple /ˈtempl/ n. 神庙
stumble /ˈstʌmbl/ vi. 绊(摔倒)；走入歧途
curiosity /ˌkjʊəriˈɒsəti/ n. 好奇心
intuition /ˌɪntjuˈɪʃn/ n. 直觉
priceless /ˈpraɪsləs/ a. 无价的；无法估价的
offer /ˈɒfə/ vt. 提供，给予
calligraphy /kəˈlɪɡrəfi/ n. 书法；美术字(体)
instruction /ɪnˈstrʌkʃn/ n. 教育；教学
serif /ˈserɪf/ n.〈印〉衬线(如字母 H 的上下四根短而细的横线)
sans serif /sænˈserɪf/ n. =sanserif 〈印〉无衬线字体
campus /ˈkæmpəs/ n. (大学)校园

* 黑体表示重点词汇和短语，白体表示一般词汇和短语

calligraph /ˈkælɪɡrɑːf/ vt. 用美术体书写
poster /ˈpəʊstə/ n. 招贴(画);海报;布告
label /ˈleɪbl/ n. 标签,标记
typeface /ˈtaɪpfeɪs/ n. 字体
vary /ˈveəri/ vt. 使……变化;使……有不同
typography /taɪˈpɒɡrəfi/ n. (书籍等的)排印;印刷版面式样
subtle /ˈsʌtl/ a. 细微的
capture /ˈkæptʃə/ vt. 捕获;引起(注意)
fascinating /ˈfæsɪneɪtɪŋ/ a. 迷人的;有极大吸引力的
application /ˌæplɪˈkeɪʃn/ n. 应用,实施
design /dɪˈzaɪn/ vt. 设计;构思
proportionally /prəˈpɔːʃənəli/ ad. 成比例地
font /fɒnt/ =fount n. 〈印〉(同样大小和式样的)一副铅字
gut /ɡʌt/ n. [~s]〈口〉勇气,胆量
destiny /ˈdestɪni/ n. 命运
karma /ˈkɑːmə/ n. 命运;因果报应
approach /əˈprəʊtʃ/ n. 途径;方式,方法

Phrases and Expressions

drop out   退出;退学
or so   ……左右;……上下
put up   提出(问题、建议等)
all set   〈口〉作好(充分)准备的
waiting list   等候者名单
find out   找出,发现;查明(真相)
figure out   想出,推断出
work out   产生结果;成功
look back   回顾,回忆
the minute (that)   一……就
turn out   结果是,(最后)证明是
later on   以后,后来
of course   当然
let down   使失望
make a difference / make all the difference   状况有(极大)改善;起作用

Unit 1　Dream & Pursuit

Proper Names

Steve Jobs /stiːv dʒɒbz/　史蒂夫·乔布斯
Reed College /riːd ˈkɒlɪdʒ/　里德大学
Stanford /ˈstænfəd/　斯坦福
Hare Krishna /ˈhɑːre ˈkrɪʃnə/　〈宗〉（印度教）克里希纳派教徒
Macintosh computer /ˈmækɪntɒʃ kəmˈpjuːtə/　麦金塔电脑

Notes on the Text

1. This text is adapted (改编) from the speech given by Steve Jobs, the founder of Apple (苹果公司创始人), at Stanford University in 2005 for the graduation commencement (毕业典礼). In the speech Steve tells three personal stories in which he advocates following your heart and doing what you love. Text A is the first story in his speech and Text B is the second.

2. **connect the dots**：理解不同经历间的关系

3. **Stanford**：A private research university located in Stanford, California, United States with a strong emphasis on scientific, technological and social science research.

4. **I learned about serif and sans serif typefaces**：serif 是指在字的笔画开始及结束的地方有额外的装饰，而且笔画的粗细会因直横的不同而有不同。相反，Sans Serif 则没有这些额外的装饰，笔画粗细大致差不多。如下图：

5. **Macintosh computer**：(or Mac) A series of several lines of personal computers designed, developed, and marketed by Apple Inc (苹果公司). The first Macintosh was introduced on January 24, 1984.

Comprehension of the Text

Answer the following questions.

1. Did the author finish his study at college?
2. When did the author drop out of Reed College?
3. Why did the author decide to drop out?

4. Did the author regret dropping out of college? Why or why not?
5. What did the author do later?
6. What do you think of the author's decision?
7. How did the author manage to support himself at Reed College as a drop-in student?
8. What did the author learn in the calligraphy class?
9. How did the author feel about the calligraphy class?
10. Did what the author learned at Reed College prove to be useful?
11. What did he do with what he had learned at the calligraphy class when designing the first Macintosh computer?
12. How do you understand "you have to trust that the dots will somehow connect in your future"?

Language Sense Enhancement

I. **Read the following paragraph until you learn it by heart. Then try to complete the following passage from memory.**

None of this had even a hope of any practical (1)_____ in my life. But 10 years later, when we were (2)_____ the first Macintosh computer, it all came (3)_____ to me. And we designed it all into the Mac. It was the first computer with (4)_____ typography. If I had never (5)_____ in on that single course in college, the Mac would have never had multiple typefaces or proportionally spaced fonts. And since Windows just (6)_____ the Mac, it's likely that no (7)_____ computer would have them. If I had never dropped out, I would have never dropped in on this calligraphy class, and personal computers might not have the (8)_____ typography that they do. Of course it was impossible to (9)_____ the dots looking forward when I was in college. But it was very, very (10)_____ looking backwards 10 years later.

II. **Read the following quotations. Learn them by heart if you can.**

Every man is the master of his own fortune.   —Richard Steel
每个人都主宰着自己的命运。   ——理查德·斯蒂尔

All that you do, do with your might; things done by halves are never done right.
        —Richard Henry Stoddard
做一切事都应尽力而为,半途而废永远不行。   ——理查德·亨利·斯托达德

Although the world is full of suffering, it is full also of the overcoming of it.
        —Hellen Keller
虽然世界多苦难,但是苦难总是能战胜的。   ——海伦·凯勒

Unit 1 Dream & Pursuit

Vocabulary

I. Fill in the blanks with the given words or phrases in the box. Change the form where necessary.

adoption	honor	birth	connect	quit
drop out	figure out	turn out	vary	capture
design	tuition	fascinating	curiosity	offer

1. They were delighted when she gave _____ to a healthy child.
2. I will always feel _____ that I had the opportunity to meet with you.
3. If you can not have children of your own, why not consider _____?
4. She attended Smith College for one year and then _____.
5. The two towns are _____ by a railway.
6. That department _____ courses in a dozen minority languages.
7. Courses _____ according to the needs of the students.
8. I can't _____ what he was hinting at.
9. The story of his adventures was _____ to listen to.
10. Would you _____ your job if you inherited (继承) lots of money?
11. The crowd looked at them with great _____.
12. The beggar _____ to be a thief.
13. We _____ butterflies with a net.
14. This school does not charge its students _____.
15. This room was _____ as a children's playroom.

II. Choose a word or a phrase from the indicated paragraph to fill in each of the following blanks. Change the form where necessary.

1. Well, fancy seeing you here! This is an _____ pleasure! (*Para. 4*)
2. He _____ his name at the end of the letter. (*Para. 4*)
3. Big houses are very _____ to maintain. (*Para. 5*)
4. He had already sold everything of _____ that he possessed. (*Para. 5*)
5. She got up and walked out of the room, and her husband _____. (*Para. 6*)
6. A _____ collection of vases was destroyed. (*Para. 6*)
7. Until she won the prize she'd led a _____ life. (*Para. 7*)
8. She set her hair the _____ her husband liked it. (*Para. 7*)
9. When I was sent to prison, I really felt I had _____ my parents _____. (*Para. 9*)
10. Exercise can _____ to your state of health. (*Para. 9*)

Structure

I. Rewrite the following sentences after the model.

Model: And since Windows just copied the Mac, no personal computer would be likely to have them.

And since Windows just copied the Mac, it's likely that no personal computer would have them.

1. I'll most likely get there at about ten o'clock.
   _____

2. We will likely be in America this time next year.
   _____

3. I am hardly likely to finish it within a week.
   _____

4. As the young man was very short of money, he was likely to apply for the dangerous job advertised in the paper.
   _____

5. As Tom is one of the best basketball players on the school team, he is most likely to be singled out for special training.
   _____

II. Complete the following sentences by translating the Chinese into English, using "would + have + p.p.".

Model: If I had never dropped in on that single course in college, _____ (Mac 就不会有这么多丰富的字体以及赏心悦目的字体间距).

If I had never dropped in on that single course in college, the Mac would have never had multiple typefaces or proportionally spaced fonts.

1. If you had told me about your problem, _____ (我会帮你的).

2. If we had not understood what he was saying, _____ (我们会叫他再解释一遍).

3. If it hadn't been for your help, I really don't know _____ (会搞成什么样子).

4. _____ (她就不会走错路), if she had studied the road map more carefully.

5. If he had not quitted school, _____ (去年6月就毕业了).

Unit 1 Dream & Pursuit

Cloze

Choose one appropriate word from the following box to fill in each of the following blanks. Each word can be used only once. Change the word form where necessary.

explanation	carefully	study	make	mistake
go	examine	about	change	from
who	paper	eager	how	that

A certain student passed all his examinations. Then he went to college to continue his (1)_____. There he put down his name for a course in geography, but after the first lecture, he did not (2)_____ to it any more.

The geography lecturer noticed (3)_____ this student was always absent and thought that he had (4)_____ to another course, so he was surprised when he saw the boy's name on the list of students (5)_____ wanted to take the geography test at the end of this year.

The lecturer had prepared a difficult examination paper, which followed his lectures very closely, and he was (6)_____ to see (7)_____ this student would answer the questions. He expected that the boy's answers would be very bad, but when they reached him soon after the exam and he examined them (8)_____, he was able to find only one small (9)_____ in them. As this surprised him very much, he (10)_____ the paper again and again but was still not able to find more than that one small mistake, so he sent for the student to question him (11)_____ his work.

When the student came into the room and sat down, the lecturer said to him, "I know that you came to my first lecture and you have been absent (12)_____ all the others. But now I have examined your (13)_____ very carefully and I have been able to find only one small mistake in it. I am anxious to know your (14)_____ for that."

"Oh, I am very worried about that mistake", answered the student. "After the examination, I realized what I ought to have done. I would not have (15)_____ that mistake if I had not been confused by your first lecture."

Translation

Translate the following sentences into Chinese.

1. It was pretty scary at the time, but looking back it was one of the best decisions I ever made.

2. And much of what I stumbled into by following my curiosity and intuition turned out to be priceless later on.

3. I learned about serif and sans serif typefaces, about varying the amount of space between different letter combinations, about what makes great typography great.

4. If I had never dropped out, I would have never dropped in on this calligraphy class, and personal computers might not have the wonderful typography that they do.

5. Again, you can't connect the dots looking forward; you can only connect them looking backwards. So you have to trust that the dots will somehow connect in your future.

Text B You've Got to Find What You Love (II)

Steve Jobs

1 My second story is about love and loss.

2 I was lucky—I found what I loved to do early in life. Woz and I started Apple in my parents' garage when I was 20. We worked hard, and in 10 years Apple had grown from just the two of us in a garage into a $ 2 billion company with over 4,000 employees. We had just released our finest creation—the Macintosh—a year earlier, and I had just turned 30. And then I got fired. How can you get fired from a company you started? Well, as Apple grew we hired someone who I thought was very talented to run the company with me, and for the first year or so things went well. But then our visions of the future began to diverge and eventually we had a falling out. When we did, our Board of Directors sided with him. So at 30 I was out. And very publicly out. What had been the focus of my entire adult life was gone, and it was devastating.

3 I really didn't know what to do for a few months. I felt that I had let the previous generation of entrepreneurs down—that I had dropped the baton as it was being passed to me. I met with David Packard and Bob Noyce and tried to apologize for screwing up so badly. I was a very public failure, and I even thought about running away from the valley. But something slowly began to dawn on me—I still loved what I did. The turn of events at Apple had not changed that one bit. I had been rejected, but I was still in love. And so I decided to start over.

4 I didn't see it then, but it turned out that getting fired from Apple was the best thing that could have ever happened to me. The heaviness of being successful was replaced by the lightness of being a beginner again, less sure about everything. It freed me to enter one of the most creative periods of my life.

5 During the next 5 years, I started a company named NeXT, another company named Pixar, and fell in love with an amazing woman who would become my wife. Pixar went on to create the world's first computer animated feature film, *Toy Story*, and is now the most successful animation studio in the world. In a remarkable turn of events, Apple bought NeXT, I returned to Apple, and the technology we developed at NeXT is at the heart of Apple's current renaissance. And Laurene and I have a wonderful family together.

6　I'm pretty sure none of this would have happened if I hadn't been fired from Apple. It was awful tasting medicine, but I guess the patient needed it. Sometimes life hits you in the head with a brick. Don't lose faith. I'm convinced that the only thing that kept me going was that I loved what I did. You've got to find what you love. And that is as true for your work as it is for your lovers. Your work is going to fill a large part of your life, and the only way to be truly satisfied is to do what you believe is great work. And the only way to do great work is to love what you do. If you haven't found it yet, keep looking. Don't settle. As with all matters of the heart, you'll know when you find it. And, like any great relationship, it just gets better and better as the years roll on. So keep looking until you find it. Don't settle.

(613 words)

Words and Phrases to Learn

employee /ˌɪmˈplɔɪiː/ *n.* 雇员，职员，员工
release /rɪˈliːs/ *vt.* 释放；放开
fire /ˈfaɪə/ *vt.* 开除，辞退
hire /ˈhaɪə/ *vt.* 雇用；租用
talented /ˈtæləntɪd/ *a.* 有天才的，有才干的
run /rʌn/ *vt.* 经营，管理
focus /ˈfəʊkəs/ *n.* 焦点；(注意、活动、兴趣等的)中心
previous /ˈpriːviəs/ *a.* 以前的
dawn /dɔːn/ *vi.* 破晓；开始；被理解
reject /rɪˈdʒekt/ *vt.* 拒绝；驳回
replace /rɪˈpleɪs/ *vt.* 替换，取代
fall in love with 爱上
remarkable /rɪˈmɑːkəbl/ *a.* 不同寻常的，值得注意的
current /ˈkʌrənt/ *a.* 现在的；目前的
convince /kənˈvɪns/ *vt.* 使确信，使信服

Comprehension Check

Choose the best answer for each of the following.

1. When the author had a different vision about the future of Apple, the Board of Directors _____.
   A. supported him   B. opposed him
   C. kept silent   D. argued with him

2. It can be inferred that _____.
   A. many people knew that the author was fired
   B. few people knew that the author was fired
   C. only David Packard and Bob Noyce knew that the author was fired
   D. only the Board of Directors knew that the author was fired
3. What made the author continue his career?
   A. His girlfriend.
   B. The Apple's development.
   C. His love of his work.
   D. The previous generation of entrepreneurs.
4. The author now thinks that being rejected by Apple was _____.
   A. unfair   B. the best thing
   C. the worst thing   D. more than he could bear
5. The author returned to Apple because _____.
   A. Apple invited him
   B. Apple bought NeXT
   C. Pixar is the most successful animation studio.
   D. *Toy Story* is the first computer animated feature film.
6. The expression "Sometimes life hits you in the head with a brick" means _____.
   A. we should not lose faith
   B. we've got to find what we love
   C. keeping looking what we love
   D. we may come across difficulties in our life

Language Practice

Fill in the blanks with words or phrases listed in the *Words and Phrases to Learn*.

1. He has _____ a restaurant since he left school.
2. I was about to pay for the shopping when it suddenly _____ on me that I had left my cheque book at home.
3. I applied for a job as a mechanic in a local garage, but I was _____.
4. We read the daily newspaper to keep up with the _____ situation.
5. That large factory has more than 1,000 _____ who make cars.
6. The zoo keepers _____ the lions from their cage.
7. It's useless trying to _____ her that she doesn't need to lose any weight.
8. Training is provided, so no _____ experience is required for the job.
9. She was _____ after she was discovered stealing from her employer.

10. She _____ a friend of her brother's.
11. Our continuing success means that we will need to _____ a hundred more staff over the coming year.
12. It is quite _____ that no one was hurt in the accident.
13. He is a _____ musician.
14. I think Dave likes to be the _____ of attention.
15. The factory _____ most of its workers with robots.

Part II Listening

Section A

Directions: In this section you will hear five short conversations. At the end of each conversation a question will be asked about what was said. Both the conversation and the question will be spoken only once. Listen carefully and choose the best answer.

1. A. At a garage.
   B. At a department store.
   C. At a car rental company.
   D. At a travel agency.
2. A. The busy streets.
   B. The crowded stores.
   C. The climate.
   D. The museums.
3. A. 750 dollars.
   B. 700 dollars.
   C. 50 dollars.
   D. 1,450 dollars.
4. A. She hasn't gone camping for several weeks.
   B. She likes to take long camping trips.
   C. She prefers not to go camping on weekends.
   D. She often spends a lot of time planning her camping trips.
5. A. He has not heard of Prof. Johnson.
   B. He has not heard of Prof. Johnson's brother.
   C. He is a good friend of Prof. Johnson's.
   D. He doesn't know Prof. Johnson's brother.

Unit 1 Dream & Pursuit

Section B

Directions: In this section you will hear a long conversation. At the end of the conversation you will hear some questions. Both the conversation and the questions will be spoken only once. After you hear a question, you must choose the best answer.

6. A. Because she can't afford an apartment off campus.
   B. Because she doesn't have to pay for her accommodation.
   C. Because all her friends are living on campus.
   D. Because it's cheaper living in a dorm on campus.
7. A. She can close the door and study in the dorm.
   B. She can make more friends living in a dorm.
   C. She can study and hang out with her roommates.
   D. She can meet interesting people on campus.
8. A. He used to live in a dorm on campus.
   B. He loves living in a dorm on campus.
   C. He likes his roommates very much.
   D. He is quite close to his roommates.

Section C

Directions: In this section you will hear a passage. At the end of the passage, you will hear some questions. The passage and the questions will be spoken only once. After you hear a question, you must choose the best answer.

9. A. It's difficult to get scholarships in Britain.
   B. The British education system is complex.
   C. It takes less time to complete degree courses in Britain than in other countries.
   D. It is very complicated to enter an undergraduate degree course in Britain.
10. A. You must be over 18 and have attended foundation courses.
    B. You must have either 3 A-levels or an IELTS score of over 5.5.
    C. You must have 3 A-levels and an IELTS score of at least 5.5.
    D. You must have 3 A-levels and have completed foundation courses.
11. A. To enable the students to be more competitive in the future.
    B. To enable the students to complete their studies within 3 years.
    C. To help international students complete their studies.
    D. To help the students to be more creative and independent.

12. A. The teachers in the university.

B. The British embassy in your country.

C. An international students organization.

D. An organization called UCAS.

Part III Speaking

Section A

Directions: Discuss the following questions in small groups.

1. What can we learn from Steve Jobs?
2. How do you like the idea of life-long education?
3. Why is it important to have a college education?

Section B

Directions: Read aloud the following passage.

The Student Walked 32 Kilometers to His New Job

A college student in Alabama, USA walked 32 kilometers in the dark to get to his new job. The story begins with Walter Carr's car breaking down the night before starting a new job at Bellhops, a furniture moving company. Carr was unable to find a ride. So, he figured out how long it would take to walk from his house to the job in Pelham—32 kilometers away. He left at midnight so that he could make it to the customer's house by 8:00 am the next morning.

Pelham police saw him walking along a highway at 4:00 am. So, they stopped to see if he needed help. After hearing his story, they took him to a restaurant for breakfast and then to a church where he could safely wait until 8:00 am. The police then took Carr to the home of customer Jenny Lamey. Lamey said that even though Carr had just walked the entire night, he refused her offer to rest. He just wanted to start working.

Jenny Lamey later wrote this on Facebook: "I just can't tell you how touched I was by Walter and his journey. He is humble, kind and cheerful, and he has big dreams! He is hardworking and tough." She then started a GoFundMe page to help Walter with money to get his car fixed. Walter Carr's story touched many others around the United States. Within a few days, people gave over $73,000 to her GoFundMe page. Carr has decided to give a part of the donations to the Birmingham Education Foundation. And he has received more offers for jobs and scholarships for schools.

Part IV Writing

Directions: Write a composition on the topic "Changing Criteria for Judging Good Students". You should write at least 100 words, and base your composition on the outline given below:

1. Years ago, to be a good student simply meant to be good at academic work.
2. But now the criteria are changing.
3. In my opinion ...

UNIT 2
Maintaining a Healthy Lifestyle

Part I   Reading

Text A   A Low Carbon Lifestyle[1]

Mukti Mitchell

1   At the moment humans are making carbon dioxide faster than plants can turn it back into oxygen. Carbon dioxide goes into the atmosphere and forms a blanket over the earth, warming it up. This causes climate change, which is threatening human life with rising sea levels, storms and floods.

2   Low carbon lifestyles create less carbon dioxide emissions. Activities that create carbon dioxide are driving cars, heating homes, generating electricity, flying planes, making goods in factories and transporting things a long way. So in a low carbon lifestyle, you live closer to work, insulate your home, holiday by train, buy national products and eat local food. It's a better life too!

3   By making lifestyle choices we can reduce our CO_2 emissions, and the new lifestyle improves our quality of life. Fresh food and daily exercise are good for your health, mood and concentration. Quality products last for years so you don't have to keep buying them again. Public transport and lift sharing relieve the stress of driving[2] and allow you to talk, read and relax. And buying local and national products creates more jobs and better wages.

4   By following these guidelines you can cut your carbon emissions without knowing what your overall levels are. However every lifestyle is different, and if you calculate your carbon emissions it is much easier to see which areas of your lifestyle have high emissions, and which are easiest

to reduce. You also get the satisfaction of seeing your reductions when you recalculate your emissions after a year. This helps you enjoy the carbon you do use without feeling guilty, because you know you are on the track. If you don't calculate your emissions there is a danger of feeling bad about every activity that emits carbon, and worrying about insignificant little actions. Feeling bad does not improve your quality of life, so is not part of this approach. This approach says ENJOY YOUR CARBON EMISSIONS, but work to a target.

5 Here are some guidelines to help cut carbon emissions and feel good at the same time:

Save here, spend there

6 You can treat your carbon quota a bit like money: If you save some here, you can spend it elsewhere. Sometimes save, occasionally splash out. If you live in a small house, work close to home, travel by bus, eat local food, buy long lasting products and go on holiday by train, you will save a lot of carbon dioxide. Occasionally feel free to drive 50 miles to an event you really enjoy. That's 20kg of CO_2 a few times a year, in a quota of several thousand kg.

Special occasions

7 At Christmas you might buy some mangoes from India. A lot of food miles, but it is a special occasion. The planet doesn't mind where you spend your carbon, if you are meeting your target.

Dull emissions, fun emissions

8 Cut out the high-carbon activities that are dull, and keep the ones that are fun. For example, driving to work every morning is dull as mud[3]. On the bus, you can read a cracking novel. If you love driving, go to a race track once a year and really drive for a day. The emissions from this would be around 200kg when a daily half-hour return trip reaches around 5,000kg over the working year.

Make the most of your carbon emissions

9 When you do use carbon, make the most of it. If you really want to go to Africa, save up your carbon quota for a few years, read some books about the place, make a deal with your boss, and go for a few months. That way you get real satisfaction out of it, and you won't need to fly back and forth twice a year. Is two weeks in a Western Hotel in Thailand any better than two weeks in Spain, which can be reached by train?

There's a place for everything

10 Even high-carbon activities have their place. Our politicians and diplomats will always have to fly. It's better to fly a rock-band across the Atlantic than fly thousands of fans to the US. Our rescue services need to burn carbon to get there in time. The only way to get into space is by rocket. And that's all OK because the planet can absorb a lot of carbon dioxide. Just not enough to waste.

11 A low carbon lifestyle is easy and fun, good for the planet, and improves your quality of life. The planet is warming up, and the majority of the world's scientists say that humans are causing it by burning fossil fuels. We are doing this partly out of ignorance, and partly because we think changing might make us unhappy. The low carbon lifestyle may help to solve both problems at once.

(792 words)

New Words

carbon /ˈkɑːbən/ n. 碳
dioxide /daɪˈɒksaɪd/ n. 二氧化物
oxygen /ˈɒksɪdʒən/ n. 氧;氧气
atmosphere /ˈætməsfɪə/ n. 大气;大气层(包围地球的气体)
blanket /ˈblæŋkɪt/ n. 毯子;覆盖物
climate /ˈklaɪmɪt/ n. 气候
threaten /ˈθretn/ vt. 恐吓,威胁
emission /iˈmɪʃn/ n. (光、热、气等的)散发;散发之物
generate /ˈdʒenəreɪt/ vt. 发生;产生
transport /trænsˈpɔːt/ vt. 运送,运输
insulate /ˈɪnsjuleɪt/ vt. 使……隔离或绝缘(尤指对热量、电流或声音)
CO_2 /ˈkɑːbən daɪˈɒksaɪd/ n. 二氧化碳
mood /muːd/ n. 心境;情绪
concentration /ˌkɒnsnˈtreɪʃn/ n. 集中;专心
last /lɑːst/ vi. 持久;持续
relieve /rɪˈliːv/ vt. 使减轻;使解除(痛苦、忧愁等)
stress /stres/ n. 压力,重压
relax /rɪˈlæks/ vi. 放松;休息
follow /ˈfɒləʊ/ vt. 按照……去做;听从;采用

* 黑体表示重点词汇和短语,白体表示一般词汇和短语

guideline /ˈgaɪdlaɪn/ n. 指导方针；准则
cut /kʌt/ vt. 削减
overall /ˌəʊvəˈrɔːl/ a. 包括一切的；全部的
calculate /ˈkælkjuleɪt/ vt. 计算；估计
guilty /ˈɡɪlti/ a. 自觉有罪的，内疚的
emit /iˈmɪt/ vt. 散发，发出
insignificant /ˌɪnsɪɡˈnɪfɪkənt/ a. 不重要的；无价值的
target /ˈtɑːɡɪt/ n. 目标
quota /ˈkwəʊtə/ n. 定额；限额；配额
Christmas /ˈkrɪsməs/ n. 圣诞节
save /seɪv/ vi. 储蓄；积攒；节省
occasionally /əˈkeɪʒnəli/ ad. 偶然地
mango /ˈmæŋɡəʊ/ n. 芒果
India /ˈɪndiə/ n. 印度（亚洲国家）
occasion /əˈkeɪʒn/ n. 时候，场合
dull /dʌl/ a. 枯燥无味的；单调的
mud /mʌd/ n. 泥；烂泥
cracking /ˈkrækɪŋ/ a. 〈口〉精彩的；棒的
novel /ˈnɒvl/ n. 小说
Africa /ˈæfrɪkə/ n. 非洲
Thailand /ˈtaɪlænd/ n. 泰国（亚洲国家）
Spain /speɪn/ n. 西班牙（欧洲国家）
politician /ˌpɒləˈtɪʃn/ n. 积极从事政治活动的人；政客
diplomat /ˈdɪpləmæt/ n. 外交官；外交家
Atlantic /ətˈlæntɪk/ n. 大西洋
rock-band /ˈrɒkbænd/ n. 摇滚乐队
fan /fæn/ n. 迷；（……的）热情崇拜者或拥护者
rescue /ˈreskjuː/ n. 援救；解救
majority /məˈdʒɒrəti/ n. 大多数；大半；大多
fossil /ˈfɒsl/ n. 化石
fuel /ˈfjuːəl/ n. 燃料
ignorance /ˈɪɡnərəns/ n. 无知，愚昧

Phrases and Expressions

at the moment　此刻,现在,目前
on the track　在正道上;未离目标;正确
splash out　随意花钱
go on holiday　去度假
cut out　〈口〉停止,放弃
race track　(赛马、赛车等的)跑道
make the most of　从……处获取尽可能多的好处
save up　储存;储蓄
make a deal with　与……达成一笔交易
back and forth　来回,往返

Proper Names

Mukti Mitchell /ˈmʊkti ˈmɪtʃl/　穆克悌·米歇尔

Notes on the Text

1. The text is adapted and abridged from *The Guide to Low Carbon Lifestyles* by Mukti Mitchell published in 2007.

2. **Public transport and lift sharing relieve the stress of driving** 公共交通以及搭便车能缓解开车的压力

3. **dull as mud**: 枯燥乏味的

Comprehension of the Text

Answer the following questions.

1. What is the harm that carbon dioxide does to the climate?
2. What are the activities that create carbon dioxide?
3. What is a low carbon lifestyle?
4. How does the new lifestyle improve our quality of life?
5. Why do we need to calculate our carbon emissions, according to the author?
6. What is the essence of the new approach, according to the author?
7. What are the guidelines given by the author to help cut carbon emissions and feel good at the same time?
8. Why does the author compare the treatment of your carbon quota to money?
9. What does the author think of buying things from distant places on special

occasions?

10. What are the author's suggestions as far as high-carbon activities are concerned?
11. What is the cause of the warming-up of the planet, according to most of the world's scientists?
12. What can help to solve the problems? Why?

Language Sense Enhancement

I. **Read the following paragraphs until you learn them by heart. Then try to complete the passage from memory.**

At the moment humans are (1) _____ carbon dioxide faster than plants can turn it back into oxygen. Carbon dioxide goes into the (2) _____ and forms a blanket over the earth, (3) _____ it up. This causes climate (4) _____, which is (5) _____ human life with rising sea levels, storms and floods.

Low carbon lifestyles create less carbon dioxide (6) _____. Activities that create carbon dioxide are driving cars, heating homes, generating electricity, flying planes, making goods in factories and transporting things a long way. So in a low carbon lifestyle you live (7) _____ to work, insulate your home, holiday by train, buy (8) _____ products and eat (9) _____ food. It's a (10) _____ life too!

II. **Read the following quotations. Learn them by heart if you can.**

Early to bed and early to rise makes a man healthy, wealthy and wise.
—Benjamin Franklin
早睡早起身体好。　　　　　　　　　　　　　　——本杰明·富兰克林
If you have a garden and a library, you have everything you need.
—Marcus Tullius Cicero
如果你有一个花园和一个图书馆,你就拥有一切。　　——马库斯·图留斯·西塞罗
Getting enough sleep can be just as important as working out.　—Ali Vincent
充足的睡眠和锻炼一样重要。　　　　　　　　　　　——阿里·文森特

Vocabulary

I. **Fill in the blanks with the given words or phrases in the box. Change the form where necessary.**

emit	relieve	calculate	majority	guilty
occasion	relax	mood	follow	threaten
at the moment	generate	save up	transport	make a deal with

1. The attacker _____ them with a gun.
2. Sulphur(硫磺,含硫的) gases were _____ by the volcano.
3. The proposal has _____ a lot of interest.
4. Such heavy items are expensive to _____ by plane.
5. I'm not really in the _____ for drinking.
6. Anxiety may be _____ by talking to a friend.
7. He lay back and let his mind _____.
8. Why didn't you _____ his advice?
9. I can't find the address _____ but I'll get it for you later.
10. The _____ of the employees have university degrees.
11. The cost of the damage caused by the recent flood has been _____ at over $2 million.
12. I'll _____ you—you wash the car and I'll let you use the computer tonight.
13. She felt _____ about not visiting her parents more often.
14. We've been _____ to go to the United States.
15. I have a suit but I only wear it on special _____.

II. Choose a word or a phrase from the indicated paragraph to fill in each of the following blanks. Change the form where necessary.

1. When they retire, they're going to move to a warmer _____. (Para. 1)
2. The government plans to _____ more jobs for young people. (Para. 2)
3. We aim to help students make more informed career _____. (Para. 3)
4. She had the _____ of seeing her book become a best-seller. (Para. 4)
5. That's not the answer but you're _____. (Para. 4)
6. My parents still _____ me like a child. (Para. 6)
7. Set yourself _____ that you can reasonably hope to achieve. (Para. 7)
8. Life in a small town could be dreadfully _____. (Para. 8)
9. It's my first trip abroad so I'm going to _____ it. (Para. 9)
10. It's awful, the way these patients were kept in _____ of what was actually wrong with them. (Para. 11)

Structure

I. Rewrite the following sentences after the model.

Model: If we make lifestyle choices we can reduce our CO_2 emissions, and the new lifestyle improves our quality of life.
By making lifestyle choices we can reduce our CO_2 emissions, and the new lifestyle improves our quality of life.

Unit 2 Maintaining a Healthy Lifestyle

1. You can unlock the door if you turn the key to the left.
   _____

2. She served as a waitress to earn a little money.
   _____

3. Phone this number and you can get hold of me.
   _____

4. If you listen to the radio every day, you can improve your English.
   _____

5. She worked hard and gained rapid promotion.
   _____

II. Complete the following sentences by translating the Chinese into English, using "partly out of/because ... partly because ...".

Model: We are doing this _____ (部分是出于无知,部分是由于我们以为改变会让我们不快乐).
We are doing this partly out of ignorance, and partly because we think changing might make us unhappy.

1. Some people are unwilling to attend the classes _____
   _____ (部分是由于没有时间,部分是由于所涉及的费用).

2. I couldn't go to sleep, _____
   (部分是由于感冒,部分是由于对第二天有所期待).

3. The newspaper would not print the story _____
   (部分是因为此事难以处理,部分是因为此事可能会引起情报部门的注意).

4. My father was severe with me, _____
   (部分是性格使然,部分是因为我是家中长子).

5. _____
   (部分因睡过头,部分因为塞车), I was late for school this morning.

Cloze

Choose one appropriate word from the following box to fill in each of the following blanks. Each word can be used only once. Change the word form where necessary.

already	by	strive	reduction	which
low-carbon	practical	to	terms	energy
feasible	tremendous	forward	establish	low

Shanghai established a low carbon economic model site in Lingang New City and

Chongming Island, promoting the integrated utilization of a low-carbon economy (1)_____ constructing a low-carbon society, business district and industrial parks. Changzhou in Jiangsu Province (2)_____ a low-carbon demonstration area, and is striving to (3)_____ low carbon-based industries featuring energy conservation and emissions (4)_____, low pollution as well as (5)_____ consumption.

They have (6)_____ set up LED lighting, wind and solar energy and an electric vehicle industry. At the same time, Nanchang, Wuxi, Hangzhou, Shenyang, Sanya, Qingdao, Chongqing and Chengdu have all put (7)_____ suggestions and objectives for the development of a (8)_____ city, and they have also made a firm position and a (9)_____ plan according to their own (10)_____ situations.

The changes green innovation has brought (11)_____ the environment are obvious. He Jiankun, director of the Low Carbon Energy Laboratory attached to Tsinghua University and vice director of the Expert Panel on Climate Change, said (12)_____ efficiency has improved and made (13)_____ achievements in (14)_____ of energy consumption reduction. Unit product energy consumption for energy-intensive products has dropped by 1 to 2 percent every year, (15)_____ is very rare in the world.

Translation

Translate the following sentences into Chinese.

1. Carbon dioxide goes into the atmosphere and forms a blanket over the earth, warming it up.

2. So in a low carbon lifestyle you live closer to work, insulate your home, holiday by train, buy national products and eat local food. It's a better life too!

3. However every lifestyle is different, and if you calculate your carbon emissions, it is much easier to see which areas of your lifestyle have high emissions, and which are easiest to reduce.

4. Here are some guidelines to help cut carbon emissions and feel good at the same time.

   _____
   _____
   _____

5. A low carbon lifestyle is easy and fun, good for the planet, and improves your quality of life.

   _____
   _____
   _____

Text B Modern Lifestyle Threatens Body and Mind

Cory Quirino

1 As our lives become so busy that even the word "hectic" seems inadequate a description, demands on a person's body, mind and spirit become greater. Modern lifestyles pose a threat to our peace of mind and put a heavy pressure on the body. The result—a body that is weaker and easier to be hurt by illnesses and a mind stressed by the business of living.

Whole, not hole

2 Do statements such as "I feel like I have a hole in my heart" or "I do not feel whole" sound familiar? The language of our times reflects the language of living. Clearly, there is a need for wholeness, the way an incomplete circle needs connection.

3 The word "holistic" came from the Greek word *holos*, which means whole. It includes the area of the physical and the non-physical. Therefore, instead of talking only about the symptom, let us look into the cause of the symptom.

Positive program

4 Taking positive steps to protect your health means: Have regular medical/health checkups. Do try to have a checkup every year. Do not wait for symptoms to appear before doing so. Do not ignore that lump in your body or that pain in your chest/back/head, etc.

5 Skin conditions reflect your overall health. Sudden appearance of raised moles should be cause for concern. Blood sugar levels and blood pressure should be controlled. The ideal weight according to weight charts can be confusing. Go by what you feel is right for you. If you are overweight and breathless when climbing stairs, you may have a heart problem.

6 Eat wisely and healthily. Your food choices directly affect your health. Stop smoking. Or, if you are a non-smoker, avoid people who smoke and stop going to smoke-filled places. Having alcoholic drinks may be a social habit, but too much drinking (more than two glasses for men, more than one for women daily) could lead to weight gain, raised blood sugar levels, wrinkles,

eye bags. If you must drink, have a full meal first.

7 Start a moderate exercise plan, one suited to your personality—walk, run, bike, swim, play badminton, dance.

Raising the spirit

8 Just as surely as there is sunrise, there is sunset. If we were to look at stress as something that comes and then goes, we can build into our system the following:
—That all worrying, upsetting situations/people/experiences can and will be resolved finally.
—That all things, whether persons or experiences, have a reason for existing/appearing in our lives.
—That it is up to you and me, to us, to deal with the feeling brought about by the experience in order to have greater insight.
—That using the insight may lead to an "Aha!" moment.

Going light

9 Physically, the body can be heavy through overeating/overdrinking. So eat less, drink less, especially alcoholic drinks or juices with sugar or sweeteners.

10 Fast. Follow a coconut water/clean water plan. With seven glasses coconut water or seven glasses clean water for one day, you can clean your body. Or take a break from any kind of cooked/processed/snack food. Replace it with fresh fruits and vegetables. Drink two tablespoons of virgin coconut oil first thing in the morning before you start the fasting. End your fast with a bowl of hot, light (non-creamy) vegetable soup.

Aha! moment

11 All through life, Aha! moments have been many. If you cannot recall them, then maybe you were not aware they happened.

12 An Aha! experience is often known as the presence of the spirit, when it is one with your mind and heart leading you to say "I am one with my true self." It is the "kind of moment when somebody simply turns on the light and your inner bulb lights up."

13 Aha! moments are precious. You can experience them if you are open-heart and spirit.

14 Here is how, as taken from Dr. Gary Zukav in *The Seat Of The Soul*:

15 Practice the art of silence. Be still, close your eyes. Admit that trust brings on the light. Keep still for 10 minutes and be aware of how energies in the form of light travel within your body. Your soul is energy, therefore it is part of the light whose source is God.

16 Love and light!

(719 words)

Words and Phrases to Learn

pose a threat to　对……构成威胁
stress /stres/ *vt.*　加压力于
reflect /rɪˈflekt/ *vt.*　反映
physical /ˈfɪzɪkl/ *a.*　身体的
symptom /ˈsɪmptəm/ *n.*　症状，征候
positive /ˈpɒzətɪv/ *a.*　积极的；正面的，肯定的
ignore /ɪgˈnɔː/ *vt.*　忽视；不理睬
concern /kənˈsɜːn/ *n.*　关心；忧虑
overweight /ˈəʊvəˈweɪt/ *a.*　超重的
moderate /ˈmɒdərət/ *a.*　适度的；中等的
resolve /rɪˈzɒlv/ *vt.*　解决
insight /ˈɪnsaɪt/ *n.*　洞察力；见识
replace with　用……替代；用……取代
recall /rɪˈkɔːl/ *vt.*　回想起；回忆起
light up　点燃；照亮

Comprehension Check

Choose the best answer for each of the following.

1. What does the author mean by "Modern lifestyles pose a threat to our peace of mind and put a heavy pressure on the body"?
   A. Our modern lives are so busy that they put greater demands on our mind and body.
   B. Our modern lifestyles are so dangerous that they might destroy us.
   C. Our modern lifestyles make holes in our hearts and minds.
   D. All of us will lose our peace of mind and become ill because of modern

Unit 2 Maintaining a Healthy Lifestyle

lifestyles.
2. Positive steps to protect our health include _____.
   A. having a physical checkup every year
   B. paying attention to skin conditions
   C. controlling blood sugar levels and blood pressure
   D. all of the above
3. Why are food choices important according to the author?
   A. Because food is something we should enjoy in our lives.
   B. Because they are directly related to our health.
   C. Because they are social habits.
   D. Because they help bring back our peace of mind.
4. Why does the author mention sunrise and sunset in Paragraph 8?
   A. Because they are what we experience every day.
   B. Because stress coming and going in our lives is just like sunrise and sunset.
   C. Because they directly affect our health.
   D. Because they pose a threat to our mind and body.
5. All of the following are elements of fasting according to the author except _____.
   A. drinking seven glasses coconut water or seven glasses clean water for one day
   B. staying away from any kind of cooked/processed/snack food
   C. ending your fast with a full meal
   D. having fresh fruits and vegetables
6. What is an Aha! moment according to the author?
   A. It's a moment you gain new energy and are filled with wisdom.
   B. It's a moment the light is turned on.
   C. It's a moment the sun rises or sets.
   D. It's a moment you are in high spirits.

Language Practice

Fill in the blanks with words or phrases listed in the *Words and Phrases to Learn*.

1. There is growing _____ about violence on television.
2. Doctors must be able to read _____ correctly.
3. Fireworks _____ the sky with their explosions of red and gold.
4. We can _____ the matter to your satisfaction.
5. The author has a keen _____ into human nature.
6. Nuclear weapons _____ everyone.
7. There was a very _____ response to our new design.

8. She _____ with horror the night that her husband was involved in the road accident.

9. He _____ the speed limit and drove very fast.

10. The doctor discovered that I'm a little _____.

11. _____ exercise is good to health.

12. The broken window has been _____ a new one.

13. The painter tried to _____ the natural life of the Tibetan people in his paintings.

14. The best way of promoting health is to do _____ exercise for half an hour every morning.

15. Don't _____ over it—we'll soon work it out.

Part II Listening

Section A

Directions: In this section you will hear five short conversations. At the end of each conversation a question will be asked about what was said. Both the conversation and the question will be spoken only once. Listen carefully and choose the best answer.

1. A. He likes to watch tragedies.
   B. He likes to watch comedies.
   C. He likes to watch thrillers.
   D. He likes to watch feature films.

2. A. He was too busy to call the woman.
   B. He called the woman but she didn't answer.
   C. He called the woman but was not successful.
   D. He forgot to call the woman last night.

3. A. Husband and wife.
   B. Doctor and patient.
   C. Boss and secretary.
   D. Repairman and customer.

4. A. He didn't work as hard as he should.
   B. He didn't pass the physics exam.
   C. He did better in an earlier exam.
   D. He found something wrong with the exam.

5. A. Henry doesn't like the color.
   B. There was no ladder in the house.
   C. Someone else painted the house.
   D. Henry painted the house himself.

Section B

Directions: In this section you will hear a long conversation. At the end of the conversation you will hear some questions. Both the conversation and the questions will be spoken only once. After you hear a question, you must choose the best answer.

6. A. On January 3rd.
   B. On December 3rd.
   C. On January 24th.
   D. On December 24th.
7. A. He prefers to sit by the window.
   B. He prefers to sit by the aisle.
   C. He prefers to sit in the middle.
   D. He prefers to sit at the back.
8. A. He will get his money back.
   B. He will get a ticket for next time.
   C. He will get a fine.
   D. He will get nothing.

Section C

Directions: In this section you will hear a passage. At the end of the passage, you will hear some questions. The passage and the questions will be spoken only once. After you hear a question, you must choose the best answer.

9. A. Because most people there don't care too much about how they dress for work.
   B. Because most people there pay great attention to how they dress for work.
   C. Because people dressed casually can easily find a job in Hungary.
   D. Because Hungary is an exception among other European countries.
10. A. Brazil.
    B. China.
    C. Russia.
    D. Australia.

11. A. In Sweden people who dress smartly are more likely to get promoted.
    B. In France people who dress smartly are more likely to get promoted.
    C. In Sweden people who dress casually are more likely to get promoted.
    D. Most people believe that whether people are dressed smartly makes no difference in their promotion.
12. A. If you're a T-shirts and jeans kind of a person, then you should go to European countries for a job.
    B. If you're a T-shirts and jeans kind of a person, then you'd better go to Asian countries for a job.
    C. If you're a T-shirts and jeans kind of a person, then you are more likely to be promoted in France.
    D. If you're a T-shirts and jeans kind of a person, then you are less likely to be promoted in Sweden.

Part III Speaking

Section A

Directions: Discuss the following questions in small groups.

1. What do you think are the activities that cause environmental degradation?
2. What does a low-carbon lifestyle contribute to the protection of the environment?
3. How do you practice the new lifestyle?

Section B

Directions: Read aloud the following passage.

Better Walking Workouts

Of all the ways to get and stay fit, walking is the easiest, safest and cheapest. It can also be a lot of fun, with attainable goals. Here are some suggestions to help you get the most out of your walking workouts.

1. Do it daily. Try to walk briskly for at least half an hour every day, or for one hour four times a week. 2. Count your steps. Get a simple pedometer or other fitness tracking device to see how many steps you take a day. 3. Add it up and speed it up. 4. Swing your arms. 5. Change your routine. Try something different. For example, speed up for a minute or two out of every five minutes. 6. Climb hills. When walking uphill, lean forward slightly—it's easier on your legs. Walking downhill can be harder on your body, especially the knees. So, slow your pace, keep your knees slightly bent and take shorter

steps. 7. Try walking poles. To enhance your upper-body workout, use lightweight, rubber-tipped trekking poles. 8. Use hand weights, with care. 9. Try backward walking. Try to go with a partner who can keep you from bumping into something and help pace you. 10. Choose shoes wisely.

Part IV Writing

Directions: Write a composition on the topic "My View on Low-Carbon Life". You should write at least 100 words, and base your composition on the outline given below:

1. 目前社会低碳生活现状；
2. 不倡导低碳生活的危害；
3. 如何实施低碳生活。

UNIT 3

Leisure & Entertainment

Part I Reading

> Text A   The Sunday Visit

Robert Klose

1 Last Sunday I made a visit to some new neighbors down the block. No specific purpose in mind, just an opportunity to sit at the kitchen table, have some tea, and chat. As I did so, it occurred to me how rare the Sunday visit has become.

2 When I was a kid in the New Jersey of the 1960s, Sunday visits were routine. Most stores were closed, almost nobody worked, and the highways, as a result, were not the desperate steeplechases they have become today. My family normally traveled eight city blocks to the home of my grandmother—the same house my father was raised in—where the adults would sit on the front porch in lawn chairs while we children played football or hide-and-seek. Every so often I'd take a breather on the stoop, where I'd pick up fragments of adult talk and bits of wisdom.

3 Everything under the sun was fodder for conversation. The weather, taxes, the state of the world, food prices, the wild nature of the current children. But there was also the mysterious things, like the time my great-uncle Stanley, remarking upon the legacy of John F. Kennedy[1], noted that President McKinley's[2] funeral had also been sad. McKinley! That one sent me scurrying to the *Encyclopedia Britannica*[3].

4 There were other destinations for our Sunday visits. My great-aunt Hattie, who lived in an apartment above a fruit store and had a dancing parrot; our relatives just over the border in Pennsylvania, a clan that included 12 cousins; my great-grandparents who lived in a house near

the Jersey City waterfront and spoke only Polish; and last, the most desired destination of Sunday visits—my uncle Gene, the only member of our extended family who had managed to accumulate significant material wealth. He had a palatial home on a New Jersey lake—a contrast to our small brick house on our densely packed Jersey City streets. Sunday visits to Uncle Gene meant unlimited swimming, fishing, and toad-hunting-heaven for a city kid.

5   The Sunday visit was something to aspire to. It was the visit to church, our reward for an hour of piety, an opportunity to take advantage of the fact that Dad was not at work. We were not in school, and there were no chores or errands that couldn't wait until Monday. Sunday was, indeed different from all the other days of the week, because everyone seemed to be on the same schedule. That means that there was one day when everyone seemed to have time for everybody else.

6   Sunday as a day of rest is, or was, so deeply rooted in the culture that it's shocking to consider that, in a short period of time, it has almost entirely lost this association. In my childhood, it was assumed that everyone would either be home or visiting someone else's home on Sunday. But now the question is, "What do you plan to DO this Sunday?" The answer can range from going to the mall to participating in a road race to jetting to Montreal for lunch. If one were to respond, "I'm making a Sunday visit to family," such an answer would feel out of date, an echo from another era.

7   I supposed I should be grateful to live in Maine, a state of small towns, abundant land, and tight relationships. Even though folks work as hard here as they do anywhere else, the state's powerfully rural feature still harbors at least remnants of the ethic of yesterday's America. People there had to depend on one another in the face of a changing economy and a challenging environment.

8   How important is the Sunday visit here in Maine? Let me illustrate by way of example. A while back a few of us adults with our children traveled to the small-town home of an elderly woman—the mother of one of the parents in our group—who had lived in that house her whole life. We had tea and cupcakes while the kids were playing in the front yard. Our hostess seemed genuinely thrilled to have us. So thrilled, in fact, that it made a headline in the morning newspaper, "Mrs. Black had Bangor guests for a Sunday visit. They had tea and cupcakes, and chatted."

9   I clipped that little statement, but have since lost it. But I know how to get another one. I just have to wait until Sunday to make my move.

(749 words)

New Words

block /blɒk/ n. 街区；一排房屋
specific /spəˈsɪfɪk/ a. 具体的；明确的
opportunity /ˌɒpəˈtjuːnəti/ n. 机会
routine /ruːˈtiːn/ n. 例行公事；日常工作
desperate /ˈdespərit/ a. 拼命的，不顾一切的
steeplechase /ˈstiːpltʃeɪs/ n. 障碍赛跑（的场地）
porch /pɔːtʃ/ n. 门廊；入口处
hide-and-seek /ˈhaɪdənˈsiːk/ n. 捉迷藏
breather /ˈbriːðə/ n. 喘息时间，短暂的休息
stoop /stuːp/ n. 俯身，弯腰
fragment /ˈfrægmənt/ n. 片断；碎片
wisdom /ˈwɪzdəm/ n. 智慧，才智
fodder /ˈfɒdə/ n. 素材
current /ˈkʌrənt/ a. 现时的，当前的
mysterious /mɪˈstɪəriəs/ a. 神秘的
legacy /ˈlegəsi/ n. 遗产
note /nəʊt/ vt. 特别提到，指出
funeral /ˈfjuːnərəl/ n. 葬礼
scurry /ˈskʌri/ vi. 急赶
destination /ˌdestɪˈneɪʃn/ n. 目的地，终点
apartment /əˈpɑːtmənt/ n. 公寓房
parrot /ˈpærət/ n. 鹦鹉
clan /klæn/ n. 〈口〉家族
waterfront /ˈwɔːtəˌfrʌnt/ n. 滨水区
Polish /ˈpəʊlɪʃ/ n. 波兰语
desire /dɪˈzaɪə/ vt. 想望，渴望
accumulate /əˈkjuːmjəleɪt/ vt. 堆积；积累
significant /sɪɡˈnɪfɪkənt/ a. 相当数量的；重要的
wealth /welθ/ n. 财富
palatial /pəˈleɪʃl/ a. 富丽堂皇的
contrast /ˈkɒntræst/ n. 对比，对照；悬殊差别
densely /ˈdensli/ ad. 密集地，稠密地
toad /təʊd/ n. 蟾蜍，癞蛤蟆
piety /ˈpaɪəti/ n. 虔诚的行为

* 黑体表示重点词汇和短语，白体表示一般词汇和短语

chore /tʃɔː/ n. 家庭杂务
errand /ˈerənd/ n. 差事
schedule /ˈʃedjuːl/ n. 日程安排(表);议事日程
shocking /ˈʃɒkɪŋ/ a. 令人震惊的
association /əˌsəʊʃɪˈeɪʃn/ n. 联想
assume /əˈsjuːm/ vt. 假定,设想
range /reɪndʒ/ vi. (在一定范围内)变动,变化
mall /mɔːl/ n. 大型购物中心
jet /dʒet/ (jetted; jetting) vi. 搭乘喷气式飞机
respond /rɪˈspɒnd/ vt. 回答,答复
echo /ˈekəʊ/ n. 回声;反响
era /ˈɪərə/ n. 时代,纪元
abundant /əˈbʌndənt/ a. 大量的,充足的,丰富的
folk /fəʊk/ n. 人,人们
rural /ˈrʊərəl/ a. 农村的,乡村的
feature /ˈfiːtʃə/ n. 特征,特点
harbor /ˈhɑːbə/ vt. 包含;怀有
remnant /ˈremnənt/ n. 残余物
ethic /ˈeθɪk/ n. 道德观;道德准则
challenging /ˈtʃælɪndʒɪŋ/ a. 挑战性的
environment /ɪnˈvaɪərənmənt/ n. 环境,四周
illustrate /ˈɪləstreɪt/ vi. 举例说明
cupcake /ˈkʌpˌkeɪk/ n. 杯形蛋糕
hostess /ˈhəʊstɪs/ n. 女主人
genuinely /ˈdʒenjuɪnli/ ad. 真诚地
thrilled /θrɪld/ a. 兴奋的
headline /ˈhedlaɪn/ n. (报刊的)大字标题;[pl.]新闻提要
clip /klɪp/ (clipped; clipping) vt. 从报刊上剪取

Phrases and Expressions

occur to   被想到
as a result   作为(……的)结果
lawn chair   〈美〉草坪躺椅
every so often   〈口〉有时,不时
pick up   (偶然地、无意地)获得(知识、消息等)
remark upon   评说,谈论
extended family   (数代同堂等的)大家庭
aspire to   渴望,追求
take advantage of   对……加以利用
be deeply rooted in   深深地根植于
range from ... to   (在一定范围内)变动,变化
participate in   参与,参加
out of date   过时的
in the face of   面对,在……面前
make one's move   有所动作,采取行动

Proper Names

New Jersey /njuː ˈdʒɜːzi/   (美国)新泽西州
Stanley /ˈstænli/   斯坦利(男子名)
John F. Kennedy /dʒɒn ef ˈkenɪdi/   约翰·F·肯尼迪
McKinley /məˈkɪnli/   麦金利
Encyclopedia Britannica /enˌsaɪkləʊˈpiːdiə brɪˈtænɪkə/   《不列颠百科全书》,《大英百科全书》
Hattie /ˈhæti/   哈蒂(女子名)
Pennsylvania /pensɪlˈveɪniə/   (美国)宾夕法尼亚州
Jersey City /ˈdʒɜːzi ˈsɪti/   泽西城(美国新泽西州城市名)
Gene /dʒiːn/   吉恩(男子名)
Montreal /ˌmɒntrɪˈɔːl/   蒙特利尔(加拿大城市)
Maine /meɪn/   (美国)缅因州
Black /blæk/   布莱克
Bangor /ˈbæŋɡə/   班戈(英国的一座城市)

Notes on the Text

1. **John F. Kennedy**: (1917 – 1963) The 35th President of the United States, serving from 1961 until his assassination(暗杀) in 1963.

2. **William McKinley**: (1843 – 1901) The 25th President of the United States. He was assassinated in 1901 and succeeded by his Vice President Theodore Roosevelt.

3. **Encyclopedia Britannica**: A general English-language encyclopedia published by Encyclopedia Britannica, Inc., a privately held company. Articles are aimed at educated adults, and written by about 100 full-time editors and more than 4,000 expert contributors. It is regarded as the most scholarly of encyclopedias.《不列颠百科全书》，又称《大英百科全书》，是一部历史悠久、享誉世界的权威性综合百科全书，所有条目均由世界各国著名学者、各领域专家撰写，对主要学科、重要人物和事件都有详尽的介绍和叙述。

Comprehension of the Text

Answer the following questions.

1. For what purpose did the author visit those new neighbors last Sunday?
2. What did the author's family do on Sundays when he was a kid?
3. What did people usually talk about during their visits?
4. What were the places the author visited?
5. Why was Uncle Gene's house a heaven for a city kid?
6. In what way was Sunday different from all the other days of the week?
7. Nowadays, what's the usual answer to the question "What do you plan to do this Sunday?"
8. Why does the author feel grateful to live in Maine?
9. How's life like in Maine?
10. How important is the Sunday visit in Maine?
11. Is the author worried about losing the clip from the newspaper?
12. What does the author mean by saying "I just have to wait until Sunday to make my move"?

Language Sense Enhancement

I. Read the following paragraphs until you learn them by heart. Then try to complete the passage from memory.

The Sunday visit was something to (1) _____. It was the visit to church, our (2) _____ for an hour of piety, an opportunity to (3) _____ the fact that Dad was not (4) _____, we were not in school, and there were no chores or errands that couldn't wait (5) _____ Monday. Sunday was, indeed (6) _____ all the other days of the week, because everyone seemed to be on the same (7) _____. That means that there was one day (8) _____ everyone seemed to have time for everybody else.

Sunday as a day of rest is, or was, so deeply (9) _____ in the culture that it's shocking to consider that, in a short period of time, it has almost entirely lost this association. In my childhood, it was (10) _____ that everyone would either be home or visiting someone else's home on Sunday.

II. Read the following quotations. Learn them by heart if you can.

Travel can be one of the most rewarding forms of introspection. —Lawrence Durrell
旅行可以是最有价值的内省形式之一。 ——劳伦斯·杜瑞尔
Movies are like an expensive form of therapy for me. —Tim Burton
电影对我来说就像是一种昂贵的治疗方式。 ——蒂姆·波顿
A picture is a poem without words. —Horace
一幅画是一首没有文字的诗。 ——贺拉斯

Vocabulary

I. Fill in the blanks with the given words or phrases in the box. Change the form where necessary.

desire	specific	opportunity	feature	accumulate
significant	challenging	environment	illustrate	current
wealth	contrast	schedule	association	abundant

1. A small closet contained his clothes and the books he had _____.
2. They suggested measures to overcome _____ difficulties.
3. There are _____ supplies of firewood in the forest.
4. This difficulty _____ my mind to find an answer.
5. They are passing new laws to prevent the pollution of the _____.
6. The book gives _____ instructions on how to make a desk.
7. In _____ to his brother, he was always considerate in his treatment of others.

8. I've been offered the _____ to work in America for a year, but I'm not sure whether to take it or not.
9. The main _____ of Southern California are the climate and the scenery.
10. Owing to difficulty in obtaining materials, we are almost three weeks behind _____.
11. His _____ is estimated at fifty million dollars.
12. The teacher _____ his lesson with pictures.
13. French bread has had positive _____ for me ever since I went on holiday to France.
14. We always _____ to live in peace with our neighbors.
15. Penicillin was an extremely _____ medical discovery.

II. Choose a word or a phrase from the indicated paragraph to fill in each of the following blanks. Change the form where necessary.

1. Going to the bank was part of the _____ of his work. (*Para. 2*)
2. They have _____ a lot of information about this area. (*Para. 2*)
3. "Your wife is charming, Doctor Manson," she quietly _____ as they sat down. (*Para. 3*)
4. At least 80 persons were injured, _____ five policemen. (*Para. 4*)
5. Life has _____ possibilities. (*Para. 4*)
6. He _____ the boy for bringing back the lost dog. (*Para. 5*)
7. These customs are _____ in tradition. (*Para. 6*)
8. Such things as family pride are _____ nowadays. (*Para. 6*)
9. The _____ of space travel has begun. (*Para. 6*)
10. I'm very _____ to you for what you have done. (*Para. 7*)

Structure

I. Rewrite the following sentences after the model.

Model: Sunday as a day of rest is, or was, deeply rooted in the culture. It's shocking to consider that, in a short period of time, it has almost entirely lost this association.

Sunday as a day of rest is, or was, **so** deeply rooted in the culture **that** it's shocking to consider that, in a short period of time, it has almost entirely lost this association.

1. I was very tired. I could hardly keep my eyes open.

2. He walked very fast. I couldn't keep up with him.
   _____

3. Jack has many friends. He can't remember all of their names.
   _____

4. She was very angry. She couldn't speak.
   _____

5. His handwriting is very illegible (难以辨认的). I can't figure out what his sentence says.
   _____

Ⅱ. Complete the following sentences by translating the Chinese into English, using "the fact that".

Model: It was the visit to church, our reward for an hour of piety, an opportunity to take advantage of _____(爸爸不用上班).
It was the visit to church, our reward for an hour of piety, an opportunity to take advantage of the fact that Dad was not at work.

1. _____(最近谁也没有见过他这一事实) disturbs everybody in the office.
2. No one disputes _____(事故本来是可以避免的事实).
3. He refused to help me, despite _____(我向他请求了好几次).
4. It is impossible to disguise _____(生意不景气的事实).
5. He was held responsible for _____(他的狗咬了邻居).

Cloze

Choose one appropriate word from the following box to fill in each of the following blanks. Each word can be used only once. Change the word form where necessary.

lie	than	hold	what	reserve
fancy	force	lose	when	realize
with	choice	close	vital	edge

Camping is uncomfortable. And yes, there's a lot to be said for getting out a credit card, (1)_____ a room in a nice hotel with a large TV in front of which to park the kid, and going out for a (2) _____ meal and a good glass of wine. But there's also something infinitely (无限地) wonderful about being so (3) _____ to nature. And just as important, there's something (4) _____ about getting young children out of their increasingly technology-padded comfort zones (科技领域) and (5) _____ them to encounter the non-cyber world (非网络世界) around them.

We (6) _____ something when we spend all our time inside a carefully constructed modernity, (7) _____ we read about daily affronts (冒犯) to the environment—yet, removed from the majesty of nature, don't fully (8) _____ what is at stake. It's a good thing to reconnect every so often (9) _____ the Great Outdoors. Lassen has no hotels. If you want to see the splendors of this landscape, you have no (10) _____ but to stay in one of the campsites nestling (偎依) on the (11) _____ of the lakes and against the sides of the mountains.

After camping in Yosemite, Teddy Roosevelt once declared that "It was like (12) _____ in a great solemn cathedral (肃穆的教堂), far vaster and more beautiful (13) _____ any built by the hand of man." That sentiment (14) _____ as true today as it did in Roosevelt's time. What a wondrous thing nature is. And (15) _____ a joy to see a child grasp that simple truth!

Translation

Translate the following sentences into Chinese.

1. As I did so, it occurred to me how rare the Sunday visit has become.

2. And last, the most desired destination of Sunday visits—my uncle Gene, the only member of our extended family who had managed to accumulate significant material wealth.

3. Sunday was indeed different from all the other days of the week, because everyone seemed to be on the same schedule.

4. The answer can range from going to the mall to participating in a road race to jetting to Montreal for lunch.

5. People there had to depend on one another in the face of a changing economy and a challenging environment.

Text B *Precious* Impresses Me

Dre Drivas

1 If I had known what *Precious* was about, I probably wouldn't have wanted to see it. It's too dark and depressing. You can't really tell a story like *Precious* successfully if you are not afraid of thrusting the sharp knife into the audience's hearts. However, screenwriter Geoffrey Fletcher and director Lee Daniels have injected some humor and hope into the film. About midway through the movie I was pretty astonished that, despite the fact

that the central character, Precious, was treated cruelly, the movie is undeniably entertaining. It attracted me. I cared. I wanted a happy ending. Even though things got even worse from that point on for her, I believe what the film believes: that the good and strength in people doesn't always prevail, but it can win eventually. I trusted in Precious's strength, even if we can barely see it at the beginning.

2 Gabourey Sidibe deserves to be chosen as a candidate for the Academy Award. I've seen her in interviews, making the rounds of all the talk shows, and she couldn't be more different than her character. I only point this out because some people unfairly think that Sidibe was just playing a version of herself in movie. The criticism might be both a tribute (赞扬) to her work and an insult(侮辱) to the girl. She's bursting with life, while Precious she played in the movie has it buried and burning inside.

3 As you can guess, a huge reason that this is an effective film is the acting. Mariah Carey is surprisingly effective as a social worker who wants some answers before she starts handing out welfare checks(福利救济金). Paula Patton who played the role of Precious's teacher essentially plays an angel, but we need one in stories like these—especially in stories with someone like Mo'Nique's evil mother. Among all the actresses, Mo'Nique's is perhaps the most powerful. I heard all the talk about how good she was, but I almost always take everything I hear in doubt. I was surprised by her work here. I mean, is this Mo'Nique?

4 Watching *Precious*, I was reminded of another film about the sufferings of women in distress, *Dancer in the Dark*. Both films are made with care. Both films contain strong performances. Both films contain a story that is increasingly cruel to its central character. I can understand the admiration for either film and I can understand the criticism toward either film. On an objective

（客观的）level, I can understand it. But movies become personal experiences and that's why I don't like *Dancer in the Dark* and will not defend it. I will surely defend *Precious*. I walked out of Lars von Trier's movie in a state of despair. I left *Precious* encouraged. There are two worlds here: one hopeless, one hopeful. I choose to live in the latter.

(492 words)

Words and Phrases to Learn

impress /ɪmˈpres/ *vt.* 给人印象，引人入胜
inject /ɪnˈdʒekt/ *vt.* 注入
prevail /prɪˈveɪl/ *vi.* 获胜；占优势 (over, against)
eventually /ɪˈventʃuəli/ *ad.* 终于，最后
deserve /dɪˈzɜːv/ *vt.* 应受，值得
candidate /ˈkændɪdeɪt/ *n.* 候选人
interview /ˈɪntəvjuː/ *n.* 采访，访谈；接见
point out 指出
burst with 充满
effective /ɪˈfektɪv/ *a.* 有力的；给人深刻印象的
hand out 分派
remind /rɪˈmaɪnd/ *vt.* 提醒；使想起
distress /dɪsˈtres/ *n.* 痛苦；危难，不幸
contain /kənˈteɪn/ *vt.* 包含；容纳
defend /dɪˈfend/ *vt.* 为……辩护

Comprehension Check

Choose the best answer for each of the following.

1. What was the author's impression on the movie *Precious* when he walked out of the cinema?
    A. It's dark and depressing.   B. It's entertaining.
    C. It's too cruel.   D. It's attractive.

2. The theme of the movie *Precious* is that _____.
    A. the good and strength in people cannot win
    B. the good and strength in people doesn't exist in human beings
    C. the good and strength in people always prevails from the beginning
    D. the good and strength in people can always win eventually

3. Why does the author think that Gabourey Sidibe deserves to be chosen as a candidate for the Academy Award?
   A. Because she was just playing a version of herself in the movie.
   B. Because she is just the same person in reality as she played in the movie.
   C. Because of her excellent performance in playing the role of Precious.
   D. Because the author doesn't like those people who criticize Gabourey Sidibe.
4. In *Precious* who plays the role of Precious's teacher?
   A. Mariah Carey.   B. Paula Patton.
   C. Mo'Nique.   D. Gabourey Sidibe.
5. The author thought of another film, *Dancer in the Dark*, while watching *Precious* because _____.
   A. both films are about the sufferings of women in distress
   B. both films contain strong performances
   C. both films contain a story that is increasingly cruel to its central character
   D. all of the above
6. The following statements are true except _____.
   A. *Dancer in the Dark* can remind the audience of their personal experience
   B. compared to *Precious*, *Dancer in the Dark* leaves the audience in a state of despair
   C. the criticism of Gabourey turned out to be a tribute to her performance
   D. one of the reasons that *Precious* is an effective film is the acting

Language Practice

Fill in the blanks with words or phrases listed in the *Words and Phrases to Learn*.

1. It was obvious that the poor woman was in _____.
2. How much liquid do you think this bottle _____?
3. I can't afford a lawyer so I shall _____ myself.
4. Jackson _____ me with his force and his kindness.
5. His appointment may _____ some new life into the committee.
6. Justice has _____; the guilty man has been punished.
7. Although she had been ill for a long time, it still came as a shock when she _____ died.
8. He certainly _____ to be sent to prison.
9. I _____ to him that this was a trouble he had brought upon himself.
10. I knew they were _____ curiosity but I said nothing.
11. His efforts to improve the school have been very _____.
12. He was the strongest _____ for the job.

13. In a television _____ last night, she denied that she had any intention of resigning.
14. Will you help me to _____ the books at the meeting?
15. The story you have just told _____ me of an experience I once had.

Part II Listening

Section A

Directions: You're going to hear five short conversations between two speakers. Then questions will be asked about what you've heard. Listen once and choose the right answer to each question you hear.

1. A. To go to the cinema and to download from the Internet.
   B. To download from the Internet and to rent at the store.
   C. To rent at the store and to go to the cinema.
   D. To go to the cinema and to watch at home.
2. A. 10:00.   B. 9:15.
   C. 8:45.   D. 9:50.
3. A. It is the tallest building in London.
   B. It overlooks the Thames River.
   C. It is located in the center of London.
   D. It is a famous tourist attraction in London.
4. A. He is going to meet his teacher.
   B. He is going to attend a class.
   C. He is going to swim with the woman.
   D. He is going to finish his homework.
5. A. Librarian and student.   B. Operator and caller.
   C. Boss and secretary.   D. Customer and repairman.

Section B

Directions: You're going to hear a long conversation between two speakers. Then three questions will be asked about what you've heard. Listen once and choose the right answer to each question you hear.

6. A. About a year.   B. Less than a year.
   C. About two years.   D. Less than two years.

7. A. He is the brother of the man's girlfriend.
   B. He keeps friends with both the man and his girlfriend.
   C. He is a very humorous person.
   D. He often invites the man to dinner.
8. A. Funny. B. Serious.
   C. Amusing. D. Pretty.

Section C

Directions: In this section you will hear a passage. At the end of the passage, you will hear some questions. The passage and the questions will be spoken only once. After you hear a question, you must choose the best answer.

9. A. A rise in divorces.
   B. An increase in childcare facilities.
   C. A rise in people's living standard.
   D. An increase in the number of working mothers.
10. A. Women earn more than men.
    B. There are more childcare facilities.
    C. It becomes difficult for men to find a job.
    D. Children have to stay at home alone.
11. A. They used to be the sole breadwinners.
    B. They used to be housewives.
    C. They used to be career women.
    D. They used to be kindergarten teachers.
12. A. Because their working mothers teach them to be independent.
    B. Because they have to take care of their siblings with their mothers at work.
    C. Because they understand it's difficult for their mother to have a career.
    D. Because they have to deal with a lot of things themselves with their mothers at work.

Part III Speaking

Section A

Directions: Discuss the following questions in small groups.

1. What do you plan to do this Sunday?
2. How do you like the idea of the Sunday visit?

3. Why is it important for the author to visit friends and relatives on Sundays?

Section B

Directions: Read aloud the following passage.

Suzhou Museum

Suzhou Museum is located at No. 204 Dongbei Street in Gusu District, ancient city of Suzhou, Jiangsu Province. It is next to the Humble Administrator's Garden. The museum was first founded in 1960 on the site of Prince Zhong's Mansion. The new exhibition building was designed by the world-famous Chinese-American architect named I. M. Pei and opened to visitors in October 2006. This museum has abundant porcelains, most notably celadon, handicraft works, calligraphies and paintings of Ming and Qing Dynasties (1368 - 1911) which fully embody the history, art and culture of Suzhou and Yangtze River Delta.

Suzhou Museum obeys the theme of "Design for China". It combines modern exhibition halls and classical gardens' architecture together. The whole structure contains three floors, which include an underground floor. The central and western parts of the museum have a second floor. The main buildings are less than 20 feet (6 meters) in height, and are surrounded by beautiful courtyards. Visitors will feel that the museum itself is like an exquisite work of art while appreciating the treasures and exhibits within.

Part IV Writing

Directions: Write a composition on the topic "My Favorite Hobby". You should write at least 100 words, and base your composition on the outline given below:

1. I have many hobbies, such as ..., but reading is my favorite hobby.
2. I like reading for three reasons.
3. Reading has become part of my life.

UNIT 4

Love

Part I Reading

Text A   How Real Is Your Love?

1 Genevieve Grossmann is a prolific secret admirer—so much so that she anonymously sends dozens of virtual gifts to her Facebook[1] friends simply to see their reactions. And with so many Valentine's Day[2] gifts to choose from—roses, kisses, flowers, chocolates—she plans to be busy today.

2 "Some people say that paying for one of these is a waste of a dollar, but I disagree," said Grossmann, 24, of West Chester, Pennsylvania. "The cost of sending a gift is a dollar; the cost of driving someone crazy? Priceless!"

3 Valentine's Day has become a hot seller when it comes to virtual gifts, a growing part of online commerce. They range from cartoonish images on social networking profiles[3] to three-dimensional-looking[4] objects that people exchange in virtual worlds and on web sites.

4 These virtual gifts hardly exist without a computer or mobile phone to display them, but as people place more value on their online presence, a bottle of champagne, diamond earrings and even lingerie have real-world prices and meaning.

5 "Sending a virtual flower is a way of showing lightweight attention and affection to someone online," said Susan Wu, a partner with Charles River Ventures in Menlo Park, California, who's been following the growth of virtual gifts. She estimates that the virtual-goods market is worth about $3 billion today. "It's become commonplace behavior on social networks."

6   Virtual goods have been a form of currency within video games and Web-based worlds such as Second Life[5] for some time. But the latest wave of gift-giving began a year ago when Facebook began selling $1 graphical icons for members to exchange. Facebook says more than 24 million gifts have been given in the past year, and about 280 million gifts are currently available. MySpace[6] offers Valentine-themed videos and other graphics users can exchange.

7   But does a collection of pixels have as much value as a physical gift? Adrienne Miller, 27, said it's "cute" to receive online trinkets from friends on holidays, "but they're not a substitute for something tangible that required some offline effort."

8   What would she do if a romantic interest gifted her a graphic of a diamond instead of the real thing? "Let's just say there wouldn't be another date," she said.

9   Nonetheless, Valentine's Day has mass appeal among social networking addicts, said Tammy Nam of Slide.com[7], the maker of interactive applications and widgets for users' profiles[8]. One of the most popular features, called the SuperPoke, lets people blow a kiss, cuddle, have a candlelit dinner, or fall in love with other members.

10   Valentine's Day resonates with people more than other holidays partly because "the concept of love and self-expression go hand in hand", Nam said.

11   Companies like Gaia Online are making a significant portion of their real world revenue stream[9] from the creation and exchange of virtual goods, said Forrester Research analyst Jeremiah Owyang. "Like real life, inanimate objects—physical or virtual—can hold value for consumers," he said.

12   Virtual entrepreneurs can also cash in on the holiday. Sales at Dianne Marshall's Second Life flower shop doubles on Valentine's Day with as many as 11,000 transactions. In the virtual world There.com, members plan on taking part in a scavenger hunt[10] and a Valentine-themed pajama party.

13   "For the younger demographic, the line between the virtual and real world is fairly blurred," said Ben Richardson, vice president of business development at There.com's parent company Makena Technologies. "The value of receiving a virtual gift can have more meaning because it has such a novel experience associated with it."

14   Giving such gifts may be easy, but they still cost real money. Grossmann said she might send her boyfriend a Valentine token today, but she doesn't expect one in return. "If I send him a free one, he'll probably retaliate," she said. "But I don't think he'll actually spend a dollar."

(651 words)

New Words

prolific / prəˈlɪfɪk / a.　丰富的；大量的
admirer /ədˈmaɪərə/ n.　赞赏者；（女人的）爱慕者，情人
anonymously /əˈnɒnɪməsli/ ad.　匿名地；不具名地
virtual /ˈvɜːtʃuəl/ a.　虚拟的
gifter /ˈɡɪftə/ n.　〈俚〉送礼人
crazy /ˈkreɪzi/ a.　发疯的；发狂的；着迷的
commerce /ˈkɒmɜːs/ n.　商业
image /ˈɪmɪdʒ/ n.　像；图像
profile /ˈprəʊfaɪl / n.　人物或事物之简介，概况
dimensional /dɪˈmenʃənl / a.　……维的
exchange /ɪksˈtʃeɪndʒ/ vt.　交换；互换
display /dɪsˈpleɪ/ vt.　展示；陈列
presence /ˈprezəns / n.　存在；在场
champagne /ʃæmˈpeɪn / n.　香槟酒
lingerie /ˈlænʒəri / n.　女内衣
lightweight /ˈlaɪtweɪt / a.　无足轻重的
affection /əˈfekʃn / n.　喜爱；爱
partner /ˈpɑːtnə / n.　合伙人；伙伴
follow /ˈfɒləʊ / vt.　关注；注视
estimate /ˈestɪmət, ˈestɪmeɪt / vt.　估计
billion /ˈbɪljən/ n. & a.　〈美〉十亿（的）
commonplace /ˈkɒmənpleɪs/ a.　平常的；平凡的
behavior /bɪˈheɪvjə/ n.　行为；举止；表现
currency /ˈkʌrənsi / n.　货币；流通
graphical /ˈɡræfɪkəl/ a.　图的；用图表示的
icon /ˈaɪkɒn/ n.　画像；图像
currently /ˈkʌrəntli/ ad.　当前；时下
available /əˈveɪləbl/ a.　可用的；可得到的
theme /θiːm/ n.　主题
pixel /ˈpɪksl/ n.　〈电子〉像素
collection /kəˈlekʃn/ n.　收集（物）
physical /ˈfɪzɪkl/ a.　有形的；实物的
cute /kjuːt/ a.　漂亮的；有吸引力的
trinket /ˈtrɪŋkɪt/ n.　廉价的小装饰物、首饰等

---

* 黑体表示重点词汇和短语，白体表示一般词汇和短语

substitute /ˈsʌbstɪtjuːt/ n. 代替者；代用品
tangible /ˈtændʒəbl/ a. 可触知的；有形的
nonetheless /ˌnʌnðəˈles/ ad. 尽管如此；然而
appeal /əˈpiːl/ n. 吸引力；感染力；号召力
addict /ˈædɪkt/ n. 有瘾的人；对某事物有强烈兴趣的人
widget /ˈwɪdʒɪt/ n. 小装置；小玩意儿
cuddle /ˈkʌdl/ vt. 拥抱
resonate /ˈrezəneɪt/ vi. 共鸣；回响
revenue /ˈrevənjuː/ n. 收入
analyst /ˈænəlɪst/ n. 分析者，分析家
inanimate /ɪnˈænɪmət/ a. 无生命的
consumer /kənˈsjuːmə/ n. 消费者；用户
entrepreneur /ˌɒntrəprəˈnɜː/ n. 企业家
double /ˈdʌbl/ vi. 加倍
transaction /trænˈzækʃn/ n. （一笔）交易；业务
scavenger /ˈskævɪndʒə/ n. 拾荒者
pajamas /pəˈdʒɑːməz/ [pl.] n. =pyjamas 睡衣裤
demographic /ˌdeməˈɡræfɪk/ a. 人口的
blur /blɜː/ vt. 使……变得模糊不清
novel /ˈnɒvl/ a. 新奇的；新颖的
associate /əˈsəʊʃɪeɪt/ vt. 将……联系起来
token /ˈtəʊkən/ n. 纪念品；表示
retaliate /rɪˈtælɪeɪt/ vi. 回报

Phrases and Expressions

so much so that　到这样的程度以至
dozens of　许多
when it comes to　涉及，至于
place much/little value on　认为……很重要/不重要
instead of　作为……的替换
hand in hand　密切关联地；手拉手
cash in on　从……中获得利益或利润
take part in　参加
in return　作为（对……的）交换；（作为对……的）报答或回报

Proper Names

Genevieve Grossmann /ˈdʒenəviːv ˈgrəʊsmæn/ 吉纳维芙·克罗斯曼
West Chester /ˈwest ˈtʃestə/ 西切斯特市（位于宾夕法尼亚州）
Pennsylvania /ˌpensɪlˈveɪnɪə/ 宾夕法尼亚
Susan Wu /ˈsuːzən ˈwuː/ 苏珊·吴
Charles River Ventures /tʃɑːlz ˈrɪvə ˈventʃə/ 查尔斯河风险投资公司
Menlo Park /ˈmenləʊ ˈpɑːk/ 门罗帕克市（位于加利福尼亚州）
California /ˌkælɪˈfɔːnɪə/ 加利福尼亚
Adrienne Miller /ˈeɪdrɪen ˈmɪlə/ 艾德丽安·米勒
Tammy Nam /ˈtæmɪ ˈnɑːm/ 泰米·纳姆
Gaia Online /ˈgaɪəˈɒnˈlaɪn/ 盖亚在线
Jeremiah Owyang /ˌdʒerɪˈmaɪə ˈəʊjɔːn/ 杰里迈亚·欧阳
Dianne Marshall /daɪˈænə ˈmɑːʃl/ 戴安娜·马歇尔
Ben Richardson /ˈben ˈrɪtʃədsən/ 本·理查森

Notes on the Text

1. **Facebook**: A social network service and website launched in February 2004. It was founded by Mark Zuckerberg.

2. **Valentine's Day**: An annual commemoration (纪念) held on February 14 celebrating love and affection between intimate companions. It is traditionally a day on which lovers express their love for each other by presenting flowers, offering confectionery (甜食), and sending greeting cards. （圣瓦伦丁节，情人节）

3. **social networking profiles**: 社交网络个人资料

4. **three-dimensional-looking**: 三维视效的

5. **Second Life**: A virtual (虚拟的) world developed by Linden Lab launched in 2003, and is accessible (能进入的) on the Internet. （一款完全模仿现实生活的社区交友型网络游戏）

6. **MySpace**: A social networking website. （全球最大的在线交友平台）

7. **Slide.com**: Interactive applications and small devices for users' **profiles**. （提供多个知名社交网站的第三方应用）

8. **the maker of interactive applications and widgets for users' profiles**: 为用户个人资料制作互动软件和小装置的制作者

9. **revenue stream**: 收入，收益

10. **a scavenger hunt**: A game in which the organizers prepare a list defining specific items, using which the participants—individuals or teams—seek to gather all items on the list—usually without purchasing them—or perform tasks or take photographs of the items, as specified. （一种寻宝游戏，可以个人或小组玩，参加游戏者会被派发一张任务清单，最先完成所有任务者获胜）

Comprehension of the Text

Answer the following questions.

1. What kind of gifts does Genevieve Grossmann anonymously send to her Facebook friends? Why does she do so?
2. What does Genevieve Grossmann think of paying for Valentine's Day gifts?
3. How have virtual gifts become a growing part of online commerce?
4. What does Susan Wu think of sending virtual gifts?
5. What are virtual goods?
6. How did the latest wave of gift-giving begin?
7. What are the differences between virtual gifts and physical gifts, according to Adrienne Miller?
8. Why does Valentine's Day have mass appeal among social networking addicts, according to Tammy Nam?
9. Why does Valentine's Day resonate with people more than other holidays, according to Nam?
10. How do companies like Gaia Online make their real world revenue stream, according to Jeremiah Owyang?
11. How can virtual entrepreneurs cash in on the holiday?
12. What does Ben Richardson think of receiving a virtual gift?

Language Sense Enhancement

I. Read the following paragraphs until you learn them by heart. Then try to complete the following passage from memory.

Valentine's Day has become a (1) _____ seller when it (2) _____ to virtual gifts, a (3) _____ part of online commerce. They range (4) _____ cartoonish images on social networking profiles (5) _____ three-dimensional-looking objects that people (6) _____ in virtual worlds and on web sites.

These virtual gifts hardly exist (7) _____ a computer or mobile phone to (8) _____ them, but as people place more (9) _____ on their online presence, a bottle of champagne, diamond earrings and even lingerie have real-world prices and (10) _____.

II. Read the following quotations. Learn them by heart if you can. You might need to look up new words in a dictionary.

My life is full because I know that I am loved.　　—From "The Elephant Man"
我的人生是圆满的，因为我知道有人爱过我。　　——《象人》

Darkness cannot drive out darkness; only light can do that. Hate cannot drive out hate; only love can do that.   —Martin Luther King, Jr.

黑暗不能驱除黑暗,只有光明可以做到;仇恨不能驱除仇恨,只有爱可以做到。

——马丁·路德·金

Love does not begin and end the way we seem to think it does. Love is a battle, love is a war, and love is a growing up.   —James A. Baldwin

爱的开始和结束不以人的意志为转移。爱是战斗,是战争,是成长。

——詹姆斯·鲍德温

Vocabulary

I. Fill in the blanks with the given words or phrases in the box. Change the form where necessary.

display	exchange	estimate	substitute	dozens of
associate	presence	behavior	addict	appeal
available	double	virtual	physical	in return

1. I always _____ the smell of the sea with my childhood.
2. The price of houses has almost _____.
3. Why dont you _____ your ad on the notice board where everyone can see it?
4. The document was signed in the _____ of two witnesses.
5. He was well-known for his violent and threatening _____ .
6. New technology has enabled development of an online "_____ library".
7. The treatment standard(诊治标准)will list those who surf online for more than 40 hours per week as Internet _____.
8. It is vital that food is made _____ to the famine areas.
9. Tofu can be used as a meat _____ in vegetarian recipes.
10. It was difficult to _____ how many trees had been destroyed.
11. He _____ the blue jumper for a red one.
12. The new fashion soon lost its _____.
13. All _____ objects occupy space.
14. I've spoken to him _____ times, but I still don't know his name!
15. _____ for your cooperation we will give you a free gift.

II. Choose a word or a phrase from the indicated paragraph to fill in each of the following blanks. Change the form where necessary.

1. I've spoken to him _____ times, but I still don't know his name! (*Para. 1*)
2. I'm afraid I have to _____ with you on that issue. (*Para. 2*)

3. He hardly seemed to notice my _____. (*Para. 4*)
4. Mark felt great _____ for his sister. (*Para. 5*)
5. Foreign travel has become _____ in recent years. (*Para. 5*)
6. She is _____ working in France. (*Para. 6*)
7. It's a long climb to the top, but well worth the _____. (*Para. 7*)
8. The problems are not serious. _____, we shall need to tackle them soon. (*Para. 9*)
9. Prosperity goes _____ with investment(投资). (*Para. 10*)
10. The film studio is being accused of _____ the singer's death. (*Para. 12*)

Structure

I. Rewrite the following sentences after the model.

Model: Genevieve Grossmann is so prolific a secret admirer that she anonymously sends dozens of virtual gifts to her Facebook friends simply to see their reactions.

Genevieve Grossmann is a prolific secret admirer—**so much so that** she anonymously sends dozens of virtual gifts to her Facebook friends simply to see their reactions.

1. We are so busy that we can't manage to take a holiday this year.

2. She was so weak that she could not walk.

3. She is so poor that she has hardly enough to live.

4. John is so tired that he could not stand up.

5. Tom is so clever that he can solve the difficult math problem in a few minutes.

II. Complete the following sentences by translating the Chinese into English, using "when it comes to something/doing something".

Model: Valentine's Day has become a hot seller _____
(当涉及虚拟礼物这种日益发展壮大的网络商务时).
Valentine's Day has become a hot seller when it comes to virtual gifts, a growing part of online commerce.

1. _____
(说到打篮球), he is the champion.

2. _____
   （至于政治）I know nothing.
3. Women are not smarter than men _____
   （至于情商）.
4. Why don't you feel the same way _____
   （当涉及非法移民时）?
5. Every investor has their own personality _____
   （当涉及投资时）.

Cloze

Choose one appropriate word from the following box to fill in each of the following blanks. Each word can be used only once. Change the word form where necessary.

laugh	realize	shy	sad	grow
arm	necessary	life	affection	offer
least	embarrassment	silent	bold	whisper

The friendship between the two lonely people developed and soon (1)_____ into a deep (2)_____ for each other. They told each other their (3)_____ stories and consoled each other. Soon they were (4)_____ enough to cry in each other's presence without any sense of (5)_____. Then one day she (6)_____ that they were deeply in love with each other. Tryan was (7)_____ but Jane was braver. One day, she looked straight into his eyes and (8)_____, "I love you."

Tryan looked away. He was (9)_____ for a long time and then he spoke, "I have been in prison, I don't think I have anything left to (10)_____ you. All I have in the world is what you see before you."

"I have enough for both of us," she said looking into his eyes, "How long are we going to live? Twenty years? Forty years? Let's live together; if nothing else, at (11)_____ we have each other's (12)_____ to cry in." No more words were (13)_____: They just fell into each other's arms and (14)_____ and cried at the same time. A new (15)_____ had begun for them.

Translation

Translate the following sentences into Chinese.

1. Genevieve Grossmann is a prolific secret admirer—so much so that she anonymously sends dozens of virtual gifts to her Facebook friends simply to see their reactions.

2. They range from cartoonish images on social networking profiles to three-dimensional-looking objects that people exchange in virtual worlds and on web sites.

3. Adrienne Miller, 27, said it's "cute" to receive online trinkets from friends on holidays, "but they're not a substitute for something tangible that required some offline effort."

4. Valentine's Day resonates with people more than other holidays partly because "the concept of love and self-expression go hand in hand", Nam said.

5. The value of receiving a virtual gift can have more meaning because it has such a novel experience associated with it.

Unit 4 Love

Text B   Cyberstepmother

Judy E. Carter

1 I've often felt that "stepparent" is a label we attach to men and women who marry into families where children already exist, for the simple reason that we need to call them something. It is most certainly an enormous "step", but one doesn't often feel as if the term "parent" truly applies. At least that's how I used to feel about being a stepmother to my husband's four children.

2 My husband and I had been together for six years, and with him I had watched as his young children became young teenagers. Although they lived primarily with their mother, they spent a lot of time with us as well. Over the years, we all learned to adjust, to become more comfortable with each other, and to adapt to our new family arrangement. We enjoyed vacations together, ate family meals, worked on homework, played baseball, rented videos. However, I continued to feel somewhat like an outsider, infringing upon foreign territory. There was a definite boundary line that could not be crossed, an inner family circle which excluded me. Since I had no children of my own, my experience of parenting was limited to my husband's four, and often I lamented that I would never know the special bond that exists between a parent and a child.

3 When the children moved to a town five hours away, my husband was understandably devastated. In order to maintain regular communication with the kids, we contacted Cyberspace and promptly set up an e-mail and chat-line service. This technology, combined with the telephone, would enable us to reach them on a daily basis by sending frequent notes and messages, and even chatting together when we were all on-line.

4 Ironically, these modern tools of communication can also be tools of alienation, making us feel so out of touch, so much more in need of real human contact. If a computer message came addressed to "Dad", I'd feel forgotten and neglected. If my name appeared along with his, it would brighten my day and make me feel like I was part of their family unit after all. Yet always there was some distance to be crossed, not just over the telephone wires.

5 Late one evening, as my husband snoozed in front of the television and I was catching up on my e-mail, an "instant message" appeared on the screen. It was Margo, my oldest stepdaughter, also up late and sitting in front of her computer five hours away. As we had done

in the past, we sent several messages back and forth, exchanging the latest news. When we would "chat" like that, she wouldn't necessarily know if it was me or her dad on the other end of the keyboard—that is unless she asked. That night she didn't ask and I didn't identify myself either. After hearing the latest volleyball scores, the details about an upcoming dance at her school, and a history project that was in the works, I commented that it was late and I should get to sleep. Her return message read, "Okay, talk to you later! Love you!"

6   As I read this message, a wave of sadness ran through me and I realized that she must have thought she was writing to her father the whole time. She and I would never have openly exchanged such words of affection. Feeling guilty for not clarifying, yet not wanting to embarrass her, I simply responded, "Love you too! Have a good sleep!"

7   I thought again of their family circle, that self-contained, private space where I was an intruder. I felt again the sharp ache of emptiness and otherness. Then, just as my fingers reached for the keys, just as I was about to return the screen to black, Margo's final message appeared. It read, "Tell Dad good night for me too." With tear-filled, blurry eyes, I turned the machine off.

(651 words)

Words and Phrases to Learn

attach /əˈtætʃ/ vt.   系；贴；装；连接
enormous /ɪˈnɔːməs/ a.   巨大的
apply /əˈplaɪ/ vt.   适用；应用
adjust /əˈdʒʌst/ vi.   适应
adapt /əˈdæpt/ vi.   适应（新环境等）
boundary /ˈbaʊndəri/ n.   分界线，边界
cross /krɒs/ vt.   穿过，越过
exclude /ɪksˈkluːd/ vt.   把……排除在外，拒绝
bond /bɒnd/ n.   联结，联系
maintain /meɪnˈteɪn/ vt.   保持，维持
combine ... with   使……与……结合（联合、混合、组合）
address /əˈdres/ vt.   写信给；向……讲话（或发表演说）
identify /aɪˈdentɪfaɪ/ vt.   认出，识别
clarify /ˈklærɪfaɪ/ vt.   澄清
embarrass /ɪmˈbærəs/ vt.   使困窘，使局促不安

Unit 4 Love

Comprehension Check

Choose the best answer for each of the following.

1. How did the author use to feel about being a stepparent?
   A. She thought "stepparent" was just a label attached to those who married someone who already had children.
   B. She felt being a stepparent was just the same as a birth parent.
   C. She felt quite interesting being a stepparent.
   D. She was glad to be a stepparent.

2. How did the author get along with her husband's four children?
   A. They disliked each other.
   B. The children regarded her as an outsider and never talked to her.
   C. They got along well with each other and spent much time together.
   D. They never spent any time together.

3. The author continued to feel somewhat like an outsider because _____.
   A. she infringed on a foreign territory
   B. she could not cross the boundary line
   C. she could not get into the family circle
   D. she had no children of her own

4. How did the father feel when the children moved away?
   A. He felt greatly relieved.
   B. He felt quite angry.
   C. He felt helpless.
   D. He felt upset.

5. The author would be especially happy when _____.
   A. she received a computer message that came addressed only to her husband
   B. she received a computer message that came addressed both to her and her husband
   C. her husband's four children moved away
   D. they set up an e-mail and chat-line service

6. Why were there tears in the author's eyes when she finished "chatting" with Margo one evening?
   A. Because she felt very sad: Margo mistook her for her father all the time.
   B. Because she felt happy: Margo was aware who she was "chatting" with.
   C. Because she felt upset: She was just a stepparent no matter how hard she tried.
   D. Because she felt tired: She and Margo "chatted" late into the night.

Language Practice

Fill in the blanks with words or phrases listed in the *Words and Phrases to Learn*.

1. Physics has made _____ progress in this century.
2. The body quickly _____ to changes in temperature.
3. I _____ a label to each bag.
4. The Ural (乌拉尔) mountains mark the _____ between Europe and Asia.
5. This policy is for British citizens—it doesn't _____ to you.
6. There is a close _____ of affection between the two sisters.
7. They wanted to _____ all boys from attending their club.
8. Our eyes slowly _____ to the dark.
9. For 200 miles, the railway _____ a bare, empty plain(平原).
10. Bad planning, _____ bad luck, led to the company's collapse.
11. A small baby can _____ its mother by her voice.
12. We need to _____ the quality of our goods but not increase the price.
13. I was really _____ when I knocked the cup of tea over onto my teacher.
14. The letter was returned because it had been wrongly _____.
15. The teacher's explanation _____ the puzzling problems.

Part II Listening

Section A

Directions: In this section you will hear five short conversations. At the end of each conversation a question will be asked about what was said. Both the conversation and the question will be spoken only once. Listen carefully and choose the best answer.

1. A. The man doesn't like playing video games.
   B. The man met all his friends in the virtual world.
   C. The man doesn't like his friends very much.
   D. The man is going to play video games with the woman.
2. A. Professor Brown's lecture is boring.
   B. Professor Brown is popular among her students.
   C. The man likes Professor Brown's lecture very much.
   D. The man is one of Professor Brown's favorite students.
3. A. The Museum of London is the largest museum in the world.
   B. Over 2 million objects are on display in the Museum of London.

C. Visitors to the Museum of London cannot see all the objects in its collection.

D. The Museum of London attracts over two million visitors each year.

4. A. Find a large room.
   B. Sell the old table.
   C. Buy two bookshelves.
   D. Rearrange some furniture.
5. A. Looking for a young lady.
   B. Looking for her watch.
   C. Looking for a young gentleman.
   D. Looking for a man wearing a watch.

Section B

Directions: In this section you will hear a long conversation. At the end of the conversation you will hear some questions. Both the conversation and the questions will be spoken only once. After you hear a question, you must choose the best answer.

6. A. He is looking for her girlfriend.
   B. He is buying his girlfriend a birthday present.
   C. He is buying himself a suit for his girlfriend's birthday.
   D. He is comparing the prices of different outfits.
7. A. She normally wears expensive clothes.
   B. She normally wears cheap clothes.
   C. She normally wears trendy clothes.
   D. She normally wears formal clothes.
8. A. Because he may find clothes within his price range there.
   B. Because he may have more choices there.
   C. Because it is a very nice clothing store.
   D. Because it sells outfits for less than $20 dollars.

Section C

Directions: In this section you are going to hear a passage. Listen to the passage three times and fill in the missing information.

With only two weeks to go before Christmas, buying (9) _____ is a high priority for a lot of people. However, these days lots of people can do their shopping in the (10) _____ of their own home with the help of the Internet.

Online shopping is becoming more and more (11) _____ for a number of reasons: Prices are often lower online, you don't have to queue up in busy shops and you can buy almost any product (12)_____ with just a few clicks of your mouse.

Computer trends are often male-dominated but this year women are expected to do more shopping on the Internet than men. It seems women are now more attracted to the (13)_____ of online shopping than they used to be.

In the past a lot of people were (14)_____ to shop online. Many were worried about the security of (15)_____ on the Internet and the reliability of the Internet. But as shopping online has become more widespread, these worries (16)_____.

However, many companies are concerned that not enough shoppers are coming through their doors. As a result, there are (17)_____ in the shops. Most shops traditionally have sales after Christmas but this year the bargains have come early in an attempt (18)_____.

Part III Speaking

Section A

Directions: Discuss the following questions in small groups.

1. Have you ever received virtual gifts from your friends or sent them such gifts? Why or why not?
2. What do you think are the differences between virtual gifts and physical ones?
3. In your opinion, what is real love?

Section B

Directions: Read aloud the following passage.

Where Is Love? How Can We Find Love?

Once a little boy wanted to meet Love. He knew it was a long trip to where Love lived, so he got his things ready with some pizzas and drinks and started off. When he passed three streets, he saw an old woman sitting in the park and watching some birds. She looked very hungry. The boy gave her a pizza. She took it and smiled at him. The smile was so beautiful that he wanted to see it again, so he gave her a Coke. She smiled once again. The boy was very happy.

They sat there all the afternoon, eating and smiling, but they said nothing. When it grew dark, the boy decided to leave. But before he had gone more than a few steps, he turned around, ran back to the old woman and gave her a hug. The woman gave him her biggest smile ever.

When the boy opened the door of his house, his mother was surprised by the look of joy on his face and asked what had made him so happy. "I had lunch with Love. She has got the most beautiful smile in the world." At the same time, the old woman's son was also surprised at his mother's pleasure and asked why.

"I ate a pizza in the park with Love," she said, "and he is much younger than I expected."

Part IV Writing

Directions: Write a composition on the topic "True Love". You should write at least 100 words, and base your composition on the outline given below:

1. Show your understanding of the meaning of true love.
2. Give a specific example.
3. Give your suggestions as to the best way to show love.

UNIT 5

Fashion

Part I Reading

Text A   Lo and Behold[1 2]

1 The other day, I saw a Louis Vuitton[3] handbag with a price tag of $750 locked inside a department store glass case, and, I confess, I wanted to have that bag. The bag was made of canvas, was covered with muddy LV signs, and resembled, in shape and size, a beach bag—none of which are especially attractive attributes. And yet, I wanted
it. Why? Why, for that matter, are so many women willing to spend a small fortune on bags decorated with Gucci[4] G's, Chanel[5] C's, and Hermes[6] H's patterns?

2 In my view, the rise of the logo as a source of appeal took off 30 years ago in response to a new kind of consumer that came into being with the investment-driven economy of the 1980's. In the past, rich people were content to know that their things were better made (and more expensive) than those of the ordinary people. Later these rich people are interested in showing off their cars and their jewels. But in the 1980s, a new group of wealthy people emerged. They all had MBAs, they wanted to show their wealth in a more efficient and brief way. Hence the birth of the logo.

3 The trend began quietly enough, making its first appearance in menswear. The first sign can be traced back to the custom-made shirt with its breast pocket that is decorated with a crocodile. The little Lacoste[7] crocodile on the breast pocket of a men's tennis shirt marked its wearer as "preppy"—a sportive type with a lot of money according to *The Official Preppy Handbook*[8], published in 1980.

4 Traditional European fashion houses like Louis Vuitton, Chanel, Prada[9], and Hermes, and

eventually, even the old-fashioned British and American companies like Burberry[10] and Coach[11], understood this and began to market their products in new ways. They did this by making their goods more instantly recognizable—aggressively promoting their distinctive aspects: the funny designs on the Hermes scarf; the leather tags on the heavy Coach bag; the old-fashioned plaid of the Burberry raincoat. Those companies that didn't understand went under.

5   As luxury manufacturers came to understand the new market, they also began to see the value in promoting themselves in even simpler ways—hence the increasing use of the logo. Logos are the quickest possible means of making clear that a product comes from a unique place. Thus, those aspiring to wealth can buy the Louis Vuitton key chain, wallet, and handbag, while those who are wealthy enough can buy the full set of Louis Vuitton luggage.

6   No sooner did the logo make an appearance on luxury goods than imitation logoed goods began to flood the market. I recall that in the 1990s one could buy a very nice imitation Gucci bag for $30 from a street vendor on the corner of 53rd and 5th in Manhattan. Since then, to fight back, the luxury manufacturers have gone to court to stop those people from imitating their products. That means that you now have to make a real effort to find the knock-offs, and, when you do, you have to pay more for them. That $30 imitation Gucci that I could have bought on 53rd and 5th 15 years ago would now cost at least $100 and take you some time to look for them on the Lower East Side.

7   You probably couldn't find a better expression of capitalistic enterprise in action than the various measures and counter measures involving logoed business, where value is continually undergoing changing. And it's amazing that I can write this and still desire a Louis Vuitton handbag. Karl Marx[12] would say that I've been fooled by the false effects of the bourgeois marketplace, the LV bag is the purest example of "exchange value"—an item entirely separated from its use value. I know I would do as well putting my stuff in a plastic bag, but that doesn't prevent me from wanting the Louis Vuitton Neverfull GM bag ($750) or the Louis Vuitton Artsy GM ($1,630).

(676 words)

New Words

lo /ləʊ/ *int.* 看哪,瞧(表示惊讶或用以唤起注意)
behold /bɪˈhəʊld/ (beheld) *vt.* 〈书〉看,瞧(多用于祈使句,用以唤起注意)

* 黑体表示重点词汇和短语,白体表示一般词汇和短语

tag /tæg/ *n.* 标签
lock /lɒk/ *vt.* 锁,锁上
confess /kən'fes/ *vt.* 承认
canvas /'kænvəs/ *n.* 帆布
muddy /'mʌdi/ *a.* 灰暗的,暗淡的
sign /saɪn/ *n.* 标记,符号
resemble /rɪ'zembl/ *vt.* 像,类似
attribute /'ætrɪbjuːt/ *n.* 属性,特性
attractive /ə'træktɪv/ *a.* 有吸引力的,引起注意的
willing /'wɪlɪŋ/ *a.* 情愿的,乐意的
decorate /'dekəreɪt/ *vt.* 装饰,装潢
fortune /'fɔːtʃuːn/ *n.* 财富,命运
logo /'ləʊgəʊ/ *n.* （公司等的）专用标识；标识图案
investment-driven /ɪn'vestmənt'drɪvn/ *a.* 投资驱动的
emerge /ɪ'mɜːdʒ/ *vi.* 出现；浮现
MBA *abbr.* = Master of Business Administration 工商管理学硕士
efficient /ɪ'fɪʃnt/ *a.* 有效的,效率高的
hence /hens/ *ad.* 因此；由此
trend /trend/ *n.* 倾向,趋势
menswear /'menzweə/ *n.* 男装
custom-made /'kʌstəm'meɪd/ *a.* 定制的
crocodile /'krɒkədaɪl/ *n.* 鳄鱼
preppy /'prepi/ *n.* 预备学校学生；（尤指在衣着、举止等方面）像预备学校学生的人
　　　　 a. 预备学校学生的；（衣着式样）刻板规矩的
market /'mɑːkɪt/ *vt.* 经营；销售
instantly /'ɪnstəntli/ *ad.* 立即,即刻
recognizable /'rekəgnaɪzəbl/ *a.* 可认出的,可辨认的
aggressively /ə'gresɪvli/ *ad.* 活跃有为地；积极进取地
promote /prə'məʊt/ *vt.* 宣传；推销（商品等）
distinctive /dɪ'stɪŋktɪv/ *a.* 区别性的,有特色的
aspect /'æspekt/ *n.* 样子；外表
scarf /skɑːf/ *n.* 围巾,披巾
plaid /plæd/ *n.* 方格花纹
luxury /'lʌkʃəri/ *n.* 奢侈,奢侈品；华贵
manufacturer /ˌmænju'fæktʃərə/ *n.* 制造商,工厂主
unique /juː'niːk/ *a.* 唯一的；独特的

imitation /ˌɪmɪˈteɪʃn/ n. 模仿,模拟
vendor /ˈvendə/ n. 小贩,摊贩
imitate /ˈɪmɪteɪt/ vt. 模仿,仿效
knock-off /ˈnɒkɒf/ n. （时装样本等的）翻印本;名牌的仿冒品
expression /ɪksˈpreʃn/ n. 表达,陈述
capitalistic /ˌkæpɪtəˈlɪstɪk/ a. 资本主义的;资本家的
enterprise /ˈentəpraɪz/ n. 企业,公司
counter /ˈkaʊntə/ a. 相反的;对立的
involve /ɪnˈvɒlv/ vt. 使卷入,连累
undergo /ˌʌndəˈɡəʊ/ (underwent, undergone) vt. 经历,经受
bourgeois /ˈbʊəʒwɑː/ n. 资产阶级

Phrases and Expressions

be decorated with 用……装饰
take off 开始;开始流行
in response to 作为(对……的)回答
come into being 形成,产生
be content to 对……满意,愿意
show off 炫耀,卖弄
be traced back to 追溯到
go under 倒闭,垮掉
fight back 还击,抵抗
make an effort 作出努力
in action 在活动中;在运转中

Proper Names

Louis Vuitton /ˈluːɪ viːˈtɒn/ 路易·威登(法国奢侈品牌)
Gucci /ˈɡuːtʃiː/ 古琦(意大利时装品牌)
Chanel /ʃɑːˈnel/ 香奈儿(法国奢侈品牌)
Hermes /ˈhɜːmiːz/ 爱马仕(法国时尚品牌)
Lacoste 鳄鱼（法国奢侈品牌）
Prada /ˈprædə/ 普拉达（意大利奢侈品牌）
Burberry /ˈbɜːbəri/ 巴宝丽（英国知名品牌）

Coach /kəʊtʃ/　寇兹（美国知名品牌）
53rd and 5th in Manhattan　曼哈顿第53大街和第5大道
Lower East Side　曼哈顿的下东区（这里多廉价商品店）
Karl Marx /kɑːrl ˈmɑːks/　卡尔·马克思
Louis Vuitton Neverfull GM　路易·威登一款产品
Louis Vuitton Artsy GM　路易·威登一款产品

Notes on the Text

1. This article was published in July, 2010 in *English Language Learning*. The present text is slightly adapted and abridged.

2. **Lo and behold**：你瞧；真怪；看（令人惊奇之事）

3. **Louis Vuitton**：One of the world's leading international fashion houses founded in 1854. It is often shortened to LV. The label is well known for its LV monogram（交织字母）, which is featured on most products, ranging from luxury trunks and leather goods to ready-to-wear shoes, watches, jewelry（珠宝；首饰）, accessories（配件）, sunglasses and books.

4. **Gucci**：An Italian fashion and leather goods label. Gucci was founded by Guccio Gucci in Florence in 1921.

5. **Chanel**：A Parisian fashion house founded by the late couturier Gabrielle "Coco" Chanel, recognized as one of the most established in haute couture（高级女子时装）, specializing in luxury goods.

6. **Hermes**：A French high fashion house established in 1837, specializing in leather, ready-to-wear, lifestyle accessories, perfumery, and luxury goods.

7. **Lacoste**：A high-end（高档的）apparel（服饰）company founded in 1933 that sells high-end clothing, footwear, perfume, leather goods, watches, eyewear, and most famously tennis shirts. The company can be recognized by its green crocodile logo.

8. *The Official Preppy Handbook*：《权威预科生手册》（主要为想跻身上流社会的年轻人做衣食住行方面的指导，后受到美国时尚界的热捧）

9. **Prada**：An Italian fashion label specializing in luxury goods for men and women. The company was started in 1913 by Mario Prada and his brother Martino as a leather goods shop.

10. **Burberry**：A British luxury fashion house founded in 1856, manufacturing clothing, fragrance, and fashion accessories. Its distinctive tartan（方格花纹）pattern has become one of its most widely copied trademarks.

11. **Coach**：An American leather goods company, founded in 1941, in a loft in Manhattan, New York, known for ladies' and men's handbags, as well as items such as

luggage, briefcases, wallets and other accessories (belts, shoes, scarves, umbrellas, sunglasses, key chains, etc.). Coach also offers watches and footwear.

12. **Karl Marx**: (1818 – 1883) A German philosopher, political economist, historian, political theorist, sociologist, and communist revolutionary, whose ideas played a significant role in the development of modern communism and socialism. His works include *Capital* (《资本论》), *The Communist Manifesto* (《共产党宣言》), etc.

Comprehension of the Text

Answer the following questions.

1. What did the author see the other day in the department store glass case?
2. What does the bag look like?
3. When did the trend of logo come into being?
4. What is the little Lacoste crocodile on a men's tennis shirt usually associated with?
5. What are the famous fashion houses in the world?
6. How do these world famous companies promote their products?
7. What are the distinctive features of the Hermes scarves, Coach bags and Burberry raincoats?
8. Why do these luxury manufacturers often use logos in their promotion?
9. What can be found on the 53rd and 5th in Manhattan along with the LV bags and Gucci bags?
10. What measures do these luxury companies take to fight back?
11. What does the writer mean by "the LV bag is the purest example of exchange value"?
12. Why does the writer say that he still wants a LV bag although he may put his stuff in a plastic bag?

Language Sense Enhancement

I. Read the following paragraph until you learn it by heart. Then try to complete the following passage from memory.

In my view the rise of the logo as a source of appeal (1)_____ 30 years ago in response to a new kind of consumer that (2)_____ with the investment-driven economy of the 1980s. In the past, rich people were (3)_____ to know that their things were better made (and more expensive) (4)_____ those of the ordinary people. Later these rich people were interested in (5)_____ their cars and their jewels. But in the 1980s, a new group of (6)_____ people emerged. They all had MBAs, and they wanted to show their wealth in a more (7)_____ and brief way. Hence the birth of the logo.

The (8)_____ began quietly enough, making its first appearance in menswear. The first sign can be (9)_____ to the custom-made shirt with its breast pocket that is (10)_____ with a crocodile.

II. Read the following quotations. Learn them by heart if you can.

Create your own style. Let it be unique for yourself and yet identifiable for others!

—Anna Wintour

创造你自己的风格，让其独属于你自己，并能被他人识别。——安娜·温图尔

Fashion fade—style is eternal. —Yves Saint Laurent

时尚易朽，风格永存。——伊夫·圣·洛朗

You can never be overdressed or overeducated. —Oscar Wilde

无论你如何打扮或接受多少教育都不过分。——斯卡·王尔德

Vocabulary

I. Fill in the blanks with the given words or phrases in the box. Change the form where necessary.

emerge	efficient	expression	enterprise	involve
undergo	resemble	confess	show off	hence
trend	promote	decorate	unique	luxury

1. Now the _____ is moving towards picking up a second language in the third or fourth year in elementary schools.
2. They are _____ their new sort of toothbrush on television.
3. People often _____ their house with holly at Christmas.
4. Do not miss this _____ opportunity to buy all six plates at half the price.
5. We'll never have enough money to be able to live in _____.
6. The travelers _____ many difficulties.
7. I _____ you are right on this point.
8. She only bought that sports car to _____ and prove that she could afford one.
9. The town was built on the side of a hill; _____ the name Hillside.
10. New political problems _____ every day.
11. We need someone really _____ who can organize the office and make it run smoothly.
12. Shelley's poems are famous for their beauty of _____.
13. They have the ability to manage their own _____.
14. We are all _____, whether we like it or not.

15. John _____ his father very much in a lot of ways.

II. **Choose a word or a phrase from the indicated paragraph to fill in each of the following blanks. Change the form where necessary.**

1. She's not beautiful, but I find her incredibly _____ because she seems so full of life and fun. (*Para. 1*)
2. He received a large _____ when his uncle died. (*Para. 1*)
3. The life of a policeman has no _____ to me. (*Para. 2*)
4. _____ your inquiries, we regret to inform you that we cannot help you in this matter. (*Para. 2*)
5. Every now and then a new plane would _____. (*Para. 2*)
6. No one knows when such a custom first _____. (*Para. 2*)
7. I think he is fairly _____ with his life. (*Para. 2*)
8. His fear of dogs can _____ an experience in his childhood. (*Para. 3*)
9. She _____ to force her mind to think of other questions. (*Para. 6*)
10. His disability _____ him from walking. (*Para. 7*)

Structure

I. **Rewrite the following sentences after the model.**

Model: Those aspiring to wealth can buy the Louis Vuitton key chain, wallet and handbag, but those who are wealthy enough can buy the full set of Louis Vuitton luggage.

Those aspiring to wealth can buy the Louis Vuitton key chain, wallet and handbag, **while** those who are wealthy enough can buy the full set of Louis Vuitton luggage.

1. Tom is very outgoing, but Ken is shy and quiet.
   _____

2. I spend two hours getting ready to go out but Jack is ready in ten minutes.
   _____

3. I do every single bit of housework but he just does the dishes now and then.
   _____

4. He gets thirty thousand pounds a year but I get only fifteen!
   _____

5. Some house plants thrive if placed near a window with plenty of sunlight, but others prefer to be in a more shady spot.
   _____

II. Complete the following sentences by translating the Chinese into English, using "no sooner ... than".

Model: _____(品牌标识刚一出现在商品上) than imitation logoed goods began to flood the market.
No sooner did the logo make an appearance on luxury goods than imitation logoed goods began to flood the market.

1. _____(她刚坐下) than the phone rang.
2. _____(我们刚动身) than a storm broke.
3. _____(我们刚摆脱麻烦) than down comes another.
4. _____(他刚到家) than his dog begins barking.
5. _____(我们刚安顿下来) than we were invited to a party.

Cloze

Choose one appropriate word from the following box to fill in each of the following blanks. Each word can be used only once. Change the word form where necessary.

cost	keep	wear	sell	which
from	good	into	with	recent
unusual	than	range	drop	sun

Fashion is moving into the 21st century. A coat that changes color with the weather, shirt strips which disappear while you are (1) _____ it, an odor(气味;臭味) free blouse that can be worn for days and days ... These are not sci-fi(科幻小说) fantasies, but the most (2) _____ developments in the fashion world, made possible by advances in fiber(纤维) technology.

Jackets by Stone Island change color in warm weather and (3) _____ between $400 and $500. Peter Siddell, a store buyer, says, "There's not much more designers can do (4) _____ clothes. They need to make new fabrics(织物;布) to (5) _____ fashion interesting."

Massimo Osti is the man who has brought these (6) _____ fabrics to the shops. Another Osti's invention is the sweatshirt (7) _____ has a logo on the chest which disappears when you breathe on it. Now there is a (8) _____ of temperature-sensitive leisurewear for golfers who like to practice in all weather. As golfers leave the warm clubhouse, their sweaters change (9) _____ white to a rainbow of colors.

Unika, a Japanese firm, has developed a synthetic(合成的) fiber called thermotron which changes sunlight (10) _____ thermal energy and keeps the wearer up to 10℃

warmer (11) _____ ordinary fiber. One ski-wear fabric turns black to absorb sunlight when the temperature (12) _____ to below zero, and changes to white above 5℃ to reflect the (13) _____.

Tights producers in the Far East and Europe have (14) _____ many tights which have been created with fragrances(香味) and insect repellent(驱虫剂). A department store in Britain reports (15) _____ sales for magnolia-fragranced tights. The fragrance lasts up to three hand-washes.

Translation

Translate the following sentences into Chinese.

1. The bag was made of canvas, was covered with muddy LV signs, and resembled, in shape and size, a beach bag—none of which are especially attractive attributes.

2. In my view the rise of the logo as a source of appeal took off 30 years ago in response to a new kind of consumer that came into being with the investment-driven economy of the 1980s.

3. They did this by making their goods more instantly recognizable—aggressively promoting their distinctive aspects: the funny designs on the Hermes scarf; the leather tags on the heavy Coach bag; the old-fashioned plaid of the Burberry raincoat.

4. No sooner did the logo make an appearance on luxury goods than imitation logoed goods began to flood the market.

5. You probably couldn't find a better expression of capitalistic enterprise in action than the various measures and counter measures involving logoed business, where value is continually undergoing change.

Text B The Life Cycle of a Fashion Trend

Denise Winterman

For years shoulder pads were fashion suicide. But they are back on the stages of London Fashion Week, back in the shops and back in our wardrobes. How did this happen?

1 They may have been in fashion in the 1980s, and during the 1990s they have been laughed at. But what was unimaginable just a few years ago has now happened—shoulder pads are back in the shops and back in our wardrobes, for the first or second time around. So how do we find ourselves handing over our money for a fashion that has passed for so long?

2 Be it music, food or cars, all trends have a life cycle and none more so than fashion trends. One of the first people to try and explain our changing attitude to what's hot and what's not was the highly-respected fashion historian James Laver. In 1937, he drew up a timeline of how a style was viewed over the years, which became known as Laver's Law. This states that a trend does not start to look attractive until 50 years after its time. If you wear something 10 years after it was in fashion, you look "ugly", 20 years after you look "ridiculous" and so on. Only after 50 years do things start turning towards the positive and you look "attractively odd".

3 According to Laver's Law, at present shoulder pads should still look ridiculous. But the fashion industry has changed greatly in the past years, and clothes are designed, produced and consumed in an entirely different way. Still, trends have a life cycle—it's just shortened. However, the trend can't be exactly the same second or third time around. Being refreshed is a necessary part of the cycle. No one wants a copy. Take shoulder-pads for instance, the way people see them today is different from the way previous generations did.

4 Welsh designer Emma Griffiths, 30, is just old enough to remember shoulder pads in the 1980s, but on her mother. "I personally think you have to look back to see forward," she says. "My collections were inspired by my early, most powerful memories. I remember the way my mum was dressed and how back then young girls were dressed like their mums. "I've taken shoulder pads and redefined them and put them on a new look. First of all, a few people were a bit shocked to see them again but could see I'd updated them and they worked in my designs. Women aren't stupid; they won't wear something if it doesn't look good."

5 What remains the same, however much the look has been changed, is the need to get the public thinking about the trend—and thinking about it in a new way if they've worn the style in the past. The best way of doing this is getting the right people to wear it. Actresses Joan Crawford and Audrey Hepburn did back in the day, and models Kate Moss and Agyness Deyn do it today. As a result, thousands of people follow their example and start to dress themselves in the same way.

6 That popularity leads to widespread acceptance and then we are back at the start. Boredom will follow and so on. Of course not everything comes back. The cycle ends for trends when they don't have any useful purposes. Fashion has to be relevant on some level, otherwise it won't get worn. Then it's not fashion any more.

7 Also, the once fixed style rules have changed in recent years. These rules are not so hard and fixed anymore. Shoulder pads are just one detail in clothes now, not the only feature. The rules don't exist like they did in the 1980s. People pick and choose details to build their own style. Take skirt lengths for example, nobody can say what the "fashionable" length is this season. They're all different, and you just choose what length works for you.

8 But the public simply has to feel ready for a trend, even if they don't always quite realize they are ready. If they are not, it's over before it even really started.

(695 words)

Words and Phrases to Learn

hand over 交出,移交
ridiculous /rɪˈdɪkjələs/ a. 可笑的,荒谬的
according to 根据,依照
at present 目前,现在
consume /kənˈsjuːm/ vt. 消费;花费
refresh /rɪˈfreʃ/ vt. 使更新;使振作精神,使恢复活力
inspire /ɪnˈspaɪə/ vt. 给……以灵感;鼓舞,激起
update /ʌpˈdeɪt/ vt. 更新,使现代化
follow somebody's example 仿效某人;学习某人
lead to 导致,通向
relevant /ˈreləvənt/ a. 有关的,有重大关系的
otherwise /ˈʌðəwaɪz/ ad. 否则,不然
fixed /fɪkst/ a. 固定的;确定了的
detail /ˈdiːteɪl/ n. 细节,详情
work /wɜːk/ vi. 奏效

Comprehension Check

Choose the best answer for each of the following.

1. According to the author, the shoulder pads become popular again because _____.
   A. women would like to be dressed like their mother
   B. people miss the old, good days
   C. these shoulder pads look attractive to women
   D. it's part of the cycle of the fashion trend

2. According to Laver's Law, how long does it take for an old fashion trend to look attractive?
   A. 10 years.   B. 20 years.   C. 30 years.   D. 50 years.

3. What has changed in the fashion industry during the past years?
   A. There is a different way of designing, production and consumption.
   B. There appears to be an unpredictable cycle of fashion in recent years.
   C. The new trend is totally different from the original style in recent years.
   D. The trend remains almost the same.

4. The following statements can explain the sentence "Being refreshed is a necessary part of the cycle" (Para. 3) except _____.
   A. at present shoulder pads should still look ridiculous
   B. the trend can't be exactly the same second or third time around
   C. no one wants a copy of the old trend
   D. the way people look at shoulder pads today is different from the older generation

5. What remains the same for the fashion trend despite all those changes?
   A. The way people design and consume the clothes.
   B. To get people to think about the trend in a new way.
   C. To get a few movie stars and models to wear the clothes.
   D. To ask their mothers to get dressed in the new style.

6. It can be inferred from the passage that _____.
   A. given a certain amount of time, all the old fashion trends can come back
   B. today there are some fixed rules in the fashion cycle
   C. the fashion cycle ends if there are no practical uses for it
   D. the shoulder pad is an important detail in clothes features now

Language Practice

Fill in the blanks with words or phrases listed in the *Words and Phrases to Learn*.

1. _____ Sarah they are not getting on very well at the moment.

2. I don't want to get married _____.
3. She _____ herself with a cup of tea.
4. His best music was _____ by the memory of his mother.
5. That's the trouble with those big powerful cars—they _____ too much fuel.
6. The data should be _____ once a week.
7. She insisted on telling me every single _____ of what they did to her in the hospital.
8. You'd better phone home, _____ your parents will start to worry.
9. It looks all right in theory, but it will not _____ in practice.
10. When Mr. Jones gets old, he will _____ his business to his son.
11. He has decided to _____ the example of his father and study law.
12. Ignoring safety rules _____ a tragic accident.
13. It's the most _____ thing I've ever heard in my life.
14. The film was _____ to what was being discussed in class.
15. He has a _____ pattern of behavior.

Part II Listening

Section A

Directions: In this section you will hear five short conversations. At the end of each conversation a question will be asked about what was said. Both the conversation and the question will be spoken only once. Listen carefully and choose the best answer.

1. A. Margaret wanted to return some magazines to the man.
   B. Margaret wanted to lend some magazines to the man.
   C. Margaret wanted to borrow some magazines from the man.
   D. Margaret wanted to get some magazines back from the man.
2. A. He went to work.
   B. He went to his friend's home.
   C. He went to the movies.
   D. He watched a film at home.
3. A. He will do a part-time job.
   B. He will go on a trip with the woman.
   C. He will go shopping at Wal-mart.
   D. He will visit his friends in Florida.

4. A. At a restaurant. B. At a hotel.
   C. At an airport. D. At a police station.
5. A. It's not as hard as expected.
   B. It's too tough for some students.
   C. It's much more difficult than people think.
   D. It's believed to be the hardest course.

Section B

Directions: In this section you will hear a long conversation. At the end of the conversation you will hear some questions. Both the conversation and the questions will be spoken only once. After you hear a question, you must choose the best answer.

6. A. He thinks he needs more exercise.
   B. He thinks he looks like Schwarzenegger.
   C. He thinks he is in good health.
   D. He thinks he should do more running.
7. A. Lifting weights.
   B. Running, biking and hiking.
   C. Cardiovascular exercises (心血管机能训练).
   D. Weight lifting and cardiovascular exercises.
8. A. Because she can't afford the time to go to the gym every day.
   B. Because she can't afford the membership fee.
   C. Because she has to go shopping every day.
   D. Because it's not convenient for her to go to the gym.

Section C

Directions: In this section you will hear a passage. Listen to the passage three times and fill in the missing information.

Here are four basic steps to staying warm. Think of COLD—C. O. L. D.

The C stands for cover. Wear a hat and scarf to keep (9)_____ from escaping through the head, neck and ears. And wear mittens instead of gloves. In gloves, the fingers are (10)_____, so the hands may not stay as warm.

The O stands for overexertion. Avoid (11)_____ that will make you sweaty. Wet clothes and cold weather are a bad mix.

L is for layers. Wearing (12)_____, lightweight clothes, one layer on top of another, is better than wearing a single heavy (13)_____ of clothing. Also, make sure outerwear is made of material that is water (14)_____ and tightly knit.

Can you guess what the D in COLD stands for? D is for dry. In other words, (15) _____. Pay attention to the places (16) _____, like the tops of boots, the necks of coats and the wrist areas of mittens.

And here are two other things to keep in mind, one for children and the other for adults. Eating snow might be fun but it (17) _____. And drinking alcohol might make a person feel warm. But what it really does is weaken (18) _____.

Part III Speaking

Section A

Directions: Discuss the following questions in small groups.

1. Do you want to possess one of these luxury products? Why?
2. What are the reasons behind the flood of the imitation logoed goods in the market?
3. Do you agree with the statement that the exchange values of the luxuries are separated from their use values?

Section B

Directions: Read aloud the following passage.

Have you noticed that you attract more attention when you wear a certain color compared to when you're wearing a different one? People are affected by colors. Colors can influence their mood. They can evoke emotions; and, I am drawn to bold colors like red, orange and bright yellow. They can change my mood almost instantly.

Red, for instance, is commonly used in restaurants' logos. Orange, on the other hand, is famously preferred by educators. Some corners of pre-schools are painted orange and in most probability, the activity room is painted in this color. In most American homes, for example, kitchens are painted yellow. This color is believed to induce appetite.

Colors are powerful. They, obviously, are not the only factor considered in fashion; however, knowing what to wear on various kinds of occasion sends the message—you have an exquisite fashion sense. In fact, it also qualifies you to leave a more favorable impression.

Part IV Writing

Directions: Write a composition on the topic "Changing Criteria for Judging Good Students". You should write at least 100 words, and base your composition on the outline given below:

1. Nowadays, more and more young people prefer to follow the fashion trend.
2. Different people have different views.
3. In my opinion ...

UNIT 6

Shopping

Part I Reading

> Text A

In Praise of Shopping[1]

Paula Marantz Cohen[2]

1 To praise shopping is to lift the last ban of academic culture. It's fine to admit to a taste for excessive drinking or a minor drug habit. Such things can qualify as "fashionable" in intellectual circles. But a willingness to spend an afternoon at the mall? Forget about it.

2 My intention is to make a change on this sort of thinking. Shopping is shopping. There are treasures at a reduced price to be found in the shopping malls of New Jersey, and small charming items mixed with conventional housewares in Pier One Imports[3]. If you want something with local features, you'll see as much in the dressing rooms of Loehmann's[4] as on the beaches of St. Tropez[5].

3 To go shopping is not necessarily to spend money, though a willingness to spend must be present to some degree. Window shopping is a contradiction in terms[6], an indirect phrase for "I hope I don't buy anything." The basic difference between going shopping and going to a museum is that, in a shop, one doesn't have to just look. Similarly, there is a difference between shopping for something and "going shopping". To shop for a pair of lime green[7] shoes to match your lime green dress is to accomplish a task. To "go shopping" is to be open to unexpected discoveries—to be an eager wanderer with a credit card.

4 Shopping has long been associated with middle-class women. The 19th century saw the development of the arcade, the first shopping mall, a covered street of shops where women could shop in a safe and pleasant setting. Soon the sociologist Thorstein Veblen[8] had coined the

term "conspicuous consumption"⁹, which gave shopping a bad name, associating it with bourgeois women with too much time on their hands.

5   Although I hope to touch on many kinds of shopping in this article, clothes shopping seems to me to be the purest example. Most people, by the time they reach their mid-twenties, have all the clothes they need, with the exception of wear and tear and weight gain. Yet individuals on relatively modest incomes spend thousands of dollars on clothes each year. This is because the things which we put on are the most concrete forms of personal expression we have. To shop for clothes is to engage in a material search for the self—for its expression and potential revision in one's culture. A character in Henry James¹⁰ *The Portrait of a Lady*¹¹ states this well: "What shall we call our 'self'? Where does it begin? Where does it end? It overflows into everything that belongs to us and flows back again. I know a large part of myself is in the clothes I choose to wear."

6   Clothes shopping appeals more to women than to men. This may be because for women it is something passed down through generations and shared through sisterhood. I learned to shop from my mother, who learned from her mother, a Russian immigrant, who began going to wholesale outlets on the lower East Side of Manhattan almost as soon as she settled in America. What did I learn from these women? I learned how to find the nicest blouse on the rack in less than two minutes, and how to look at a pair of shoes and know whether they'll hurt as soon as I walk a block. In department store dressing rooms, other women feel free to help me decide whether the skirt I'm trying on is too tight. In a word, we learn these things through the female line¹², and shopping qualifies as a folk art and culture.

7   To understand culture one must live among its things—acquire them, get rid of them, and acquire them again in an endless cycle of both adopting and rejecting conventional items and tastes. Shopping is a quest. It is never over until we're over. The knights didn't kill the dragon once and be done with it. They went out to find another dragon. And I can always use another pair of shoes.

(674 words)

New Words

lift /lɪft/ *vt.* 撤销(命令)
ban /bæn/ *n.* 禁止；禁令
academic /ˌækəˈdemɪk/ *a.* 传统的,拘泥刻板的；学术的
taste /teɪst/ *n.* 爱好,兴趣

* 黑体表示重点词汇和短语,白体表示一般词汇和短语

excessive /ɪkˈsesɪv/ *a.* 过多的；过分的
minor /ˈmaɪnə/ *a.* 较少的；较次要的
intellectual /ˌɪntəˈlektʃuəl/ *n.* 知识分子
circle /ˈsɜːkl/ *n.* （具有共同兴趣、利益的人们形成的）圈子
willingness /ˈwɪlɪŋnɪs/ *n.* 情愿，乐意，自愿
treasure /ˈtreʒə/ *n.* 财富，珍宝
charming /ˈtʃɑːmɪŋ/ *a.* 迷人的；可爱的
item /ˈaɪtəm/ *n.* 条，项；注意或关心的对象
conventional /kənˈvenʃənl/ *a.* 惯例的；常规的
houseware /ˈhauswer/ *n.* 家用器皿
local /ˈləʊkl/ *a.* 地方（性）的；当地的
contradiction /ˌkɒntrəˈdɪkʃn/ *n.* 矛盾
term /tɜːm/ *n.* 词语；名称
similarly /ˈsɪmɪləli/ *ad.* 相似地，类似地
lime /laɪm/ *n.* 酸橙树；酸橙
match /mætʃ/ *vt.* 和……相配；和……相称
accomplish /əˈkɒmplɪʃ/ *vt.* 完成（任务等）；达到（目的）
arcade /ɑːˈkeɪd/ *n.* 有拱顶的走道（两旁常设商店）
sociologist /ˌsəʊsɪˈɒlədʒɪst/ *n.* 社会学家
coin /kɔɪn/ *vt.* 创造；杜撰（新词语等）
conspicuous /kənˈspɪkjuəs/ *a.* 明显的，显著的
consumption /kənˈsʌmpʃn/ *n.* 消费
bourgeois /ˈbʊəʒwɑː/ *a.* 资产阶级的
individual /ˌɪndɪˈvɪdʒuəl/ *n.* 个人
relatively /ˈrelətɪvli/ *ad.* 相对地；比较而言
modest /ˈmɒdɪst/ *a.* 适中的；适度的
income /ˈɪnkʌm/ *n.* 收入；收益
concrete /ˈkɒnkriːt/ *a.* 具体的；有形的
material /məˈtɪəriəl/ *a.* 物质的，实体的
potential /pəˈtenʃl/ *a.* 潜在的；可能的
revision /rɪˈvɪʒn/ *n.* 修订；修改
character /ˈkærɪktə/ *n.* 人物，角色
state /steɪt/ *vt.* 陈述
overflow /ˌəʊvəˈfləʊ/ *vt.* 多得使……无法容纳；从……中溢出
sisterhood /ˈsɪstəhʊd/ *n.* 姐妹关系；姐妹情谊
immigrant /ˈɪmɪɡrənt/ *n.* 移民
wholesale /ˈhəʊlseɪl/ *a.* 批发的

outlet /ˈaʊtlet/ n. 经销店
settle /ˈsetl/ vi. 安顿下来
blouse /blaʊz/ n. 女衬衫；宽大短外套
rack /ræk/ n. 货架
female /ˈfiːmeɪl/ a. 女性的；妇女的
acquire /əˈkwaɪə/ vt. 取得，获得
adopt /əˈdɒpt/ vt. 采用，采纳
quest /kwest/ n. （长时间的）寻找；追求
knight /naɪt/ n. （欧洲中世纪的）骑士，武士
dragon /ˈdrægən/ n. 龙

Phrases and Expressions

admit to　承认；供认（事实、错误等）
qualify as　具备合格条件；把……归做
dressing room　化妆室；（运动场等的）更衣室；梳妆室
to some degree　有点，稍微；从某种程度上来说
credit card　信用卡
associate ... with　（在思想上）把……和……联系在一起
touch on　谈到，论及
with the exception of　除……之外
wear and tear　磨损
weight gain　体重增加
engage in　从事，参加
appeal to　吸引
pass down　传递，传下来
in a word　总之，简言之
folk art　民间艺术
get rid of　摆脱，除去，处理掉
be done with　结束

Proper Names

Paula Marantz Cohen /ˈpɔːlə mərænts ˈkəʊən/ 葆拉·马兰士·科恩
Thorstein Veblen /ˈtɔːsteɪn ˈveblən/ 托尔斯坦·凡勃伦
Henry James /ˈhenri dʒeɪmz/ 亨利·詹姆斯
lower East Side of Manhattan （纽约）曼哈顿区下东区

Notes on the Text

1. This article is published in May, 2010 in *English Language Learning*. The present text is slightly adapted and abridged.

2. **Paula Marantz Cohen**: A distinguished Professor of English at Drexel University where she teaches courses in literature, film and creative writing.

3. **Pier One Imports**: A Fort Worth, Texas-based retailer specializing in imported home furnishings and decor, particularly furniture, table-top items, decorative accessories and seasonal decor. (美国一家专营装饰品和礼品的零售店) The chain operates over 1,000 stores under the name **Pier 1 Imports** in the United States, Canada, Mexico and Puerto Rico.

4. **Loehmann's**: A chain of off-price department stores in the United States. Loehmann's is best known for its "Back Room", where women interested in fashion can find designer clothes at prices lower than in department or specialty stores. In recent years, Loehmann's has expanded its offerings to include shoes, accessories, and men's products. (美国一家大型服装折扣店)

5. **St. Tropez**: A town 104km to the east of Marseille, in the Var department of the Provence-Alpes-Côte d'Azur region of southeastern France. It is also the principal(主要的)town in the canton(行政区) of St. Tropez. It is located on the French Riviera, and it is known today for its famous and extremely wealthy summertime guests. (圣特罗佩斯,法国度假胜地,位于地中海沿岸)

6. **contradiction in terms**: A combination of words whose meanings are in conflict with one another. (自相矛盾的说法)

7. **lime green**: Also known as lime or lime-green, is a color three-fourths of the way between yellow and green (closer to yellow than to green), so named because it is a representation of the color of the citrus fruit(柑橘类的水果)called limes.

8. **Thorstein Veblen**: (1857 – 1929) A Norwegian-American sociologist and economist and a primary mentor, along with John R., Commons, of the institutional economics movement. Besides his technical work he was a popular and witty critic of capitalism, as shown by his best known book *The Theory of the Leisure Class* (1899).

> 9. **conspicuous consumption**: 炫耀性消费,挥霍
> 10. **Henry James**: (1843 – 1916) An American-born writer, regarded as one of the key figures of 19th-century literary realism. James spent the last 40 years of his life in England, becoming a British subject in 1915, one year before his death. He is primarily known for the series of novels in which he portrays the encounter of Americans with Europe and Europeans.
> 11. ***The Portrait of a Lady***: A novel written by Henry James.
> 12. **female line**: 母系,女性

Comprehension of the Text

Answer the following questions.

1. According to the author, what's the public view on praising shopping?
2. What does the author intend to change?
3. What does "window shopping" mean?
4. How is shopping for something different from going shopping?
5. Why is clothes shopping the best example among many kinds of shopping?
6. Why do people with little income still spend a lot of money on clothes?
7. Who seem to like clothes shopping more, men or women?
8. Why does clothes shopping appeal more to women?
9. What does the author learn from those women in shopping?
10. Is shopping part of the culture we are living in?
11. How does one understand a culture better?
12. According to the author, is there an end to shopping?

Language Sense Enhancement

I. **Read the following paragraph until you learn it by heart. Then try to complete the passage from memory.**

Although I hope to (1) _____ many kinds of shopping in this article, clothes shopping seems to me to be the purest example. Most people, by the time they (2) _____ their mid-twenties, have all the clothes they need, with the (3) _____ of wear and tear and weight gain. Yet individuals on relatively (4) _____ incomes spend thousands of dollars on clothes each year. This is because the things which we (5) _____ are the most concrete forms of (6) _____ expression we have. To shop for clothes is to (7) _____ a material search for the self—for its expression and

(8) _____ revision in one's culture. A (9) _____ in Henry James *The Portrait of a Lady* states this well: "What shall we call our 'self'? Where does it begin? Where does it end? It overflows into everything that (10) _____ us and flows back again. I know a large part of myself is in the clothes I choose to wear."

II. Read the following quotations. Learn them by heart if you can.

The quickest way to know a woman is to go shopping with her.
—Marcelene Cox
了解一个女人最快的方法就是和她一起去逛街。 ——玛瑟琳·考克斯
Whoever said money can't buy happiness simply didn't know where to go shopping.
—Bo Derek
那些说金钱无法买到快乐的人,只是不知道该上哪买东西。 ——波·德瑞克
Too many people spend money they haven't earned, to buy things they don't want, to impress people they don't like. —Will Smith
太多人花费他们还没挣到的钱,去买他们不需要的东西,来取悦他们不喜欢的人。
——威尔·斯密斯

Vocabulary

I. Fill in the blanks with the given words or phrases in the box. Change the form where necessary.

excessive	get rid of	charming	engage in	material
potential	minor	with the exception of	acquire	adopt
consumption	accomplish	modest	income	touch on

1. People on fixed _____ are hurt by price increases.
2. His report did not _____ the issue.
3. An _____ dosage (剂量) of this drug can result in injury to the liver.
4. Let's _____ this old furniture.
5. He left most of his money to his sons; his daughter only received a _____ share of his wealth.
6. _____ Harry, all the boys were anxious to go.
7. Her colorful character makes her very _____.
8. I have no time to _____ gossip (闲聊).
9. A warm house and good food are _____ comforts.
10. She was the first to realize the _____ danger of their situation.
11. The collector has _____ a fine collection of impressionist paintings (印象派绘画).

12. After careful consideration, the president decided to _____ her suggestion.
13. We need to cut down on our fuel _____ by having fewer cars on the road.
14. The students _____ the task in less than ten minutes.
15. Prices tended to rise year by year, but at a _____ rate.

II. Choose a word or a phrase from the indicated paragraph to fill in each of the following blanks. Change the form where necessary.

1. George would never _____ being wrong. (*Para. 1*)
2. It takes six years to _____ a doctor. (*Para. 1*)
3. I suggest that he put an advertisement in the _____ paper. (*Para. 2*)
4. He can be trusted _____. (*Para. 3*)
5. They tried to assure him of their _____ to work. (*Para. 3*)
6. Your tie should _____ your shirt. (*Para. 3*)
7. In the children's minds summer _____ picnics. (*Para. 4*)
8. He _____ in the country after his retirement. (*Para. 6*)
9. The skill has _____ over four generations. (*Para. 6*)
10. The _____ for gold was long and difficult. (*Para. 7*)

Structure

I. Rewrite the following sentences after the model.

Model: This may be because for women it is something that is passed down through generations and shared through sisterhood.

This may be because for women it is something **passed down** through generations and shared through sisterhood.

1. You have to pay duties on goods that are imported from abroad.

2. Is there anything that has been planned for tonight?

3. Most people who had been invited to the party were old friends.

4. I hate to see letters that are written in pencil.

5. The firm's latest product, which was launched only six months ago, has already taken up a significant share of the market.

Unit 6 Shopping

II. Complete the following sentences by translating the Chinese into English, using "as ... as".

Model: If you want something with local features, you'll see _____
_____ (Loehmann's 试衣间里带有地方特色的商品和圣特佩罗斯海滩上的一样多).

If you want something with local features, you'll see <u>as much in the dressing rooms of Loehmann's as on the beaches of St. Tropez</u>.

1. There is _____ (这个瓶子里装的水与那个瓶子里的一样多).
2. I'm _____ (做菜的手艺没有她好).
3. The village gardens are _____ (和过去一样好).
4. It's _____ (这里的天气和罗马一样暖和).
5. Buildings here are _____ (这里的建筑不如别处的高).

Cloze

Choose one appropriate word from the following box to fill in each of the following blanks. Each word can be used only once. Change the word form where necessary.

or	problem	everything	enjoy	like
power	while	addiction	specific	sad
hook	that	better	forget	after

Shopaholics (购物狂), also called compulsive spenders, are like any addicted person who is hooked on something. They are (1) _____ on shopping. They really like shopping and usually buy things (2) _____ they don't need. Even though they don't have enough money, they buy (3) _____ they want.

The question is: why do they have this (4) _____? There isn't a (5) _____ answer. Some people go shopping when they are (6) _____, worried, upset or lonely and they want to feel (7) _____. They use this activity as a way to (8) _____ their problems. Shopaholics say that they feel more important and better (9) _____ they buy something.

We are used to thinking that women (10) _____ shopping more than men; but according to some studies, that's not true. Men really (11) _____ shopping because they feel they have (12) _____ and control. Also, men usually buy big items (13) _____ women spend their money on clothes, cosmetics, decorations for their houses, (14) _____ things for family.

Shopaholism (购物癖) seems to be a harmless addiction, but the fact is it can cause many (15) _____.

Translation

Translate the following sentences into Chinese.

1. To go shopping is not necessarily to spend money, though a willingness to spend must be present to some degree.

2. Window shopping is a contradiction in terms, an indirect phrase for "I hope I don't buy anything".

3. Although I hope to touch on many kinds of shopping in this article, clothes shopping seems to me to be the purest example.

4. Most people, by the time they reach their mid-twenties, have all the clothes they need, with the exception of wear and tear and weight gain.

5. To understand culture one must live among its things—acquire them, get rid of them, and acquire them again in an endless cycle of both adopting and rejecting conventional items and tastes.

Text B Shopping Can Be Fun—Honest!

Karmen Kooyers

1 The girls' night adventure usually begins with a simple trip to the shopping mall. I usually resist shopping. I do not wander and look around in stores. My mode of operation is continual forward movement—I snatch what I need, check out and escape.

2 On this particular weekend, however, we were visiting relatives in Ohio over the holidays. We had spent a relaxing day wandering around and playing games. After supper, I mentioned that I needed a new jacket. My niece said she knew of a department store in the mall having a great sale.

3 "Let's go," I said suddenly without thinking, to the surprise of everyone around me. My plan for this trip was to walk into the store, select a great jacket at an irresistible price, check out and depart. It would take a half hour at the most.

4 Then we—my sister-in-law, niece, two daughters, and I—arrived at the department store, with its wide aisles spreading in all directions, each aisle overflowing with clothing and other goods at a reduced price.

5 I suspected that my usual method of speed shopping would not work. My suspicion was confirmed when my companions spread out in four different directions and began searching through the clothing racks. I realized I was stuck there for a while.

6 After searching through jackets and not finding the bargain I had expected, I walked around in the aisles, looking for my family. I found my sister-in-law in a dressing room, talking with her teenage daughter, who declared that the jeans her mom had chosen to try on were "boring".

7 "At my age, this is what I can wear," my sister-in-law said. Her daughter disagreed and hurried off to select some alternatives.

8 This I have to see, I thought. My niece soon returned with flowery skirts, wide blouses and jeans dotted with jewels.

9 "I can't wear those!" My sister-in-law cried.

10 "Yes, you can, Mom! Try them on," her daughter urged.

11 My sister-in-law rolled her eyes and threw me a "get me out of this" look.

12 "Come on," I made fun of her. "Try them on." I was eager to see her in something so out of character. Unwillingly, she tried on the clothes.

13 "You look so cute," her daughter cheered her on. I agreed. This mother of six children was a vision of sparkles and color. She laughed and assured us these clothes were not her style.

14 "But they could be," I said, "You look great."

15 My niece dashed away and soon returned with something for me to try, a bright skirt and a black blouse with a soft boa collar.

16 "Oh, no," I said. I would never wear something like that.

17 "Oh, yes," my sister-in-law said, "Great."

18 I took my courage and tried them on. I hardly dared look in the mirror.

19 "It's great! You look cute!" My niece said.

20 Well. No one had called me "cute" in quite some time. Maybe not since I was a teenager.

21 I stared at the mirror. Who was this woman with the soft boa collar turning without a care around her neck? Not quite me, but I was attracted by the complete change of my appearance.

22 My niece showed more choices in front of my sister-in-law and me, and we tried on the crazy combinations, laughing at ourselves, excited that we actually fitted into the pieces.

23 In the end, most of the clothes went back on the racks. My sister-in-law bought the "boring" jeans. But we each also selected one "very unusual for us" item.

24 We may be middle-aged women, but we still have sparks of daring within us. We still know how to act on impulse. And we still find being called "cute" simply irresistible.

(653 words)

Words and Phrases to Learn

attract /əˈtrækt/ vt.　吸引,引起……的注意
mention /ˈmenʃn/ vt.　提及,说起
know of　知道……情况
to somebody's surprise　令某人惊讶的是
depart /dɪˈpɑːt/ vi.　离开,出发
suspect /səˈspekt/ vt.　推测;怀疑
confirm /kənˈfɜːm/ vt.　证实,肯定
spread out　(人群等)散开;伸展,延伸
bargain /ˈbɑːgɪn/ n.　廉价货
alternative /ɔːlˈtɜːnətɪv/ n.　两者挑一;取舍
urge /ɜːdʒ/ vt.　力劝;鼓励
make fun of　开玩笑
assure /əˈʃʊə/ vt.　使确信,使放心
fit into　合身,合适
resist /rɪˈzɪst/ vt.　抵制,抗拒

Comprehension Check

Choose the best answer for each of the following questions.

1. What did the author propose to do while speaking to her relatives on the holiday weekend?
   A. Wander about in the neighborhood.
   B. Play games.
   C. Spend a relaxing holiday.
   D. Buy a new jacket.

2. We can infer from the passage that the author's usual attitude towards shopping is _____.
   A. enthusiastic   B. indifferent
   C. resentful   D. resistant

3. What did the author plan to do in the department store?
   A. Just buy what she needs in a short time.
   B. Take a close look at those bargains on the holiday.
   C. Select a great jacket whatever the price.
   D. Spend the whole night in the store.

4. The author's niece brought them some flowery skirts and wide blouses because _____.

A. she wanted to make fun of them

B. she thought they would look great in these clothes

C. she thought that they should change their style

D. she would like to encourage them to try on something boring

5. When the author looked into the mirror, she _____.

   A. didn't like the way she was dressed

   B. wanted to get out of the store as soon as possible

   C. was attracted by the complete change of her appearance

   D. became a teenager like her niece

6. It can be inferred from the passage that _____.

   A. The author's sister-in-law and the author will not wear those unusual clothes

   B. The author's niece seems to know of all the stores with a great sale

   C. girls' night adventure usually begins with a simple trip to the shopping mall

   D. love for beauty exists in all age groups

Language Practice

Fill in the blanks with words or phrases listed in the *Words and Phrases to Learn*.

1. _____ the door was unlocked.
2. I can _____ you of my full support for your plan.
3. I have no reason to _____ her honesty.
4. If you _____ someone, you laugh at them unkindly or you cause others to laugh at them.
5. He _____ the picture into the frame.
6. She found it difficult to _____ his charms.
7. The latest information _____ my belief that he is to blame.
8. They _____ when they entered the field and began to search the ground.
9. I _____ you all to take the time to read at least three novels on the list.
10. I bought a coat for only $5 at the sales; it was a real _____.
11. I'm afraid I have no _____ but to ask you to leave.
12. Lanny _____ that he had a Van Gogh (凡·高的作品) in the dining-room.
13. He said that he _____ a hotel that might suit them.
14. Before you _____, let me give you a piece of advice.
15. The local government is trying to _____ high-tech companies to the area.

Part II Listening

Section A

Directions: In this section you will hear five short conversations. At the end of each conversation a question will be asked about what was said. Both the conversation and the question will be spoken only once. Listen carefully and choose the best answer.

1. A. They make the film even more romantic.
   B. They are different from those of other films.
   C. They are not good by present standard.
   D. They are really very good.
2. A. Basketball.   B. Football.
   C. Tennis.   D. Swimming.
3. A. He encourages the woman to do shopping at Harrods.
   B. Harrods sometimes sells luxury goods at discount prices.
   C. Not everyone can afford to do shopping at Harrods.
   D. People can always find good bargains at Harrods.
4. A. He has got a heart attack.
   B. He was unharmed.
   C. He was badly hurt.
   D. He has recovered from the shock.
5. A. To attend a party at a classmate's home.
   B. To do homework with her classmate.
   C. To attend an evening class.
   D. To have supper out with her classmate.

Section B

Directions: In this section you will hear a long conversation. At the end of the conversation you will hear some questions. Both the conversation and the questions will be spoken only once. After you hear a question, you must choose the best answer.

6. A. He loves hip hop but he hates pop music.
   B. Pop music is the last thing he will listen to.
   C. He listens to nothing but hip hop.
   D. Hip hop is his favorite music.

7. A. She was influenced by her friends.
   B. She often hears it on the radio.
   C. She often listens to pop music CDs.
   D. She loves those pop stars.
8. A. They have ended their partnership.
   B. They have stopped selling their CDs.
   C. They were great artists.
   D. They were very popular.

Section C

Directions: In this section you are going to hear a passage. Listen to the passage three times and fill in the missing information.

The world's most famous footballer, David Beckham, is leaving his club, Real Madrid, to sign for the American side, LA Galaxy.

Why has the (9)_____ England captain decided to leave the most high-profile club in the world to play in a country where football isn't popular? Beckham says he likes the (10)_____ of playing football in the USA and wants to build a bridge between America and the rest of the sporting world by making football a major sport. He's already set up a soccer academy for children in Los Angeles to help (11)_____ the game.

Some people think that David Beckham decided to move because he's been unhappy at Real Madrid. He hasn't won any (12)_____ trophies during his four-year service there and he seems to have fallen out of (13)_____ with the manager, Fabio Capello: Beckham has spent most of the season on the bench.

But Beckham has no (14)_____ about his time in Madrid. He said that playing with people like Zinedine Zidane, from France, and Ronaldo, from Brazil, has been (15)_____.

David Beckham's already played for (16)_____ in the world: Manchester United and Real Madrid. He's been captain of England and now he could become (17)_____. If he manages to conquer America then, some say, he'll be (18)_____ since the Beatles.

Part III Speaking

Section A

Directions: Discuss the following questions in small groups.

1. Do you like shopping? Why do you shop?
2. Do you agree that the clothes we put on are different forms of personal expression?

3. What are the other things in a culture other than shopping that can help us understand that culture better?

Section B

Directions: Read aloud the following passage.

I saw a lady in the subway station today. She was quarreling with the security guard, because she was not willing to put her handbag into the security inspector. "It's expensive!" she shouted, "The machine's gonna scratch it!" I noticed the logo on that handbag when I passed by. Yeah, it was of a luxury brand and looked quite new. And judging from the lady's reaction, I guess it's authentic. But if you check out the lady's other items and her behavior, it's not so difficult to see that her income may not be very high. So it's highly probable that the handbag really cost her a fortune, maybe the money she saved from her every meal. And apparently it was also costing her this precious commuting time and at the same time her good mood.

"Sad." I thought. My mother once told me, "Never buy anything that you can't really afford to use." It's not only about money. It's about everything that you give up for it. I'm totally happy with my handbag that I bought online. It's not expensive. It's not of any luxury brand. But it's of great quality and designed in just the way I like it. That's enough.

When you buy things to use, you own the things. When you buy things to worship, they own you. And I don't want to pay to be a slave.

Part IV Writing

Directions: Write a composition on the topic "Online Shopping". You should write at least 100 words, and base your composition on the outline given below.

1. Nowadays an increasing number of people are fond of purchasing goods online.
2. Different people have different ways of shopping.
3. In my opinion ...

UNIT 7

Job & Occupation

Part I Reading

Text A   Nursing[1]

John McLane

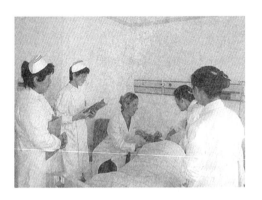

1   To most Americans nurses are creatures that exist in hospitals and doctors' offices, or take care of those in assisted living facilities or nursing homes[2]. While it is true that the majority of those working in the field are found in these places, and thus are concentrated in the larger towns and cities, a nurse can find work nearly anywhere, particularly in this time of massive nursing shortages.

2   As demand increases for the small pool of practicing nurses, prospective employees are finding that higher wages and greater flexibility in scheduling are normal. Once you have your certification, you can create your own position to a degree rarely found in the service sector, and you can do so while practicing skills that are greatly useful to yourself, your loved ones, and your entire community.

3   Each state in America has its own Board of Nursing[3] which sets the exact policies for local education and licensing. While most states do not recognize each other's nursing licenses yet, a degree or diploma from an accredited nursing school is accepted anywhere in the country. Generally, there are two levels of nursing licensure, the Licensed Practical Nurse (LPN)[4] or Licensed Vocational Nurse (LVN)[5], and the Registered Nurse (RN)[6].

4   The LPN/LVN licensure usually requires about a year of course work, with these programs frequently offered through junior colleges, community colleges, or vocational schools[7]. This level

of nurse is frequently employed in large facilities such as hospitals and nursing homes, though they may also be found in small doctors' offices or in some home health situations. The LPN/LVN is a skilled provider, but has limits placed on their scope of practice and thus generally has a lower salary than the RN. However, LVN/LPNs are in demand, and many nurses are either content to practice at this level or use it as a launching pad[8] to RN licensure.

5 The RN is what is most commonly thought of when people speak of nurses. Traditionally, many RNs were trained in programs run by hospitals, these being three years in length and known as diploma programs. Diploma programs have been largely replaced with college-based schools of nursing which offer either a two-year Associates Degree[8] (ADN) or a four-year Bachelors Degree[9] (usually BS or BSN). Both types of degree enable students to take the licensure exam known as the National Council Licensure Examination[10] (NCLEX). Upon passing this exam, students are able to obtain a license to practice as an RN.

6 If your area has no hospital or nursing homes nearby, never fear. The range of alternative jobs is great. Schools frequently need a part-time nurse for the students, and local knowledge is always a plus. Local doctors will need help in their offices. Home care services provide nursing care to patients who need it but can not stay in the hospital indefinitely. These services offer perhaps the greatest flexibility, with you choosing your patient load and arranging visit times around your schedule.

7 Local and State government employ rural Public Health Nurses who help educate, track and treat disease, and serve as local resources to the community. Many businesses employ nurses to treat their staff. Insurance companies use nurses to review cases, often at home over the Internet.

8 With another couple of years of education leading to a Nurse Practitioner[11] or Nurse Midwife[12] degree, you can establish your own practice in some states. Best of all, all of these roles put you in direct contact with your neighbors and community in a role that is appreciated and admired.

9 Nursing school is a large investment of time and money, but the return is immense. Nursing teaches you skills that you will use to others' benefits for as long as you live, and that will make you a valuable, contributing member of your family, church, community, and nation. Nursing allows for good pay and flexibility within your job, and a great sense of job security. After all, no matter how bad or good things get, people will always need help, and people will always need nurses.

(682 words)

New Words

creature /ˈkriːtʃə/ n. 人；动物；生物
assist /əˈsɪst/ vt. 援助，帮助
facility /fəˈsɪləti/ n. 设施，设备；场所
concentrate /ˈkɒnsəntreɪt/ vt. 集中；集结
massive /ˈmæsɪv/ a. 可观的；巨大的
shortage /ˈʃɔːtɪdʒ/ n. 缺乏；不足
demand /dɪˈmɑːnd/ n. 需要；需求
pool /puːl/ n. 集中使用的物资、服务等
prospective /prəsˈpektɪv/ a. 将来的；预期的
flexibility /ˌfleksəˈbɪləti/ n. 机动性；灵活性
schedule /ˈʃedjuːl/ vt. 排定；安排
certification /ˌsɜːtɪfɪˈkeɪʃn/ n. 证书；证明
degree /dɪˈɡriː/ n. 程度
rarely /ˈreəli/ ad. 很少；难得
sector /ˈsektə/ n. 部门
community /kəˈmjuːnəti/ n. 社区；社区居民
set /set/ vt. 制定（规则等）；决定
policy /ˈpɒləsi/ n. 政策；方针
license /ˈlaɪsəns/ vt. 发许可证给
                 n. 许可证
recognize /ˈrekəɡnaɪz/ vt. （正式）承认
diploma /dɪˈpləʊmə/ n. 文凭
accredited /əˈkredɪtɪd/ a. 官方认可的；公认的
level /ˈlevl/ n. 级别；层次
licensure /laɪˈsenʃə/ n. 许可证的颁发
vocational /vəʊˈkeɪʃənl/ a. 职业的
registered /ˈredʒɪstəd/ a. 注册的；登记过的
program /ˈprəʊɡræm/ n. 课程；教学大纲
frequently /ˈfriːkwəntli/ ad. 时常；经常地
provider /prəˈvaɪdə/ n. 供给者
scope /skəʊp/ n. 范围
content /kənˈtent/ a. 满足的；满意的
launch /lɔːntʃ/ vt. 发射；发动

---

* 黑体表示重点词汇和短语，白体表示一般词汇和短语

pad /pæd/ *n.* 衬垫
commonly /ˈkɒmənli/ *ad.* 通常地
train /treɪn/ *vt.* 训练；培养
length /leŋθ/ *n.* 长度
enable /ɪˈneɪbl/ *vt.* 使……能够；使……成为可能
obtain /əbˈteɪn/ *vt.* 获得；达到
practice /ˈpræktɪs/ *vi.* （医生、律师等）开业，从事职业
range /reɪndʒ/ *n.* 范围；行列
alternative /ɔːlˈtɜːnətɪv/ *a.* 可供选择的
plus /plʌs/ *n.* 有利的事情；好处
indefinitely /ɪnˈdefɪnətli/ *ad.* 无限期地
load /ləʊd/ *n.* 工作量
arrange /əˈreɪndʒ/ *vt.* 安排
track /træk/ *vt.* 跟踪；追踪
treat /triːt/ *vt.* 治疗
resource /rɪˈsɔːs/ *n.* [常作~s]资源
staff /stɑːf/ *n.* 全体员工
insurance /ɪnˈʃʊərəns/ *n.* 保险
review /rɪˈvjuː/ *vt.* 复审；再检查
couple /ˈkʌpl/ *n.* （一）对；数个
establish /ɪˈstæblɪʃ/ *vt.* 设立；建立
contact /ˈkɒntækt/ *n.* 接触；联络
appreciate /əˈpriːʃieɪt/ *vt.* 感激；欣赏
admire /ədˈmaɪə/ *vt.* 赞美；钦佩；喜欢，爱慕
investment /ɪnˈvestmənt/ *n.* 投资；投资的对象
return /rɪˈtɜːn/ *n.* 收益
immense /ɪˈmens/ *a.* 巨大的；广大的
valuable /ˈvæljuəbl/ *a.* 有价值的，宝贵的
contributing /ˈkɒntrɪbjuːtɪŋ/ *a.* 贡献的；起作用的
security /sɪˈkjʊərəti/ *n.* 安全；保证

Phrases and Expressions

in demand 有需要；销路好
think of 想起
be known as 被称为
best of all 最好的
allow for 考虑到；顾及
after all 毕竟

Proper Names

John McLane /ˈdʒɒn məˈkleɪn/ 约翰·麦克雷恩

Notes on the Text

1. The text is adapted from "*Nursing: A Perfect Backwoods Career*" on http://www.backwoodshome.com.
2. **assisted living facilities or nursing homes**：辅助生活护理院或疗养院
3. **Board of Nursing**：护士局
4. **Licensed Practical Nurse（LPN）**：领照实习护士
5. **Licensed Vocational Nurse（LVN）**：领照职业护士
6. **Registered Nurse（RN）**：注册护士
7. **junior colleges, community colleges, or vocational schools**：初级学院、社区学院或职业院校
8. **launching pad**：（导弹、火箭等的）发射台；起点；跳板
8. **Associates Degree**：副学士学位
9. **Bachelors Degree**：学士学位
10. **National Council Licensure Examination**：全国联合委员会注册护士执照考试
11. **Nurse Practitioner**：执业护士、护师
12. **Nurse Midwife**：接生护士

Comprehension of the Text

Answer the following questions.

1. What is most Americans' idea of nurses?

2. What can a nurse do when he/she has his/her certification according to the author?
3. In America, who sets the exact policies for local nursing education and licensing?
4. Do states in America recognize each other's nursing licenses?
5. How many levels of nursing licensure are there generally? What are they?
6. What is the difference between LPN/LVN and RN?
7. How can students in college-based schools of nursing become registered nurses?
8. Where else can nurses find jobs besides hospitals or nursing homes according to the author?
9. How can a nurse establish his/her own practice in some states in America?
10. What does the author think of the roles of nurses who contact their neighbors and community directly?
11. What does the author think of nursing school?
12. Why does the author think that a nurse is a valuable, contributing member of a family, church, community and nation?

Language Sense Enhancement

I. **Read the following paragraph until you learn it by heart. Then try to complete the passage from memory.**

Nursing school is a large (1)_____ of time and money, but the (2)_____ is immense. Nursing teaches you (3)_____ that you will use to others' benefits for (4)_____ you live, and that will make you a (5)_____, contributing member of your family, church, community, and nation. Nursing allows for good (6)_____ and (7)_____ within your job and a great sense of job (8)_____. After all, no matter how bad (9)_____ good things get, people will always need help, and people will always need (10)_____.

II. **Read the following quotations. Learn them by heart if you can.**

Pleasure in the job puts perfection in the work.　　　　　　—Aristotle
工作中的快乐使工作变得完美。　　　　　　　　　　　　——亚里士多德
If you do what you love, you'll never work a day in your life.　—Marc Anthony
如果你喜欢你所做的事,你就会一天都不觉得自己在工作。　——马克·安东尼
The end crowns the work.　　　　　　　　　　　　　　　—Shakespeare
最后的结果决定了工作的成败。　　　　　　　　　　　　——莎士比亚

Vocabulary

I. Fill in the blanks with the given words or phrases in the box. Change the form where necessary.

facility	obtain	appreciate	content	recognize
establish	demand	train	concentrate	schedule
treat	be known as	enable	policy	arrange

1. The library has _____ for the disabled.
2. There's an increased _____ for organic produce these days.
3. Many voters are displeased with the government's _____.
4. Power is largely _____ in the hands of a small elite.
5. The train is _____ to arrive at 8:45, but it's running 20 minutes late.
6. The company _____ a close working relationship with a similar firm in France.
7. He _____ his position with the help of friends.
8. She spent a few years _____ teachers to use new technology.
9. I will never be _____ with my performance.
10. The international community has refused to _____ the newly independent nation state.
11. These drugs were frequently used to _____ the disease.
12. I have _____ to meet Tom at the station.
13. Computerisation should _____ us to cut production costs by half.
14. We really _____ all the help you gave us last weekend.
15. These chocolate bars _____ something else in the U.S., but I can't remember what.

II. Choose a word or a phrase from the indicated paragraph to fill in each of the following blanks. Change the form where necessary.

1. Man is a reasoning _____. (Para. 1)
2. The long hot summer has led to serious water _____. (Para. 1)
3. Scientists disagree about how the universe was _____. (Para. 2)
4. The government has _____ strict limits on public spending this year. (Para. 3)
5. Good secretaries are always _____. (Para. 4)
6. She _____ as a lawyer for many years. (Para. 5)
7. I stopped and asked a man the way, but he wasn't _____ to the area and he couldn't tell me. (Para. 6)
8. We've got to _____ these articles we have learnt. (Para. 7)

9. She had not been _____ her mother when she moved into the flat last month. (*Para. 8*)
10. I do like him—_____, he is my brother. (*Para. 9*)

Structure

I. Rewrite the following sentences after the models.

Model 1: It is true that the majority of those working in the field are found in these places ... yet a nurse can find work nearly anywhere, particularly in this time of massive nursing shortages.

While it is true that the majority of those working in the field are found in these places ... a nurse can find work nearly anywhere, particularly in this time of massive nursing shortages.

Model 2: Although most states do not recognize each other's nursing licenses yet, a degree or diploma from an accredited nursing school is accepted anywhere in the country.

While most states do not recognize each other's nursing licenses yet, a degree or diploma from an accredited nursing school is accepted anywhere in the country.

1. I am willing to help, yet I do not have much time available.

2. I accept that she's not perfect in many respects, yet I do actually like the girl.

3. Although I fully understand your point of view, I do also have some sympathy with Ben's.

4. Although respected, he is not liked.

5. I admit his good points, yet I can see his shortcomings.

II. Complete the following sentences by translating the Chinese into English, using the Absolute Construction(独立结构).

Model: Traditionally, many RNs were trained in programs run by hospitals, _____ (这些课程长达三年,被称为文凭课程).

Traditionally, many RNs were trained in programs run by hospitals, <u>these being three years in length and known as diploma programs.</u>

1. He wrote a lot of novels, _____ (有许多被翻译成外国语).
2. _____ (没有别的事可讨论), we all went home.
3. _____ (如果情况如此的话), you have no grounds for dismissing him.
4. _____ (由于没有公共汽车), we had to walk home.
5. She ran up to me, _____ (秀发在风中飘扬着).

Cloze

Choose one appropriate word from the following box to fill in each of the following blanks. Each word can be used only once. Change the word form where necessary.

but	reach	latest	to	growth
that	traditionally	what	every	unchanged
independence	though	at	those	children

Women are on their way to holding more than half of all American jobs. The (1)_____ government report shows that their share of nonfarm jobs nearly (2)_____ fifty percent in September.

Not only have more and more women entered the labor market over the years, (3)_____ also the recession has been harder on men. In October the unemployment rate for men was almost eleven percent compared (4)_____ eight percent for women.

Industries that (5)_____ use a lot of men have suffered deep cuts. For example, manufacturing and building lost more jobs last month. But health care and temporary employment services have had job (6)_____. Both of those industries employ high percentages of women.

Thirty years ago, women earned sixty-two cents for every dollar (7)_____ men earned. Now, for (8)_____ who usually work full time, women earn about eighty percent of (9)_____ men earn. And women hold fifty-one percent of good-paying management and professional jobs.

Yet a study said men still hold about nine out of (10)_____ ten top positions at the four hundred largest companies in California. The results have remained largely (11)_____ in five years of studies from the University of California, Davis. Also, a new research paper in the journal *Sex Roles* looks (12)_____ the experiences of women who are the main earners in their family. Rebecca Meisenbach at the University of Missouri in Columbia interviewed fifteen women. She found they all valued their (13)_____ and many enjoyed having the power of control, (14)_____ not all wanted it. But they also felt pressure, worry and guilt. Part of that was because of cultural expectations that working women will still take care of the (15) _____. Also, men who are not the main earners may feel threatened.

Translation

Translate the following sentences into Chinese.

1. To most Americans, nurses are creatures that exist in hospitals and doctors' offices, or take care of those in assisted living facilities or nursing homes.

2. As demand increases for the small pool of practicing nurses, prospective employees are finding higher wages and greater flexibility in scheduling are normal.

3. Best of all, all of these roles put you in direct contact with your neighbors and community in a role that is appreciated and admired.

4. Nursing school is a large investment of time and money, but the return is immense.

5. Nursing allows for good pay and flexibility within your job, and a great sense of job security.

Text B My First Job

Compiled by Daniel Levine

Two high achievers explain why it's not what you earn ... it's what you learn.

The Bookseller

By Ann Carry (news anchor of the NBC News "Today" show)

1 I was 15 when I walked into McCarley's Bookstore in Ashland, Ore., and began scanning titles on the shelves. The man behind the counter, Mac McCarley, asked if I'd like a job. I needed to start saving for college, so I said yes.

2 I worked after school and during summers for minimum wage, and the job helped pay for my freshman year of college. I would work many other jobs: I brewed coffee in the student union during college, was a hotel maid and even made maps for the U. S. Forest Service. But selling books was one of the most satisfying.

3 One day a woman asked me for books on cancer. She seemed fearful. I showed her almost everything we had in stock and found other books we could order. She left the store less fearful, and I've always remembered the pride I felt in having helped her.

4 Years later, as a television reporter in Los Angeles, I heard about an immigrant child who was born with his thumb attached, weblike, to the rest of his hand. His family could not afford corrective surgery, and the boy lived in shame, hiding his hand in his pocket. I persuaded my boss to let me do the story. After my story was broadcast, a doctor and a nurse called, offering to perform the surgery for free.

5 I visited the boy in the recovery room after the operation. The first thing he did was hold up his repaired hand and say, "Thank you." I felt a great sense of reward.

6 At McCarley's Bookstore, I always sensed I was working for the customers, not the store. Today it's the same. NBC News pays my salary, but I feel as if I work for the viewers, helping them make sense of the world.

Shoe Salesman

By Jack Welch (former chairman and CEO of General Electric Company)

7   I had three jobs growing up in Salem, Mass., and they all helped shape my life. When I was about 12, I started serving tea at a nearby country club. All the kids in the neighborhood did it, and I liked it a lot. I got to watch people who were generally pretty well-off businessmen and doctors—talk about deals, and see how they behaved with each other. It was like being a fly on the wall at a meeting.

8   I got another job at Parker Brothers games, drilling small holes in pieces of cork for a game called Dig. I liked Parker, but not the job. It lasted about a month, and I concluded that I never wanted to do anything like that again, ever.

9   The third job was at a Thom McAn shoe store. I often met people from all walks of life, and the challenge was exciting. I'd start bringing them different kinds of shoes and get right down there and put them on their feet. If they didn't like a certain shoe, I always tried to be thinking ahead to a pair they might like better.

10   This job helped teach me an important business lesson: it's all about closing the sale. I never wanted to let a customer get out of that store without buying a pair of shoes. It was like stepping up to the plate in a baseball game. Every time someone walked into that store, I was going to bat and taking a swing. I'd get a seven-cent commission for every pair I sold, 25 cents for the slow movers, such as those that were out of stock or of an odd color.

11   Today I believe that the worst fault in running a big company is to manage its size rather than using that size. The advantage of size is the resources it gives you to go to bat often. You have to take risks in business. If you take a risk and fail, get up to bat and swing again.

From *Reader's Digest*

(689 words)

Words and Phrases to Learn

scan /skæn/ vt. 浏览；扫描
minimum /ˈmɪnɪməm/ a. 最低的，最小的
stock /stɒk/ n. 备料，库存
order /ˈɔːdə/ vt. 定购，定货
surgery /ˈsɜːdʒəri/ n. 外科手术
shame /ʃeɪm/ n. 羞耻，羞愧
persuade /pəˈsweɪd/ vt. 劝；说服
broadcast /ˈbrɔːdkɑːst/ (broadcast 或 broadcasted) vt. （用电台或电视）广播，播出
perform /pəˈfɔːm/ vt. 做；执行，履行
make sense of 理解；弄懂
behave /bɪˈheɪv/ vi. 举止，行为；表现
conclude /kənˈkluːd/ vt. 断定；决定；推断出
challenge /ˈtʃælɪndʒ/ n. 挑战
odd /ɒd/ a. 奇特的
rather than 不是……（而是）；与其……（不如）

Comprehension Check

Choose the best answer for each of the following questions.

1. Why did Ann Carry take the job of selling books at McCarley's Bookstore?
   A. Because she had much free time.
   B. Because the job offered a high salary.
   C. Because she needed to save for college.
   D. Because she liked the bookstore very much.

2. What did Ann Carry learn from her past working experiences?
   A. You should work hard for the boss because he/she pays your salary.
   B. If you work for the customers or audience, you'll feel proud and a great sense of reward.
   C. How much you earn is quite important.
   D. You should persuade your boss to give you a chance.

3. Which of the following statements is **NOT** true according to the story "The Bookseller"?
   A. Ann Carry tried quite a few different jobs before working for NBC News.
   B. The woman left the bookstore less fearful because she got much help from Ann Carry.
   C. It was due to Ann Carry's help that the immigrant boy had his hand repaired.

D. The corrective surgery cost the boy's family a lot of money.
4. Jack Welch had all the following jobs except _____.
   A. being a bookseller
   B. serving tea at a country club
   C. digging holes for a game
   D. selling shoes at a shoe store
5. Why did Jack Welch think it was like being a fly on the wall at a meeting when he served tea at a country club?
   A. Because he was an unnoticed observer of the customers of the club.
   B. Because there were many flies on the wall of the country club.
   C. Because those well-off businessmen and doctors behaved just like flies on the wall.
   D. Because he felt himself small like a fly compared to those well-off businessmen and doctors.
6. What can be inferred from Jack Welch's story?
   A. Getting commissions for every sale is quite important.
   B. What's important in business is to take risks and close the deal.
   C. Businessmen and doctors are better-off than other people.
   D. Drilling holes is more boring than selling shoes.

Language Practice

Fill in the blanks with words or phrases listed in the *Words and Phrases to Learn*.

1. I've read the letter twice, but I can't _____ it.
2. She will have to learn to _____ properly.
3. _____ the newspaper article quickly and make a note of the main points.
4. I took her on one side to ask about her _____ behavior.
5. This operation has never been _____ in this country.
6. We talked late into the night, but nothing was _____.
7. A lot will depend on how she responded to the _____.
8. Eighteen is the _____ age for entering most nightclubs.
9. We don't have any green jackets in _____ at present.
10. The tennis championship is _____ live to several different countries.
11. She was full of _____ about having deceived her friend.
12. I think I'd like to stay at home this evening _____ going out.
13. He has an injury which can only be cured by _____.
14. We want to _____ them to redesign the whole machine.
15. These boots can be _____ directly from the maker.

Part II Listening

Section A

Directions: In this section you will hear five short conversations. At the end of each conversation a question will be asked about what was said. Both the conversation and the question will be spoken only once. Listen carefully and choose the best answer.

1. A. He wanted to say hello to the woman.
   B. He wanted the woman to go to Las Vegas with him.
   C. He wanted to borrow the woman's car.
   D. He wanted to give the woman a surprise.
2. A. Nov. 18th.   B. Nov. 30th.
   C. Nov. 20th.   D. Nov. 28th.
3. A. He is checking out.   B. He is cancelling his reservation.
   C. He is checking in.   D. He is ordering his meal.
4. A. The woman doesn't think it is exciting to travel by air.
   B. They will stay at home during the holidays.
   C. They are offered some plane tickets for their holidays.
   D. They'll be flying somewhere for their vacation.
5. A. In a hotel room.   B. At a restaurant.
   C. In an office.   D. At home.

Section B

Directions: In this section you will hear a long conversation. At the end of the conversation you will hear some questions. Both the conversation and the questions will be spoken only once. After you hear a question, you must choose the best answer.

6. A. She is going through security check at the airport.
   B. She is having an X-ray examination at the hospital.
   C. She is doing shopping at a supermarket.
   D. She is having a job interview.
7. A. Because he found a bomb in the woman's bag.
   B. Because he found something valuable in the woman's bag.
   C. Because he found something strange in the woman's bag.
   D. Because he found a bottle of water in the woman's bag.

8. A. Because it may get poisoned.
   B. Because it can be made into a bomb.
   C. Because it may cause some unnecessary trouble.
   D. Because it may explode at any time.

Section C

Directions: In this section you will hear a passage. At the end of the passage, you will hear some questions. The passage and the questions will be spoken only once. After you hear a question, you must choose the best answer.

9. A. 4.   B. 3.
   C. 2.   D. 5.
10. A. The modern double-decker buses can accommodate more people.
    B. The modern double-decker buses are more convenient for people with disabilities.
    C. The modern double-decker buses are longer and can fit more people.
    D. The modern double-decker buses are more beautiful and more spacious.
11. A. Trams were phased out in London.
    B. Trams were replaced with buses.
    C. A new tram system was built in South London.
    D. A new tram system was built in most parts of London.
12. A. To take the underground.
    B. To use different types of public transport.
    C. To buy a travel card.
    D. To take the double-decker bus.

Part III Speaking

Section A

Directions: Discuss the following questions in small groups.

1. What do you think of being a nurse?
2. What kinds of jobs would you like to have in the future?
3. What do you think are the important qualities that lead a person to success in his/her career?

Section B

Directions: Read aloud the following passage.

Kate Wants to Be a Nurse

Kate wants to be a nurse and work with sick people. She knows they need her help. When Kate goes to the hospital, she always sees many people there. Last summer Kate broke her leg. The pain was very great and she could not even walk. Her parents took her to the hospital by car, and she had to stay there for about one month. She could not leave her bed for the first few days, so she was not very happy.

One day a nurse came to Kate's bed and said with a smile, "You will be better soon. You can walk again, so don't think about bad things. Try to be happy!" The nurse was very kind and they became friends. After Kate left the hospital she thought a lot about the kind nurse. She now understands that the work of a nurse is very important, because they can often give hope to sick people.

Kate is now thinking about her own future. She often talks with her parents about it. Kate knows what she should do to be a good nurse, and she is studying very hard at school.

Part IV Writing

Directions: Write a composition on the topic "My Ideal Job". You should write at least 100 words, and base your composition on the outline given below.

1. Different people choose different jobs as their ideal careers.
2. As for me, I have made up my mind to be ...
3. What should I do to prepare myself for my ideal job?

UNIT 8

Science & Technology

Part I Reading

Text A Only Disconnect[1]

Wyatt Mason

1 Shortly after my wife and I decided to rent a New Hampshire summer house in 2007, we made an annoying discovery. Temporary Internet access wasn't going to be possible. We could get it, sure, but hesitated at the one-year contract required. We couldn't justify the expense and decided we would do without: surely our three acres of apple trees and old stone walls and wooded walks would offer us enough things to do.

2 And yet, when news of our decision reached friends and family, it was as if we'd announced that we no longer intended to wear pants. We tried to explain to them that we hadn't become Luddites[2] and it was only a few months. Nothing to get mad about.

3 The withdrawal period from home Internet was not without some pretty peculiar behavior.[3] In those initial unconnected late-spring weeks, we would wake to birdsong and breakfast on our screened-in porch[4] with its view of the apple trees in bloom. And once a day, or maybe twice a day, or at worst three times a day, and surely never more than four times a day, and only once that I can recall five times a day, I would make my way down the 0.8 mile to our little town library, where the Wi-Fi flowed 24/7 and in-boxes filled[5]. New problems still came up. The hours of the library itself were limited. The signal reached outside the building but not into our car. And the occasional rain made it inconvenient for me to wander about outside the library. All these set me on the road to improper ways of getting on line.[6]

4 I did, I confess, begin to take advantage of our new neighbors, in search of e-mail. I did drive with suspicious slowness down leafy lanes, laptop open in the passenger seat, pulling into driveways where I had no honest business. Idling in front of a house where there was an unprotected network signal, I did master the art of holding a map in my left hand and looking stealthily at its surface while pointing and clicking and connecting with my hidden right hand.

5 By the time July rolled in and I was gardening and taking photos with my laptop camera of my proud crop of organic kale, I noticed a WiFi signal I'd not seen before, faint, but promising. I let the machine lead me from the garden and deep into the woods, where I found the signal strength I sought. Did I get my e-mail? Yes. I also got stung by a hornet in the process. At the time it seemed fair enough.

6 When summer ended, several things changed. First, we decided we liked the house and New Hampshire so much that we signed a lease to live there full time. This brought up the inevitable question: now that we knew we would be there for 12 months, should we get Internet at home? Even though my wife found all my digital hunter-gathering a little out of the ordinary (I had begun to cruise library parking lots in other towns), we both agreed on a decision: we wouldn't get the thing. As it turned out, we had in fact come to prefer the atmosphere around the house without the Web. Moreover, our mornings were free and clear. We seemed to go into the day and our work with more focus, as if that should have been a surprise.

7 Over the next two years, living there and then moving to another house more isolated still, we remained without Internet. I even wrote an online column three days a week for a year without an Internet connection.

8 Last spring, my wife and I took offices in an old textile mill down the road from us. Big, quiet spaces in which she can paint and I can write. There's no cell service, no mail delivery, no nothing. A worker's paradise. Until a couple of months ago, that is. My little community decided, unknown to us, to install free WiFi that would cover the whole area.

(681 words)

New Words

rent /rent/ vt. 租借,租用
annoying /əˈnɔɪɪŋ/ a. 讨厌的,恼人的
access /ˈækses/ n. 通道,入口;接近,进入
hesitate /ˈhezɪteɪt/ vi. 犹豫,踌躇;不情愿
contract /ˈkɒntrækt/ n. 合同
justify /ˈdʒʌstɪfaɪ/ vt. 证明……正当(或有理);为……辩护
expense /ɪkˈspens/ n. 价钱,花费,费
acre /ˈeɪkə/ n. 英亩
wooded /ˈwʊdɪd/ a. 长满树木的
walk /wɔːk/ n. 走道
reach /riːtʃ/ vt. 传到;达到;及到
announce /əˈnaʊns/ vt. 宣布;宣告
pants /pænts/ n. [pl.] 长裤
withdrawal /wɪðˈdrɔːəl/ n. 退缩;逃避现实
peculiar /pɪˈkjuːliə(r)/ a. 奇怪的;特有的,独具的,独特的
initial /ɪˈnɪʃl/ a. 最初的, 开始的
view /vjuː/ n. 景色,风景
Wi-Fi /ˈwaɪ faɪ/ abbr. =Wireless Local Area Network 无线局域网
in-box /ˈɪnbɒks/ n. 收件箱
limited /ˈlɪmɪtɪd/ a. 有限的
signal /ˈsɪɡnəl/ n. 信号;标志
occasional /əˈkeɪʒənəl/ a. 偶尔的,间或发生的
inconvenient /ˌɪnkənˈviːniənt/ a. 不方便的
improper /ɪmˈprɒpə/ a. 不适当的,不合适的
suspicious /səˈspɪʃəs/ a. 猜疑的;可疑的;(of)表示怀疑的
leafy /ˈliːfi/ a. 叶子覆盖着的
lane /leɪn/ n. (乡间)小路(巷)
laptop /ˈlæptɒp/ n. 便携式电脑,笔记本电脑
passenger /ˈpæsɪndʒə/ n. 乘客,旅客
driveway /ˈdraɪvweɪ/ n. 私人车道
idle /ˈaɪdl/ vi. 懒散
stealthily /ˈstelθɪli/ ad. 隐秘地,暗中地
surface /ˈsɜːfɪs/ n. 表面;面
click /klɪk/ vi. 咔哒一声地敲击

---

* 黑体表示重点词汇和短语,白体表示一般词汇和短语

garden /ˈgɑːdn/ vi. 从事园艺
organic /ɔːˈgænɪk/ a. 有机(体)的,有机物的
kale /keɪl/ n. 无头甘蓝类,甘蓝类蔬菜
faint /feɪnt/ a. 模糊的;微弱的
promising /ˈprɒmɪsɪŋ/ a. 有希望的,有前途的
sting /stɪŋ/ (stung) vt. 刺,蜇,叮
hornet /ˈhɔːnɪt/ n. 大黄蜂
lease /liːs/ n. 租约,租契
inevitable /ɪˈnevɪtəbl/ a. 不可避免的,必然(发生)的
digital /ˈdɪdʒɪtl/ a. 数字的
cruise /kruːz/ vt. 航游于,巡航于
prefer /prɪˈfɜː/ vt. 更喜欢,宁愿
atmosphere /ˈætməsfɪə/ n. 气氛
moreover /mɔːˈəʊvə/ ad. 再者,此外
isolate /ˈaɪsəleɪt/ vt. 使隔离,使孤立
online /ˈɒnlaɪn/ a. 联机的,在线的
column /ˈkɒləm/ n. 专栏(文章)
paradise /ˈpærədaɪs/ n. 天堂,乐园
install /ɪnˈstɔːl/ vt. 安装,安置

Phrases and Expressions

do without   没有……也行
intend to   想要,打算,计划
get mad about   〈口〉对……大为恼火
in (full) bloom   (盛)开着花
at worst   在最坏的情况下
make one's way   前进,行进
come up   产生
in search of   寻找;寻求
pull into   把(车、船等)驶入
bring up   提出
now that   既然,由于
out of the ordinary   不寻常的
parking lot   〈美〉停车场
agree on   商定;达成

as it turned out   结果
take office   就职
textile mill   纺织厂
cell service   手机服务
mail delivery   邮递

Proper Names

Wyatt Mason /ˈwaɪət ˈmeɪsn/   怀亚特·梅森
New Hampshire /njuː ˈhæmpʃɪə/   （美国）新罕布什尔州
Luddite /ˈlʌdaɪt/   勒德分子

Notes on the Text

1. This text is adapted from *Only Disconnect* by Wyatt Mason. The title *Only Disconnect* is an imitation of E. M. Forster's epigraph（格言，警句）in his novel *Howards End*—"*Only connect*".（本文标题戏仿英国小说家E·M·福斯特的代表作《霍华德庄园》中的名句"Only connect!"）

2. **Luddites**：勒德分子，反对技术进步的人，源自英国雷斯特郡一工人的名字，此人约于1779年捣毁两台织袜机。

3. The withdrawal period from home Internet was not without some pretty peculiar behavior. 这种远离互联网的归隐生活让我养成了一些古怪习惯。

4. **screened-in porch**：装了纱门或纱窗的侧廊、游廊

5. ... **where the Wi-Fi flowed 24/7 and in-boxes filled**：24/7 is an abbreviation which stands for "24 hours a day, 7 days a week", usually referring to a business or service available at all times without interruption.（小镇图书馆提供）全天候无线局域网服务，我的收件箱也是满满的。

6. All these set me on the road to improper ways of getting on line. 这些不便之处让我开始用不怎么妥当的新方法（去上网）。

Comprehension of the Text

Answer the following questions.

1. What did the author and his wife find out when they moved to a new house in New Hampshire?
2. Why didn't the author install the Internet at home?

3. How did their friends react to their decision?
4. What was their life like at the beginning with no interruption of the Internet?
5. What became unusual about the author as time passed?
6. What was the author doing outside the library?
7. According to the author, what were improper ways of getting on line?
8. How did the author take advantage of his neighbors in search of the email?
9. According to the author, he got stung by a hornet in search of the Wi-Fi signal. Was it worth that?
10. What decisions did the author and his wife make when the summer ended?
11. What's the reason behind the decision that they wouldn't install the Internet at home?
12. Up to now, are they happy with the life without Internet?

Language Sense Enhancement

I. **Read the following paragraphs until you learn them by heart. Then try to complete the following passage from memory.**

When summer ended, several things changed. First, we decided we liked the house and New Hampshire so much that we (1)_____ a lease to live there full time. This (2)_____ the inevitable question: (3)_____ we knew we would be there for 12 months, should we get Internet at home? Even though my wife found all my digital hunter-gathering a little (4)_____ (I had begun to cruise library parking lots in other towns), we both (5)_____ a decision: we wouldn't get the thing. As it (6)_____, we had in fact come to (7)_____ the atmosphere around the house without the Web. (8)_____, our mornings were free and clear. We seemed to go into the day and our work with more (9)_____, as if that should have been a surprise.

Over the next two years, living there and then moving to another house more (10)_____ still, we remained without Internet. I even wrote an online column three days a week for a year without an Internet connection.

II. **Read the following quotations. Learn them by heart if you can.**

People think computers will keep them from making mistakes. They're wrong. With computers you make mistakes faster.　　　　　　　　　　　　　—Adam Osborne

人们以为计算机能防止人们犯错。其实，它使人们犯错更快。　　—亚当·奥斯本

Technology is, of course, a double edged sword. Fire can cook our food but also burn us.　　　　　　　　　　　　　　　　　　　　　　　　　　—Jason Silva

科技当然是一把双刃剑，正如火可以用来烹饪也能把我们烧伤。　—詹森·席尔瓦

Progress is the activity of today and assurance of tomorrow.　　　—Emerson

今日之进步,是明日之保障。
——爱默生

Vocabulary

I. **Fill in the blanks with the given words or phrases in the box. Change the form where necessary.**

idle	peculiar	make one's way	prefer	in bloom
now that	bring up	faint	in search of	justify
install	moreover	initial	announce	inevitable

1. These are matters that you can _____ in committee.
2. Nothing can _____ your cheating on an exam.
3. Instead of working, Jack was _____ away his time.
4. The plumber(水管工) is coming tomorrow to _____ the new washing machine.
5. I had a _____ hope that the manager might have succeeded in his attempt.
6. An argument was _____ because they disliked each other so much.
7. I _____ the quiet countryside to the noisy cities.
8. Bicycling is a good exercise; _____, it doesn't pollute the air.
9. My _____ surprise was soon replaced by delight.
10. She _____ the winner of the competition to an excited audience.
11. The garden looks lovely when the roses are _____.
12. You ought to have a good rest _____ you've finished the work.
13. I have my own _____ way of doing things.
14. They _____ towards the centre of the town.
15. They started off at once _____ the missing girl.

II. **Choose a word or a phrase from the indicated paragraph to fill in each of the following blanks. Change the form where necessary.**

1. Only a few people have _____ to the full facts of the case. (*Para. 1*)
2. If we can't afford a car, we'll just have to _____. (*Para. 1*)
3. He did not _____ to ask her to sit beside him. (*Para. 1*)
4. He pays me _____ visits. (*Para. 3*)
5. He _____ that he had never seen her before. (*Para. 4*)
6. Passengers stood up as the train _____ the station. (*Para. 4*)
7. It _____ that she was a friend of my sister. (*Para. 6*)
8. The talk was conducted in a friendly _____. (*Para. 6*)
9. Scientists _____ the virus(病毒) causing the epidemic(流行病). (*Para. 7*)
10. He's going to _____ an air-conditioner in the house. (*Para. 8*)

Structure

I. Rewrite the following sentences after the model.

Model: I did drive with suspicious slowness down leafy lanes, laptop open in the passenger seat *when I pulled into driveways.*

I did drive with suspicious slowness down leafy lanes, laptop open in the passenger seat, *pulling into driveways.*

1. As he was unable to afford a car, he bought a bicycle.

2. Because he didn't know what to do, he telephoned the police.

3. It rained three days on end so that it completely ruined our holiday.

4. After he had finished his work, he went out and had a drink.

5. While I was standing in the middle of the crowd, I could plainly feel the sense of anger and hatred.

II. Complete the following sentences by translating the Chinese into English, using "as …".

Model: _____(结果是), we had in fact come to prefer the atmosphere around the house without the Web.

<u>As it turned out</u>, we had in fact come to prefer the atmosphere around the house without the Web.

1. He is absent, _____(就像经常的那样).
2. He is a teacher, _____ (从他的举止可以清楚地看出来).
3. _____ (不出所料), he performed the task with success.
4. David, _____ (如你所知), has not been well lately.
5. _____ (正如我在信中所提到的那样), I am taking the examination in July.

Cloze

Choose one appropriate word from the following box to fill in each of the following blanks. Each word can be used only once. Change the word form where necessary.

space	attract	post	join	despite
live	now	age	including	enjoy
look	keep	become	oldest	computer

Who's the oldest person you know on Twitter (微博)? 50? 60? Try 104, the age of what is believed to be the (1) _____ Twitter user in the world. Her name was Ivy Bean.

Last August a woman by the name of Ivy Bean (2) _____ something of an Internet phenomenon by joining Facebook at the old (3) _____ of 103. (4) _____, she's popular and well known by (5) _____ the new social network (网络), Twitter, (6) _____ the fact that she's now 104-year-old.

Bean (7) _____ in a care home (养老院) in Bradford, Britain. She wasn't alone in trying to (8) _____ up with new technology. Other people there had been taking (9) _____ courses too.

Bean's first tweet (微博消息) to the outside world was, "I'm (10) _____ Twitter and having my photo taken—and I'm (11) _____ forward to Deal or No Deal." Since then she had (12) _____ every few hours with news (13) _____ how she's playing with her friend Mabel and watching *The Sound of Music*. Her interesting insights into the life of a 104-year-old lady have (14) _____ over 5,000 followers in the (15) _____ of two days.

Translation

Translate the following sentences into Chinese.

1. We couldn't justify the expense and decided we would do without: surely our three acres of apple trees and old stone walls and wooded walks would offer us enough things to do.

   _____
   _____
   _____

2. I did, I confess, begin to take advantage of our new neighbors, in search of email. I did drive with suspicious slowness down leafy lanes, laptop open in the passenger seat, pulling into driveways where I had no honest business.

3. Idling in front of a house where there was an unprotected network signal, I did master the art of holding a map in my left hand and looking stealthily at its surface while pointing and clicking and connecting with my hidden right hand.

4. By the time July rolled in and I was gardening and taking photos with my laptop camera of my proud crop of organic kale, I noticed a Wi-Fi signal I'd not seen before, faint, but promising.

5. Even though my wife found all my digital hunter-gathering a little out of the ordinary (I had begun to cruise library parking lots in other towns), we both agreed on a decision: we wouldn't get the thing.

Text B How to Live Without a Cell Phone

Mario

1   Considering I travel quite a bit for work and personal reasons, it might be somewhat surprising that I am getting rid of my cell phone. That's what this article is for—to explain why I've stopped using my cell phone. And who knows, maybe it will inspire some of you to live without a permanent cell phone. Here are five reasons why I got rid of my cell phone contract.

Cell phones are distracting.

2   I spend 12 ~ 14 hours a day being completely connected via either phone or my computer. There's email, Twitter, Facebook, Instant Messenger, my mum, etc. I constantly get interrupted by something. The only time I am myself and with my own thought is when I am running errands or traveling from one distraction to the next. But not when I am carrying my cell phone. By taking away my cell phone, I now have at least 1 ~ 2 hours a day where nobody can get a hold of me and my brain can function without interruption. I can think again.

Cell phones cause brain cancer.

3   While this is not confirmed, many doctors and scientists predict that cell phone radiation ought to have some negative effects on our brains. To me it's common sense—having those levels of radiation near my brain can't be good. Just like breathing smoke into your lungs can't be healthy.

Cell phones are expensive.

4   Since I also used my cell phone for email, my monthly bill was usually around $80 (all those government fees were ridiculous). If I put $80 every month into my savings account for the next 30 years and earn 4% interest, I will have saved more than $55,000.

Digital phone service is dirt cheap.

5   I use Vonage at home. It costs me $35 a month and I can call whoever I want from wherever

I want—including my friends and family in Germany. Also, if I really wanted to, I could take my phone and line to wherever I go. (Yes, I can take my Vonage phone to Germany, hook it into my parents' Internet connection and talk to you with my Portland number). Your cable company would be happy to supply you with a digital phone line for $20 ~ $30 a month. You can even try using Skype which is only a few dollars a month. It should be noted that because of my International calling, just having cell phone service was never enough.

You can have a cell phone without the contract or monthly payment.

7　I am cheating a bit here, but I did sign up for an AT&T GoPhone. It costs me 10 cents a minute with no monthly fee. I bought a $100 worth of minutes, which I am hoping will last me for a year. I also signed up for a separate text messaging service, where for $5 a month (taken right out of $100 balance) a month I get 200 text messages. My new phone is not nearly as cool as my old phone and I am paying every time I use it, so I won't carry it with me or use it as often as my old phone. Less distraction, same emergency backup, healthier brain cells.

How do you do it?

8　First, wait until your cell phone contract is up, and then cancel it. If your contract isn't up for a long time, try to find an excuse that can help to end your contract.

9　Second, sell your old cell phone on eBay. I will get $150 for mine, which will actually pay for my new cell phone and service for over a year.

10　Third, get a Pay-As-You-Go Phone. Virgin Mobile, Boost Mobile, AT&T, T-Mobile all have cheap phones. I got a Nokia 2610 for $19. It works with a SIM card, so I can even use it in Europe if I want to.

11　Lastly, tell your close friends your number and let everybody else know that you are stopping your cell phone service.

12　That's it. I might post more about this, as my life without cell phone begins. Do you see any advantages to still having a permanent cell phone plan?

(697 words)

(http://themarioblog.com/how-to-live-without-a-cell-phone/)

Words and Phrases to Learn

somewhat /'sʌmwɒt/ *ad.* 稍微,有点
permanent /'pɜːmənənt/ *a.* 永久(性)的,固定的
via /'vaɪə/ *prep.* 经由,经过,通过
interrupt /ˌɪntə'rʌpt/ *vt.* 打断,打扰;中止,阻碍
function /'fʌŋkʃn/ *vi.* 运行,起作用
predict /prɪ'dɪkt/ *vt.* 预言,预测,预告
radiation /ˌreɪdɪ'eɪʃn/ *n.* 放射物;辐射
have an effect on 对……产生影响
monthly /'mʌnθli/ *a.* 每月的,每月一次的
savings account 储蓄存款户头
interest /'ɪntrɪst/ *n.* 利息
hook /hʊk/ *vt.* 钩住;连接
sign up for 登记注册,登记报名
emergency /ɪ'mɜːdʒənsi/ *n.* 紧急情况,突然事件,非常时刻
post /pəʊst/ *vt.* 邮寄;贴出

Comprehension Check

Choose the best answer for each of the following questions.

1. The purpose of the author writing the article is _____.
   A. to explain the reason why he stopped his cell phone
   B. to persuade other people to live without a mobile
   C. to warn against the harm a cell phone might do to our brain
   D. to save money

2. With a constant connection to a phone or a computer, the author found that _____.
   A. he's busy with traveling and errands
   B. his brain functioned better
   C. he was kept updated whenever he was
   D. he lost himself

3. According to the passage, the following statements are true except _____.
   A. cell phones constantly distract me from the work I was doing
   B. cell phones can do harm to our brains
   C. scientists have confirmed that cell phones can do harm to our brains
   D. the expenses for cell phone could be very high

4. The author recommended that _____.
   A. we should exchange our cell phone for a new one on eBay
   B. one-year contract was the best choice for the cell phone users
   C. we should use the digital phone service because it was cheap and convenient
   D. all of the above
5. You can live a life without a cell phone by _____.
   A. getting a Pay-As-You-Go Phone from Virgin Mobile, Boost mobile, AT&T, T-Mobile, etc.
   B. keeping your cell phone number secret
   C. finding an excuse that can help to end your cell phone contract
   D. finding a buyer online who can pay for your new cell phone
6. We can infer that this passage might be _____.
   A. a newspaper article   B. a blog
   C. a magazine article   D. a personal diary

Language Practice

Fill in the blanks with words or phrases listed in the *Words and Phrases to Learn*.

1. The names of the members of the team will _____ today.
2. The pilot of the aircraft was forced to make an _____ landing on Lake Geneva.
3. I'd like to transfer $300 from my _____ to my checking account (支票帐户).
4. The rent on his apartment was his biggest _____ expense.
5. She's _____ more confident than she used to be.
6. It is impossible to _____ the future accurately.
7. The radiation leak (放射物泄漏) _____ a disastrous _____ on the environment.
8. With nuclear power, there is always the fear that there will be an escape of harmful _____.
9. I got a loan from the bank at 10% _____ per year.
10. The television was _____ normally until yesterday.
11. I don't want to _____ you. Go on with your story.
12. This flight is routed to Chicago _____ New York.
13. He _____ the trailer(拖车) to his car.
14. After doing odd jobs (打零工) for a week, he got a _____ position as a secretary in the office.
15. Many men _____ the army because they can not get ordinary jobs.

Unit 8 Science & Technology

Part II Listening

Section A

Directions: In this section you will hear five short conversations. At the end of each conversation a question will be asked about what was said. Both the conversation and the question will be spoken only once. Listen carefully and choose the best answer.

1. A. He thinks it is sensible for John to quit his job.
   B. He thinks it is risky for John to quit his job.
   C. He thinks it is ridiculous for John to quit his job.
   D. He thinks it is unbelievable for John to quit his job.
2. A. At 10:00. B. At 10:05.
   C. At 10:15. D. At 10:30.
3. A. In the center of London.
   B. In the center of Britain.
   C. In the center of Regent's Park.
   D. In the center of Hyde Park.
4. A. To the school. B. To a friend's house.
   C. To the post office. D. Home.
5. A. It was boring. B. It was entertaining.
   C. It was touching. D. It was encouraging.

Section B

Directions: In this section you will hear a long conversation. At the end of the conversation you will hear some questions. Both the conversation and the questions will be spoken only once. After you hear a question, you must choose the best answer.

6. A. He is reluctant to help the woman.
   B. He knows how to fix the woman's computer.
   C. He knows everything about computers.
   D. He doesn't know much about computers.
7. A. Because it is the only solution to her computer problems.
   B. Because it always solves his computer problems.
   C. Because it is the fastest way to fix the woman's computer.
   D. Because the woman doesn't know how to re-start her computer.

8. A. The woman likes surfing the Internet.

   B. The woman regrets having the man fix her computer.

   C. The man is sorry for being unable to help the woman.

   D. The man is going to contact the Internet company.

Section C

Directions: In this section you will hear a passage. At the end of the passage, you will hear some questions. The passage and the questions will be spoken only once. After you hear a question, you must choose the best answer.

9. A. An extra 6 hours will accumulate.

   B. An extra day will accumulate.

   C. An extra 28 days will accumulate.

   D. An extra 29 days will accumulate.

10. A. Women are allowed to ask their boyfriends to marry them.

    B. Women are allowed to get married to the men they love.

    C. Men are allowed to say no to women who propose to them.

    D. Men are allowed to have a day off.

11. A. He will be punished by working an extra day.

    B. He will be punished by paying some money.

    C. He will not be allowed to propose to anyone.

    D. He will not be allowed to get married any more.

12. A. Getting extra pay on February 29th.

    B. Going on a trip on February 29th.

    C. Having a day off on February 29th.

    D. Going to work on February 29th.

Part III Speaking

Section A

Directions: Discuss the following questions in small groups.

1. Do you have Internet access at home? What do you usually do online?
2. Can you describe what our life would be like without Internet?
3. Do you think modern science and technology have brought us many problems? If so, give some examples.

Section B

Directions: Read aloud the following passage.

Great Inventions

There have been many great inventions that have changed the way we live. The first one is still very important today—the wheel. This made it easier to carry heavy things and to travel long distances. For hundreds of years after that, there were few inventions that had as much effect as the wheel did.

In the second half of the 19th century, many great inventions were made; among them were the camera, the light and the radio. These are all a big part of our lives today. In the first half of the 20th century, we saw many great inventions. For example, the helicopter in 1909, movies with sound in 1926, the computer in 1928, and jet planes in 1930. This was also a time when a new material was first made. Nylon was made in 1935. It changed the kinds of clothes people wore. By this time, many people had a very good life. People had a desire to explore the world again. They began looking for ways to go into space. Russia made the first step. Then the United States took the second step. Since then other countries, including China and Japan, have done so too. In 1969, two Americans walked on the moon. This is certainly just the beginning. New inventions will someday allow us to do things we have never dreamed of.

Part IV Writing

Directions: Write a composition on the topic "How Can the Computer Change Our Life?" You should write at least 100 words, and base your composition on the outline given below.

1. People depend more and more on the computer.
2. Although computers can be very helpful to those who use them wisely, they may bring about some problems to our life.
3. In my opinion ...

UNIT 9

Health

Part I Reading

Text A The Healing Power of Music[1]

1 Music has long been recognized for its healing value. Ages ago, David[2] was called to play for King Saul[3] to help drive away His Majesty's "evil spirits". Today, music is known for its ability to affect mood, trigger memories and encourage loving associations.

2 But did you know that certain forms of music—particularly classical—can help you tap into your own natural ability to heal your heart?

3 It's for this reason that many healthcare practitioners, cardiologists included, have begun turning to the power of music. They have come to believe that the melody, pitch and beat of music can change a patient's state of being by making his body quiet and allowing him to rest mentally.

4 Sound unbelievable? Maybe so. But calming, soothing music is considered one of the ultimate mind-body tools. "No question about it, music is a very powerful way to connect the mind and the body. And when they're connected, the real process of healing begins," says Stephen Sinatra, a cardiologist at the New England Heart & Longevity Center in Manchester, Connecticut, who is a firm believer in the mind-body connection.

5 "Music can be like meditation," explains Sinatra. "Some people who practice yoga, for example, will put on soft music. So whether you're doing yoga or meditating, the music in itself can have a positive influence on your blood pressure."

6 That means *lowering* your blood pressure. In fact, research shows that music can help lower heart beat and blood pressure by reducing the stress hormones, adrenalin and cortisol.

7 "From a psychological evaluation, we found that classical music tends to be comforting. This is because the sympathetic nerve is suppressed by the sound of classical music," noted Dr. Umemura Honda in a 1998 medical journal article. On the other hand, "rock music and noise tend to cause discomfort," he said.

8 Music was also found to reduce stress in patients having brain operations. In a study of 30 patients, two German doctors from Hannover Medical School monitored stress hormones, blood pressure and heart beat. They found that the patients who were not exposed to music "showed rising levels of cortisol in their blood, which means high stress levels, while cortisol in patients examined with music remained stable. Blood pressure was much lower listening to music." What's more, "patients with a high level of fear did appear to benefit particularly from the music," the doctors noted.

9 Cardiologist Sinatra has also seen the power of music at work. "I used to play music when I did heart operations because it calmed my patients. I use music in my office all of the time to help calm my patients—and myself—and I know more doctors who are using music for this reason."

10 What about music's ability to lower cholesterol? While there's no data to show that music can reduce the stuff that can go on to cause heart disease, Sinatra believes that any time you reduce stress, you reduce your risks for heart disease—the leading killer of both men and women.

11 Interestingly, music also can reduce the "white coat syndrome"[4], by which blood pressure rises when a patient visits his/her doctor, even if it's for a routine checkup.

12 How does music cause such positive, physical changes? Most scores of classical music, for example, range between 60 beats per minute and 140 beats per minute, which stimulates the rhythm of the heart beat, thereby causing relaxation and tranquility in the body, says Sinatra. What's more, he adds, "some researchers believe that such scores can take you back to the safety of the womb if you have a good experience in utero—the mother was kind to you, wasn't angry with you and this nice energy was passed on to the fetus. It's all unconscious, of course, and only a hypothesis at that."

13 Lastly, music doesn't involve a logical thought process, says Sinatra. When listening to music, you use your "right brain", which thinks in terms of images. "It's the creative and imaginative place in your mind that is responsible for dreams and expressive forms of art like

music and painting. I'm convinced that the right brain should be exercised to truly allow healing to take place," he says.

14 Sinatra encourages his patients to listen to the following pieces of classical music to help keep their blood pressure in check, their heart disease-free and their lives long-lived:
- Bach[5]—Brandenberg Concerto #4, 2nd movement[6]
- Bach—Orchestral Suite #2, Sarabande[7]
- Gustav Holst[8]—The Planets: "Venus"[9]
- Ravel[10]—Mother Goose Suite, 1st movement[11]

(765 words)

New Words

healing /ˈhiːlɪŋ/ a. （可）使愈合的；有疗效的
Majesty /ˈmædʒɪsti/ n. 陛下（对帝王、王后等的尊称）
evil /ˈiːvl/ a. 邪恶的
spirit /ˈspɪrɪt/ n. 神灵，幽灵，鬼怪
trigger /ˈtrɪɡə/ vt. 触发，引起
classical /ˈklæsɪkl/ a. 古典的；古典主义的
tap /tæp/ vt. 开发；着手利用
practitioner /prækˈtɪʃənə/ n. 从事者，实践者；开业医生
cardiologist /ˌkɑːdɪˈɒlədʒɪst/ n. 心脏病专科医生
melody /ˈmelədi/ n. 曲子；曲调
pitch /pɪtʃ/ n. 音高
beat /biːt/ n. （音乐的）拍子；节拍
being /ˈbiːɪŋ/ n. 身心
unbelievable /ˌʌnbɪˈliːvəbl/ a. 难以置信的
soothing /ˈsuːðɪŋ/ a. 安慰的；抚慰的
ultimate /ˈʌltɪmɪt/ a. 终极的，最后的；根本的
tool /tuːl/ n. 工具
longevity /lɒnˈdʒevɪti/ n. 长寿
firm /fɜːm/ a. 坚定的
meditation /ˌmedɪˈteɪʃn/ n. 沉思；冥想
yoga /ˈjəuɡə/ n. 瑜伽
lower /ˈləuə/ vt. 使……降低；减少

* 黑体表示重点词汇和短语，白体表示一般词汇和短语

hormone /ˈhɔːməʊn/ n. 〈生化〉荷尔蒙
adrenalin /əˈdrenlɪn/ n. 〈生化〉肾上腺素
cortisol /ˈkɔːtɪsɒl/ n. 〈生化〉皮质(甾)醇
psychological /ˌsaɪkəˈlɒdʒɪkl/ a. 心理的；心理学的
evaluation /ɪˌvæljuˈeɪʃn/ n. 评估；评价
sympathetic /ˌsɪmpəˈθetɪk/ a. 〈解〉交感神经的
nerve /nɜːv/ n. 〈解〉神经
suppress /səˈpres/ vt. 压制；抑制
journal /ˈdʒɜːnl/ n. 期刊，杂志；日报
discomfort /dɪsˈkʌmfət/ n. 不适
monitor /ˈmɒnɪtə/ vt. 监督；监视
stable /ˈsteɪbl/ a. 稳定的
benefit /ˈbenɪfɪt/ vi. 得益；得到好处
cholesterol /kəˈlestərɒl/ n. 〈生化〉胆固醇
data /ˈdeɪtə/ n. 数据；资料
stuff /stʌf/ n. 东西；物质
risk /rɪsk/ n. 风险，危险
leading /ˈliːdɪŋ/ a. 首位的，最主要的
syndrome /ˈsɪndrəʊm/ n. 〈医〉综合症；症候群
routine /ruːˈtiːn/ a. 常规的
checkup /ˈtʃekʌp/ n. 健康检查
score /skɔː/ n. 〈音〉总谱
stimulate /ˈstɪmjuleɪt/ vt. 刺激；激励
rhythm /ˈrɪðəm/ n. 节奏；旋律
thereby /ˌðeəˈbaɪ/ ad. 因此；从而
relaxation /ˌriːlækˈseɪʃn/ n. 松弛；放松；缓和
tranquility /træŋˈkwɪləti/ n. 宁静
womb /wuːm/ n. 子宫
in utero /ɪnˈjuːtərəʊ/ ad. & a. 〈拉〉在子宫内(的)；尚未出生(的)
fetus /ˈfiːtəs/ n. 胎儿
unconscious /ʌnˈkɒnʃəs/ a. 无意识的
hypothesis /haɪˈpɒθɪsɪs/ n. 假设
involve /ɪnˈvɒlv/ vt. 需要；包含
logical /ˈlɒdʒɪkl/ a. 逻辑的；符合逻辑的
imaginative /ɪˈmædʒɪnətɪv/ a. 想象的；虚构的
expressive /ɪksˈpresɪv/ a. 表现的；表达的
exercise /ˈeksəsaɪz/ vt. 训练；锻炼

concerto /kənˈtʃɜːtəʊ/ n. 〈音〉协奏曲
orchestral /ɔːˈkestrəl/ a. 管弦乐队的
suite /swiːt/ n. 〈音〉组曲

Phrases and Expressions

drive away　赶走
turn to　求助于
put on　放录音
in itself　本质上；就其本身而言
tend to　趋向；往往会
be exposed to　暴露于；遭受
range between ... and　（在一定幅度或范围内）变动
what is more　而且
pass on　传递
in terms of　根据；按照
be responsible for　是……的原因；对……负责
take place　发生
in check　受抑制的(地)，有控制的(地)

Proper Names

David /ˈdeɪvɪd/　大卫
King Saul /sɔːl/　索罗王
Stephen Sinatra /ˈstiːvn ˈsɪnɑːtrə/　史蒂芬·西纳特拉
New England Heart & Longevity Center　新英格兰心脏与长寿中心
Manchester /ˈmæntʃestə/　（英国城市）曼彻斯特
Connecticut /kəˈnetɪkət/　（美国）康涅狄格州
Umemura Honda　本田梅村
Hannover /hɑːˈnəʊvər/ Medical School　汉诺威医学院
Bach /bɑːk/　巴赫
Brandenburg /ˈbrændənbɜːg/　勃兰登堡
Sarabande /ˈsærəbænd/　萨拉班德舞曲
Gustav Holst /ˈgʊstɑːv həʊlst/　古斯塔夫·霍尔斯特
Ravel /ˈrɑːvel/　拉威尔

Notes on the Text

1. The text is adapted from *The Healing Power of Music* on http://health.howstuffworks.com/wellness.
2. **David**: The second king of the United Kingdom of Israel according to the Hebrew Bible. He is depicted as a righteous king as well as a warrior, musician and poet. (《圣经》中以色列的第二任国王)
3. **King Saul**: The first king of the United Kingdom of Israel (reigned 1047–1007 BCE) according to the Hebrew Bible. (《圣经》中以色列的第一任国王)
4. **white coat syndrome**: A situation where patients have high blood pressure in the doctor's office but nowhere else. (白大褂性综合征)
5. **Bach**: 巴赫(1685—1750),德国作曲家、管风琴家
6. **Brandenberg Concerto #4, 2nd movement**:《勃兰登堡协奏曲》,第四号,第二乐章
7. **Orchestral Suite #2, Sarabande**: 管弦乐组曲第二号,《萨拉班德舞曲》
8. **Gustav Holst**: 古斯塔夫·霍尔斯特(1874—1934),英国作曲家
9. **The Planets**: "Venus":《行星:金星》
10. **Ravel**: 拉威尔(1875—1937),法国著名作曲家、钢琴家
11. **Mother Goose Suite, 1st movement**:《鹅妈妈》管弦乐组曲,第一乐章

Comprehension of the Text

Answer the following questions.

1. Why was David called to play for King Saul?
2. What can music do today?
3. Why have healthcare practitioners begun turning to music, according to the author?
4. What have healthcare practitioners come to believe?
5. What does Stephen Sinatra think of music?
6. Why is music like meditation, according to Doctor Sinatra?
7. What does Dr. Umemura Honda think of classical music and rock music?
8. What was the finding of the two German doctors in their study of 30 patients?
9. Why did Sinatra play music when he did heart operations?
10. What is "white coat syndrome"?
11. How does music cause positive, physical changes, according to Sinatra?
12. Does music involve a logical thought process, according to Sinatra?

Language Sense Enhancement

I. Read the following paragraphs until you learn them by heart. Then try to complete the passage from memory.

"From a psychological evaluation, we found that classical music (1)_____ to be comforting. This is because the sympathetic nerve is (2)_____ by the sound of classical music," noted Dr. Umemura Honda in a 1998 medical journal article. On the other (3)_____, "rock music and noise tend to cause (4)_____," he said.

Music also was (5)_____ to reduce stress in patients having brain operations. In a study of 30 patients, two German doctors from Hannover Medical School (6)_____ stress hormones, blood pressure and heart beat. They found that the patients who were not (7)_____ to music "showed rising levels of cortisol in their blood, which (8)_____ high stress levels, (9)_____ cortisol in patients examined with music remained stable. Blood pressure was (10)_____ lower listening to music."

II. Read the following quotations. Learn them by heart if you can.

Good health is not something we can buy. However, it can be an extremely valuable savings account.   —Anne Wilson Schaef

健康不是我们所能买到的东西，它是我们极其珍贵的储蓄账户。

——安妮·威尔逊·沙夫

The only way to keep your health is to eat what you don't want, drink what you don't like, and do what you'd rather not.   —Mark Twain

保持身体健康的唯一办法，就是吃点你不想吃的，喝点你不想喝的，以及做点你不愿做的事情。   ——马克·吐温

An ounce of prevention is worth a pound of cure. 预防为主，治疗为辅。

Vocabulary

I. Fill in the blanks with the given words or phrases in the box. Change the form where necessary.

range between ... and	stable	risk	firm	ultimate
stimulate	heal	benefit	routine	drive away
be responsible for	monitor	exercise	tend to	be exposed to

1. People who stole did not _____ from ill-gotten gains.
2. Certain plants have _____ powers.
3. The new findings suggest that women ought to _____ their cholesterol (胆固醇) levels.

4. The rioters (骚乱者) fired shots in the air to _____ news photographers.
5. He is a _____ believer in traditional family values.
6. We _____ get cold winters and warm, dry summers in this part of the country.
7. Your _____ goal as an athlete is to represent your country.
8. The children's ages _____ 5 _____ 15.
9. You're getting fat; you should _____ more.
10. About 800,000 children _____ poisons each year.
11. A good teacher should ask questions that _____ the children to think.
12. The fault was discovered during a _____ check.
13. Last month's bad weather _____ the crop failure.
14. The hospital said he was in a _____ condition following the operation.
15. Smoking can increase the _____ of developing heart disease.

II. **Choose a word or a phrase from the indicated paragraph to fill in each of the following blanks. Change the form where necessary.**

1. The book is now _____ as a classic. (*Para. 1*)
2. It's _____ that you should feel upset when you first leave home. (*Para. 2*)
3. She had _____ see the problem in a new light. (*Para. 3*)
4. You should see her wardrobe—it's _____ —she's got about fifteen pairs of shoes. (*Para. 4*)
5. We must take _____ steps to deal with the problem. (*Para. 5*)
6. This drug is used to _____ blood pressure. (*Para. 6*)
7. On the one hand they'd love to have kids, but _____, they don't want to give up their freedom. (*Para. 7*)
8. I feel that I have _____ greatly _____ her wisdom. (*Para. 8*)
9. It's possible to _____ the virus to others through physical contact. (*Para. 12*)
10. The child has a very _____ imagination. (*Para. 13*)

Structure

I. **Rewrite the italicized parts in the following sentences after the model.**

Model: Many healthcare practitioners, cardiologists included, have begun turning to the power of music *for this reason.*

It's for this reason that many healthcare practitioners, cardiologists included, have begun turning to the power of music.

1. All this happened *on Monday night*.
   _____

2. I met Li Ming *at the railway station* yesterday.
   _____

3. *Mary and James* are standing behind the door.
   _____

4. He didn't come to school *because he was ill*.
   _____

5. *Tom* met an old beggar in the street yesterday.
   _____

II. Complete the following sentences by translating the Chinese into English, using "whether or".

Model: So _____ （不管你是在练瑜伽还是在沉思）, the music in itself can have a positive influence on your blood pressure.

So <u>whether you're doing yoga or meditating</u>, the music in itself can have a positive influence on your blood pressure.

1. I show everything on my face, _____ （无论我生气还是高兴）.
2. _____ （不管你乐意不乐意）, I'm going out tonight.
3. _____ （不管我们现在做还是以后做）, it's got to be done some time.
4. _____ （无论他是对是错）, he will have my support.
5. Let's face it—you're going to be late _____ （不管你是乘汽车去还是坐火车去）.

Cloze

Choose one appropriate word from the following box to fill in each of the following blanks. Each word can be used only once. Change the word form where necessary.

gift	with	from	used	regular
good	that	to	in	weight
not	owner	risk	fairly	benefit

Valentine's Day is the single biggest day for chocolate sales in the United States. More than 36 million boxes of chocolates are given as (1)_____ on Valentine's Day, and that's only in the U. S. VOA's Carol Pearson looks at whether all this chocolate can actually be (2)_____ for you.

Recent studies show that chocolate is good for you—dark chocolate, that is—but (3)_____ milk or white chocolate or dark chocolate eaten (4)_____ milk.

Sam Aboulhosn is the (5)_____ of the Schakolad Chocolate Factory in Crystal City, Virginia. "This is the dark chocolate. Our dark is 73 percent pure cocoa." Studies have shown (6)_____ dark chocolate can lower the blood pressure of people suffering from mild high blood pressure. Other studies have shown dark chocolate increases "good" cholesterol and reduces the (7)_____ of heart disease.

That's because dark chocolate contains chemicals, antioxidants(抗氧化剂)—called flavonoids—that cause the body (8)_____ make more nitric oxide(氧化氮). Nitric oxide widens the blood vessels and prevents plaque(斑块)(9)_____ building up. Flavonoids are found in other foods: including tea, onions, broccoli, soybeans and wine, but cocoa that is (10)_____ to make dark chocolate is extraordinarily rich (11)_____ antioxidants.

Research in antioxidants is still (12)_____ new and there's a lot yet to learn. Experts say it is still too soon to make a bar of chocolate a (13)_____ part of your diet, especially if you are watching your (14)_____. Dr. David Katz has been studying the positive effects of eating dark chocolate. He warns about overeating. "If you eat too much, then the (15)_____ no longer win out." Chocolate contains a lot of fat. Too much chocolate could cause you to gain weight, which would not be good for your blood pressure.

Translation

Translate the following sentences into Chinese.

1. Today, music is known for its ability to affect mood, trigger memories and encourage loving associations.

2. But did you know that certain forms of music—particularly classical—can help you tap into your own natural ability to heal your heart?

3. From a psychological evaluation, we found that classical music tends to cause comfort.

4. Interestingly, music also can reduce the "white coat syndrome", by which blood pressure rises when a patient visits his/her doctor, even if it's for a routine checkup.

5. How does music cause such positive, physical changes?

Unit 9 Health

Text B   100 Candles on Her Next Cake

Jane E. Brody

1   Esther Tuttle is nearing the end of the 10th decade of a very productive life. If all continues to go well, on July 1, 2011 she will join the rapidly growing group of centenarians, whose numbers in the United States have increased to 96,548 in 2009 from 38,300 in 1990, according to the Census Bureau.

2   At age 92, Mrs. Tuttle wrote a memoir with the title "No Rocking Chair for Me" showing a good memory of events, names, dates and places.

3   Although 30 years younger than her, I couldn't remember the kinds of details that are fresh in her active mind. I can only hope, should I live that long, to be as active and physically healthy as she is.

4   What, I asked, is the secret to her long life? Is it genetics? Perhaps, but it's hard to say. Her parents died at ages 42 and 50, leaving her an orphan at age 11, along with three brothers and sisters, one of whom did live to 96.

5   Genes do play a role in a long life. Dr. Nir Barzilai, a geneticist at the Albert Einstein College of Medicine in New York, reports that centenarians are 20 times as likely as the ordinary person to have a long-lived relative. But a Swedish study of identical twins separated at birth and growing up apart showed that only about 20 to 30 percent of a long life is genetically determined. Lifestyle seems to be the more critical factor.

6   As Mrs. Tuttle said, "I am blessed and I've worked on it. You've got to work, be cheerful and look for something fun to do. It's a whole attitude. If you respect what the doctors tell you to do, you can live a long life, but you have to do it. You can't ignore the advice."

7   Throughout her long life, she's dealt calmly with hardships and gone pleasantly over difficulties. And she has kept to a plan of a careful diet, hard work, regular exercise and a very long list of community service, all while raising three children.

8   Like many if not most other centenarians, according to the findings of the New England Centenarian Study at Boston University, Mrs. Tuttle has many friends, healthy self-esteem and

strong relations with family and community. She continues to enjoy her youthful loves for the theater and opera.

9   A study of centenarians in Sardinia found that they tend to be physically active, have large social networks and keep strong relations with family and friends. They are also less likely to be more depressed than the ordinary 60-year-old.

10   Tuttle could be a model for that study's findings. Each morning, she does an hour of yoga and other floor exercises, then dresses and goes out on the street or to the top of her Manhattan apartment building for a half-hour walk before breakfast. Her usual breakfast: orange juice, oatmeal, a banana and black coffee. Then she works at her desk, mostly corresponding with her 11 grandchildren, 21 great grandchildren and 1 great-great-grandchild, now 3. "So many birthdays—one or two a month," she said.

11   Lunch may be soup or meat, a "very thin" piece of bread, with tea or fruit. The afternoon includes an hour's nap and another walk, often combined with grocery shopping.

12   At 6:30 every evening, she enjoys a cocktail before a home-cooked dinner of perhaps lamb, pork chops, roast chicken or "a very good stew" she makes herself. Mrs. Tuttle, whose husband, Ben, died in 1988, lives with a dear friend, Allene Hatch, 84, an artist and author known as Squeaky. "Most days I do the cooking, and Squeaky cleans up afterward," Tuttle comments.

13   Stay-at-home evenings are spent reading or watching "a good movie" on television, she said.

14   As good as her health is, it is not perfect. She describes herself as "a bionic woman from the waist up", with an artificial breast to replace the cancerous one removed 20 years ago, a heart pacemaker installed about a decade ago, a hearing aid and contact lenses.

15   Nor has she always enjoyed a wealthy lifestyle. Though born into a well-to-do family, her parents' early death (the children were taken in by an aunt with limited income) and her decision to be an actress led to a hard existence that continued through the early years of her marriage and life on a farm with three small children and no electricity. According to one study, survivors of painful life events learn to deal better with stress and poverty and are more likely to live to 100.

16   Instead of pains, there are many measures one can take to have a long, healthy and productive life. Why do we live to 100 if those last years will be destroyed by physical and emotional pain?

(804 words)

Words and Phrases to Learn

decade /'dekeɪd/ n. 十年
productive /prə'dʌktɪv/ a. 富有成效的
fresh /freʃ/ a. 新的；新近的
play a role 扮演角色；起作用
identical /aɪ'dentɪkl/ a. 相同的
separate /'sepəreɪt/ vt. 分开；隔开
determine /dɪ'tɜːmɪn/ vt. 决定；确定
critical /'krɪtɪkl/ a. 关键的
cheerful /'tʃɪəfl/ a. 快活的，高兴的
depressed /dɪ'prest/ a. 沮丧的；忧愁的
correspond with 和……通信
artificial /ˌɑːtɪ'fɪʃl/ a. 人工的；假的
remove /rɪ'muːv/ vt. 清除；消除
poverty /'pɒvəti/ n. 贫困，贫穷
measure /'meʒə/ n. ［常 pl.］措施，办法

Comprehension Check

Choose the best answer for each of the following questions.

1. What is a centenarian?
   A. A person who is ten years old.
   B. A person who is a hundred years old.
   C. A person who will be born on July 1, 2011.
   D. A person who has a very productive life.

2. What does the author hope if she could live as long as Mrs. Tuttle?
   A. To be as active and healthy as Mrs. Tuttle.
   B. To join the growing group of centenarians in the United States.
   C. To have a productive life.
   D. To remember the details of the events, names, dates and places in her life.

3. What is the secret to her long life, according to Mrs. Tuttle?
   A. A whole attitude.
   B. Hard work.
   C. God's blessing.
   D. Genes.

4. What are the common features of centenarians, according to the findings of several studies of centenarians?

A. They tend to be physically active.

B. They have strong relations with family, friends and community.

C. They are less likely to be depressed.

D. All of the above.

5. All the following statements about Mrs. Tuttle are true except _____.

   A. she has good and perfect health

   B. she had a hard existence through the early years of her marriage and life on a farm

   C. she is a walking example of centenarians

   D. she wrote a book of her own life and experiences

6. Which of the following statements would the author agree with?

   A. It is good to have a long life even if the later years will be destroyed by physical and emotional pains.

   B. Genes are the number one factor in a long life.

   C. Lifestyle and attitude to life are critical to a long life.

   D. A wealthy lifestyle in one's early years is the secret to a long life.

Language Practice

Fill in the blanks with words or phrases listed in the *Words and Phrases to Learn*.

1. The doctor's waiting room was bright and _____ with a yellow carpet and curtains.
2. My time spent in the library was very _____.
3. It was impossible to _____ the stain from the tablecloth.
4. What further _____ can we take to avoid shoplifting?
5. She felt very _____ about the future.
6. Your decision is _____ to our future.
7. Prices have risen steadily during the past _____.
8. The tests are _____ to those carried out last year.
9. I've been _____ several experts in the field.
10. The media(媒体) _____ in influencing people's opinions.
11. Police tried to _____ the two men who were fighting.
12. We set out to _____ exactly what happened that night.
13. In 1991 almost 36 million Americans were living below the _____ line.
14. The events of last year are still _____ in people's minds.
15. He was born with only one ear, but surgeons have fitted him with an _____ one.

Unit 9 Health

Part II Listening

Section A

Directions: In this section you will hear five short conversations. At the end of each conversation a question will be asked about what was said. Both the conversation and the question will be spoken only once. Listen carefully and choose the best answer.

1. A. Students can make friends with people from all over the world.
   B. Students can communicate in different languages.
   C. Students can meet lots of minority students.
   D. Students can learn different cultures in the world.
2. A. He doesn't want another cup of tea.
   B. He is fond of drinking tea.
   C. They should prepare some more tea.
   D. They are out of tea now.
3. A. It is the largest library in the world.
   B. It consists of three large libraries.
   C. It is the largest library in London.
   D. It has a large collection of over 150 million books.
4. A. Skating.
   B. Swimming.
   C. Boating and swimming.
   D. Boating and skating.
5. A. The woman does not want to go to the movies.
   B. The man is too tired to go to the movies.
   C. The woman wants to go to the movies.
   D. The man wants to go out for dinner.

Section B

Directions: In this section you will hear a long conversation. At the end of the conversation you will hear some questions. Both the conversation and the questions will be spoken only once. After you hear a question, you must choose the best answer.

6. A. Ask Mr. Lee to call back.
   B. Ask Mr. Lee to meet him.

C. Tell Mr. Lee that he will call again.

D. Tell Mr. Lee that he will visit him tomorrow.

7. A. He's having a meeting.

   B. He's staying at the hotel.

   C. He's leaving a message.

   D. He's meeting some clients.

8. A. Tomorrow morning before 10:00.

   B. Tomorrow morning after 10:00.

   C. Tomorrow afternoon.

   D. Tomorrow evening.

Section C

Directions: In this section you will hear a passage. At the end of the passage, you will hear some questions. The passage and the questions will be spoken only once. After you hear a question, you must choose the best answer.

9. A. Long, long ago.　　　　　　B. 900 years ago.

   C. Long before 900.　　　　　 D. In 4000.

10. A. English.　　　　　　　　　B. Japanese.

    C. Persian.　　　　　　　　　D. Indian.

11. A. The one when one man played 400 games.

    B. The one played by radio.

    C. The one played by two persons at the same table.

    D. The one played by post.

12. A. When one player says "Check".

    B. When one player says "Check mate".

    C. When one player has nothing to say.

    D. When the Queen can not move any longer.

Part Ⅲ　Speaking

Section A

Directions: Discuss the following questions in small groups.

1. Besides healing the heart, what else do you know music can do?

2. What can we do to keep physically and mentally healthy?

3. In your opinion, which one is more important, health or wealth? Please give your reasons.

Section B

Directions: Read aloud the following passage.

Train your mind

　　Everyone knows you must exercise regularly to keep good health. Indeed, staying physically fit is a big part of our culture. We consider that healthy people are attractive people. Since most of us want to be attractive, there is no shortage of exercise clubs, training videos, magazines and books offering to help us stay physically fit. Unfortunately, however, our culture doesn't place the same emphasis on mental fitness. Although we tend to like men and women with strong, healthy-looking bodies, we don't have the same degree of respect or attraction for smart, educated, mentally healthy people. This is a pity, because there are great rewards for people who have developed the ability to think well. If your mind is well trained and flexible, you will be able to understand a great deal of what happens around you. And if you are also well educated—that is, if you understand basic science, mathematics, music, art, literature, history and so on—you will find it much easier to make good decisions throughout your life. Over the long run, this leads to a sense of control over your destiny and a much better life than otherwise.

Part IV Writing

　　Directions: Write a composition on the topic "Good Health". You should write at least 100 words, and base your composition on the outline given below.

1. Importance of good health.
2. How to keep healthy.
3. My own practices.

UNIT 10

Transportation

Part I Reading

> Text A   Well, America: Is the Car Culture Working?[1]

David E. Shi[2]

1 Soaring gas prices this summer have angered people, but no one seems to be driving less. Like Granny in Jan and Dean's[3] 1964 song "The Little Old Lady from Pasadena"[4], we can't keep our foot off the accelerator.

2 We are crazy about our cars—and always have been. "The American", William Faulkner[5] lamented in 1948, "really loves nothing but his automobile." His words retain their force over a half-century later. There are now more than 200 million cars in the United States. In Los Angeles there evidently are more registered cars than people. Some families spend more on their monthly car payments than on their home mortgage. We dream of cars as we dream of lovers. They express our fantasies; they fulfill our desires.

3 Our intense love affair with cars began as soon as they were invented. Since its first appearance in the 1890s, the automobile has embodied deep-seated cultural and emotional values that have become an integral part of the American Dream[6]. All of the romantic mythology associated with the frontier experience has been transferred to the car culture.

4 Americans have always cherished personal freedom and mobility, individualism and masculine force. The advent of the horseless carriage combined all these qualities and more. The automobile traveled faster than the speed of reason; it promised to make everyone a pathfinder to a better life. It was the vehicle of personal democracy, acting as a social leveling force, granting more and more people a wide range of personal choice—where to travel, where to work and live,

where to seek personal pleasure and social recreation.

5 A century ago, automobiles were viewed as friends of the environment; they were much cleaner than horses. In 1900, for example, New York City horses deposited over 2.5 million pounds of manure and 60,000 gallons of urine on the streets. About 15,000 dead horses also had to be removed from the city streets each year. The motorcar promised to eliminate such animal waste.

6 But it was one thing to praise the individual freedom offered by the horseless carriage when there were a few thousand of them spread across the nation; it is quite another matter when there are 200 million of them. In 1911 a horse and buggy paced through Los Angeles at 11 miles per hour. In 2000, an automobile makes the rush hour trip averaging four miles per hour. American drivers are stuck in traffic for eight billion hours a year. Young graduates entering the workforce in the summer of 2000 will spend four years of their lives behind the wheel.

7 Yet despite heavy traffic, polluted air, and rising gas prices, Americans have not changed their driving or car ownership patterns. Suburban commuters have resolutely stayed in their vehicles rather than join car pools or use public transportation. Teens continue to fill high-school parking lots with automobiles. And the Sunday driver remains a peculiarly American phenomenon. America's love affair with the car has matured into a marriage—and an addiction. We refuse to consider other transportation options. As one popular bumper sticker resolutely declares, "You'll Get Me Out of My Car When You Pry My Cold, Dead Foot from the Accelerator."

8 The automobile retains its firm hold over our psyche because it continues to represent a metaphor for what Americans have always prized: the seductive ideal of private freedom and personal mobility.

9 Our solution to rush hour gridlock is not to demand public transportation but to transform our immobile automobile into a temporary office, bank, restaurant, bathroom, and stereo system. We talk on the phone, eat meals, cash checks and listen to music and audio books in them.

10 A company that records audio books reports that two of its most popular selections among commuters are Henry David Thoreau's[8] *Walden; Or, Life in the Woods*[9] and Mark Twain's[10] *Huckleberry Finn*. An interstate highway is not exactly a path to Walden Pond[11], nor does a BMW much resemble Huck's raft, but Americans remain firmly committed to the open road—even if only in our imaginations.

(683 words)

New Words

soar /sɔː/ vi. （物价、失业人数等）猛增,剧增
accelerator /əkˈseləreɪtə/ n. （汽车等的）加速装置;油门踏板
lament /ləˈment/ vi. 悲叹
retain /rɪˈteɪn/ vt. 保持,保留
register /ˈredʒɪstə/ vt. 登记,注册
mortgage /ˈmɔːgɪdʒ/ n. 抵押贷款,按揭
fantasy /ˈfæntəsi/ n. 幻想,白日梦
fulfill /fʊlˈfɪl/ vt. 实现;满足
desire /dɪˈzaɪə/ n. 愿望,欲望
intense /ɪnˈtens/ a. 强烈的,剧烈的
embody /ɪmˈbɒdi/ vt. 体现
deep-seated /ˈdiːpˈsiːtɪd/ a. 根深蒂固的
integral /ˈɪntɪgrəl/ a. 构成整体所必需的;组成的
mythology /mɪˈθɒlədʒi/ n. 神话
frontier /ˈfrʌntɪə, frʌnˈtɪə/ n. 边远地区
transfer /trænsˈfɜː/ (transferred; transferring) vt. 转移;迁移
cherish /ˈtʃerɪʃ/ vt. 珍惜,珍爱
mobility /məʊˈbɪləti/ n. 流动(性)
individualism /ˌɪndɪˈvɪdʒuəlɪzəm/ n. 个人主义(行为);个性
masculine /ˈmæskjəlɪn/ a. 男性的;男子气概的
advent /ˈædvənt/ n. 出现,到来
pathfinder /ˈpɑːθˌfaɪndə/ n. 探路者,探索者
vehicle /ˈviːɪkl/ n. 车辆;（用来表达思想、情感的）工具,手段
democracy /dɪˈmɒkrəsi/ n. 民主
level /ˈlevl/ vt. 把……拉平;使相等,使平等
grant /grɑːnt/ vt. 同意,准予,授予
recreation /ˌrekrɪˈeɪʃn/ n. 娱乐,消遣
deposit /dɪˈpɒzɪt/ vt. 使沉积
manure /məˈnjʊə/ n. 粪肥
gallon /ˈgælən/ n. 加仑
urine /ˈjʊərɪn/ n. 尿
eliminate /ɪˈlɪmɪneɪt/ vt. 消灭,消除
buggy /ˈbʌgi/ n. 四轮单马轻便马车
pace /peɪs/ vi. 踱步

＊黑体表示重点词汇和短语,白体表示一般词汇和短语

commuter /kəˈmjuːtə/ n. （市郊间）乘公交车辆上下班者;经常乘车往返者
phenomenon /fɪˈnɒmɪnən/ n. [pl.] phenomena 现象
mature /məˈtʃʊə/ vi. 成熟;长成
addiction /əˈdɪkʃn/ n. 瘾;入迷
option /ˈɒpʃn/ n. 自由选择
pry /praɪ/ vt. 撬开;使劲分开
psyche /ˈsaɪki/ n. 灵魂
represent /ˌreprɪˈzent/ vt. 代表
metaphor /ˈmetəfə/ n. 比喻的说法
prize /praɪz/ vt. 珍视,重视
seductive /sɪˈdʌktɪv/ a. 诱惑的
gridlock /ˈgrɪdlɒk/ n. 交通全面大堵塞
transform /trænsˈfɔːm/ vt. 改变,转变
interstate /ˌɪntəˈsteɪt/ a. 州与州之间的
raft /rɑːft/ n. 木筏
committed /kəˈmɪtɪd/ a. 坚定的

Phrases and Expressions

keep off　（使）不接近
nothing but　只有,只不过
dream of　梦想
love affair　强烈爱好
act as　扮演;担当
It is one thing ... ; it is (quite) another thing ...　……是一回事;……是另一回事
rush hour　高峰时间;（上下班时的）交通拥挤时间
car pool　〈美〉合伙用车

Proper Names

Jan /dʒæn/　简（Jane, Janet 的昵称）
Dean /diːn/　迪安
Pasadena /ˌpæsəˈdiːnə/
1. 帕萨迪纳（美国加利福尼亚州洛杉矶东北郊的住宅卫星城市）
2. 帕萨迪纳（美国德克萨斯州城市,在休斯敦以东）
William Faulkner /ˈwɪliəm ˈfɔːknə/　威廉·福克纳

Los Angeles /lɒs ˈændʒɪliːz/ 洛杉矶
New York City /ˌnjuː ˈjɔːk ˈsiti/ 纽约(市)
Henry David Thoreau /ˈhenri ˈdævɪd ˈθɔːrəʊ/ 亨利·大卫·梭罗
Walden Pond /ˈwɔːldən pɒnd/ 沃尔登湖
Mark Twain /ˈmɑːk ˈtweɪn/ 马克·吐温
Huckleberry Finn /ˈhʌklberi ˈfɪn/ 哈克贝利·费恩

Notes on the Text

1. This article is published on Sunday, July 9, 2000 in *the Philadelphia Inquirer*. The present text is slightly adapted and abridged.

2. **David E. Shi**: President of Furman University in Greenville, S.C.

3. **Jan and Dean**: American folk rock singers.

4. **The Little Old Lady from Pasadena**: A song written by Don Altfeld, Jan Berry and Roger Christian, and recorded by 1960s American folk rock singers, Jan and Dean. The song reached number three on the Billboard Hot 100 chart in 1964.

5. **William Faulkner**: (1897 -1962) American novelist and short story writer.

6. **American Dream**: The belief of Americans that their country offers opportunities for a good and successful life. For minorities and immigrants, the dream also includes freedom and equal rights. (追求平等和物质富足的美国理想)

7. **bumper sticker**: 汽车的保险杠张贴物

8. **Henry David Thoreau**: (1817 - 1862) American naturalist, essayist, philosopher and poet.

9. *Walden; or, Life in the Woods*: An American book written by Henry David Thoreau. Published in 1854, it details Thoreau's experiences over the course of two years in a cabin he built near Walden Pond, amidst woodland owned by his friend and mentor Ralph Waldo Emerson, near Concord, Massachusetts. (《沃尔登》或《林中生活》)

10. **Mark Twain**: (1835 - 1910) Pseudonym (笔名) of Samuel Langhorne Clemens, American humorist, lecturer and essayist. He is noted for his novels *Adventures of Huckleberry Finn* (1885), called "the Great American Novel", and *The Adventures of Tom Sawyer* (1876).

11. **Walden Pond**: A lake located in Concord, Massachusetts, the United States. Henry David Thoreau lived on the shores of the pond for two years starting in the summer of 1845. His account of the experience was recorded in *Walden, or, Life in the Woods*, and made the spot famous.

Comprehension of the Text

Answer the following questions.

1. Do American people drive less because of the soaring gas prices?
2. How many cars are there in the United States now?
3. What status do cars enjoy?
4. When did American people begin to love their cars?
5. What does the automobile embody?
6. What did the automobile promise Americans?
7. What role does the automobile play in American people's life?
8. Why were automobiles viewed as friends of the environment a century ago?
9. Is it good to have 200 million cars spreading across the nation? Why or why not?
10. Are people willing to consider other transportation options?
11. Why do people refuse to give up driving their cars?
12. How does one solve the problem of gridlock during the rush hour according to the author?

Language Sense Enhancement

I. **Read Paragraph 2 until you learn them by heart. Then try to complete the following passage from memory.**

We are (1) _____ about our cars—and always have been. "The American", William Faulkner lamented in 1948, "really loves nothing (2) _____ his automobile." His words (3) _____ their force over a half-century (4) _____. There are now more than 200 million (5) _____ in the United States. In Los Angeles there (6) _____ are more registered cars (7) _____ people. Some families spend more on their monthly car payments than (8) _____ their home mortgage. We (9) _____ of cars as we dream of lovers. They express our fantasies; they (10) _____ our desires.

II. **Read the following quotations. Learn them by heart if you can.**

The cars we drive say a lot about us. —Alexandra Paul
什么人开什么车。 ——亚历姗卓拉·保罗

There are three things men always talk about—women, sports, and cars.
—Mario Lopez
男人总是谈论三件事:女人、运动和汽车。 ——马里奥·洛佩兹

There's a lot of stress ... but once you get in the car, all that goes out the window.
—Dan Brown
生活中有许多压力,但你一上车,它们都飞出窗外。 ——丹·布朗

Vocabulary

I. Fill in the blanks with the given words or phrases in the box. Change the form where necessary.

register	dream of	fulfill	evidently	grant
pace	despite	commuter	option	represent
transform	nothing but	retain	eliminate	recreation

1. Last night I did _____ watch TV.
2. In the United States most married women do not _____ their maiden names.
3. A part of the program was _____ to save time.
4. He bought a new car and _____ it in his name.
5. He _____ around the room nervously, waiting for the results of the tests.
6. His favorite _____ are golf and playing computer games.
7. I enclosed a resume for your consideration and would be grateful if you would _____ me an interview.
8. When he was young he _____ traveling around the world.
9. _____, there is no one at home. The lights are out.
10. A school fails if it does not _____ the needs of its students.
11. _____ the cold wind, they went out without their coats.
12. The word "love" is often _____ by a heart.
13. The train was packed with sweaty complaining _____.
14. The beautiful dress _____ the girl into a pretty young lady.
15. When I left school, I wanted to travel, but I didn't have any money. I had no _____ but to work.

II. Choose a word or a phrase from the indicated paragraph to fill in each of the following blanks. Change the form where necessary.

1. She _____ a guide for the group. (*Para. 4*)
2. They are _____ about old motorbikes. (*Para. 2*)
3. Standing under the scorching sun, he was sweating from the _____ heat. (*Para. 3*)
4. Why do men _____ enjoying themselves with getting drunk? (*Para. 3*)
5. She is _____ as a strong candidate for the job. (*Para. 5*)
6. People who send their children to _____ schools must pay fees. (*Para. 8*)
7. Many students find _____ jobs during their summer holidays. (*Para. 9*)
8. It was a _____ song of the 1960s. (*Para. 10*)
9. You _____ your mother very closely. (*Para. 10*)
10. The fax is the most useful machine to be _____ since the telephone. (*Para. 3*)

Structure

I. Rewrite the following sentences after the model.

Model: An interstate highway is not exactly a path to Walden Pond. And a BMW does not much resemble Huck's raft.

An interstate highway is not exactly a path to Walden Pond, **nor does** a BMW much resemble Huck's raft.

1. He was not very intelligent. And he did not work very hard.
   _____

2. She will not leave. And she will not allow him to continue treating her badly.
   _____

3. The meal didn't cost much. And it was not very good.
   _____

4. We don't know all of our enemies. And we can not be sure of all our friends.
   _____

5. He has never experimented with the new method. And he does not intend to.
   _____

II. Complete the following sentences by translating the Chinese into English, using "rather than".

Model: Suburban commuters have resolutely stayed in their vehicles _____
_____ (而不是拼车或乘坐公共交通工具).

Suburban commuters have resolutely stayed in their vehicles <u>rather than join car pools or use public transportation.</u>

1. He is my sister's friend, _____ (而不是我的朋友).
2. He is a writer _____ (而不是个老师).
3. We would do anything _____ (而不是让他受到伤害).
4. He would prefer a week on a big ship _____ (而不想坐飞机旅行).
5. I would play football _____ (而不是去游泳).

Cloze

Choose one appropriate word from the following box to fill in each of the following blanks. Each word can be used only once. Change the word form where necessary.

place	efficient	produce	purpose	cross
similar	contribute	bring	accident	suffer
traffic	quality	compare	process	walk

In the year 1913, Henry Ford introduced the assembly line in car manufacturing. Very quickly, other strong nations copied the (1) _____ and soon, cars were being (2) _____ by the thousands each day all over the world from Japan to Malaysia to Europe and America. The car was invented in the first (3) _____ to make travelling faster, more (4) _____ and more comfortable as (5) _____ to the older modes of transportation like the horse-drawn carriage, the bull cart, or the elephant in India. Today, however, the original (6) _____ of the car may not be as accurate anymore. In Central London for instance, it can take as long to (7) _____ a street as it did in the year 1900. Back then, the horse-drawn carriages traveled at 8 mph. The cars in the (8) _____ jams in London today will not be doing much more. The situation is (9) _____ in other major cities in the world such as New York, Paris, Brisbane and Lagos in Nigeria.

The increased use of motor vehicles all over the world has (10) _____ to the creation of massive jams. In New York, rush hour jams can (11) _____ traffic to a standstill for hours. Jams in Hong Kong can stretch so long that one might just as well (12) _____. The congestion on roads today has also contributed to more serious (13) _____ that can involve many vehicles piling up one against another. Apart from that, people stuck in their vehicles in a serious jam every single day of their working lives, can be expected to (14) _____ from stress and anxiety. The (15) _____ of life as they would perceive it then is bound to be negatively affected.

Translation

Translate the following sentences into Chinese.

1. Since its first appearance in the 1890s, the automobile has embodied deep-seated cultural and emotional values that have become an integral part of the American Dream.

   _____
   _____
   _____

2. It was the vehicle of personal democracy, acting as a social leveling force, granting more and more people a wide range of personal choice—where to travel, where to work and live, where to seek personal pleasure and social recreation.

3. It was one thing to praise the individual freedom offered by the horseless carriage when there were a few thousand of them spread across the nation; it is quite another matter when there are 200 million of them.

4. As one popular bumper sticker resolutely declares, "You'll Get Me Out of My Car When You Pry My Cold, Dead Foot from the Accelerator."

5. Our solution to rush hour gridlock is not to demand public transportation but to transform our immobile automobile into a temporary office, bank, restaurant, bathroom, and stereo system.

Text B Bike Sharing

1 In the last ten years bike sharing systems have quickly become an almost essential feature to cities worldwide, and it is rare now to visit an urban center that doesn't have some manner of communal cycling infrastructure in place. It makes sense; an increase in bicycles has proven time and again to be an overwhelming positive force on a city, its inhabitants, and its relationship to the wider world as a whole. But recently, the bike hasn't always been so warmly  received. According to a report by the guardian, cyclist numbers in China have plummeted from 63% of Beijing commuters in 1980 to just 12% today.

2 Elsewhere however, the outlook is decidedly brighter, with bike sharing infrastructure popping up left right and center. While those ubiquitous racks of bicycles on your city's sidewalks may seem like a modern addition, the concept of a bike sharing system goes all the way back to 1960's Amsterdam. Given that the city is notorious for its high volume of cyclists, it is not surprise that in 1965 a group of activists founded an initiative called the white bikes'. Painted white and deposited at various locations around the city, the guerrilla cycling scheme was quickly abandoned after many of the vehicles were stolen or dumped, but the core concept caught the imagination of others.

3 It wasn't until 1995 however that another city—this time Copenhagen—attempted to replicate the project. Entitled "bycyklen", the system used coin operated machines to manage its public bicycles. Not without its own troubles (like theft and vandalism) the scheme nevertheless started a revolution that has today grown into a worldwide phenomenon of green transport.

4 The benefits of an efficient, cost effective bike sharing system to a city and its people are endless. Not only does it drastically reduce traffic congestion, it takes a huge chunk out of the overall air pollution, carbon footprint and noise profile of a region. It's common knowledge regular exercise has a notably positive effect on our mental health and wellbeing, and a recent study by Portland state university suggests that cyclists are by far the happiest of commuters. It develops a city's tourism sector by granting a quick and cheap means of transport to visitors, but more than this, it builds a sense of community between locals around a shared activity, bringing people together whose paths may never have otherwise crossed.

5 The design of these systems vary, but share the simple core concept of checking bikes in or out for allotted periods of time by means of strategically placed bike racks. Since their debut however, the technology has come on in leaps and bounds. Many schemes, such as Citi Bikes in

New York or London's Santander cycles use solar powered stations, with more advanced iterations featuring automatic locking and digital tracking. London's bikes recently debuted its "blaze laserlights": green, bicycle shaped lasers that project onto the path a few feet ahead of the vehicle, making other travelers aware of approaching bicycles.

6   Recently, sports giant NIKE helped launch Portland's new bike sharing initiative, "biketown"; smart bicycles whose vibrant orange color way helps them stand out in a crowd. Unlike other systems, biketown's technology is embedded into the bicycles themselves. Rather than interact with a central station, each bike is equipped with a solar powered screen, GPS, and tracking system. These advancements technologies that support the bicycles are slowly but surely making the schemes safer, faster, more democratic and just plain easier to use.

7   At present, the driving force in the field is, surprisingly, China. With densely populated cities, soaring levels of pollution and an automotive market larger than the US, China's cities are quickly turning to two wheeled alternatives in an attempt to solve its transport crisis. The name on everybody's lips is "ofo", a cycling startup thus named because of the word's literal similarity to a bicycle. Founded by 25-year-old Dai Wei, the company is distinguished by its use of bright yellow cycles, and is leading the charge of China's two-wheeled revolution. What makes them stand out however is that users can hop on and off anywhere they like, without needing to find a nearby docking station.

8   Users of the scheme are guided to the nearest ofo bike by means of an accompanying app. Once found, the app provides them with a four digit code to unlock the bike's back wheel. The technology takes the hassle out of regular bike-sharing schemes, which often sees cyclists travelling out of their way to find a docking station that isn't already full. As long as the bike is parked in a legal and safe spot, it's all good. The system has proven so popular that it's even bringing 500 of its units to Cambridge in the UK where cyclists will pay a flat fee of 50p per journey—no matter the distance.

9   While it's always exciting to see advancement in human carrying drones and driverless cars, it's still heartening to see that trusty old bicycles are proving themselves favorites when it comes to getting from A to B. With the success of ofo, citibikes and others like them, it's hard to see them putting the brakes on anytime soon.

(928 words)

(https://www.designboom.com/design/bike-sharing-design-ofo-citibike-03-15-2017/)

Words and Phrases to Learn

essential /ɪˈsenʃl/ *a.* 基本的；必要的；本质的；精华的
overwhelming /ˌəʊvəˈwelmɪŋ/ *a.* 势不可挡的；压倒的；无法抗拒的
plummet /ˈplʌmɪt/ *vi.* 垂直落下；骤然跌落
abandon /əˈbænd(ə)n/ *vt.* 遗弃；放弃
nevertheless /ˌnevəðəˈles/ *adv.* 然而；尽管如此；不过；仍然
congestion /kənˈdʒestʃn/ *n.* 阻塞；拥挤；充血
allot /əˈlɒt/ *vt.* 分配；拨给；分派
leaps and bounds 跃进；突飞猛进
stand out 突出；显眼；引人注目
embed /ɪmˈbed; em-/ *vt. & vi.* 把……嵌入；栽种；深留（记忆中）
distinguish /dɪˈstɪŋgwɪʃ/ *vt.* 区别；辨认；使显著
automotive /ˌɔːtəˈməʊtɪv/ *a.* 汽车的；自动的
hop /hɒp/ *v.* 单足跳跃；跳行；双足或齐足跳行
accompany /əˈkʌmpəni/ *vt.* 陪伴；伴随……发生；补充
put the brakes on 阻止某事物

Comprehension Check

Choose the best answer for each of the following.

1. The concept of bike sharing system dates back to _____.
   A. 1960's Amsterdam
   B. 1970's London
   C. 1980's Beijing
   D. 1990's Copenhagen

2. What are the positive effects of bike sharing system?
   A. Reducing traffic congestion.
   B. Building a sense of community
   C. Improving our mental health and well-being
   D. All of the above.

3. Why is bike sharing called green transport?
   A. Because bikes are painted green.
   B. Because bike sharing is environmentally friendly.
   C. Because they are easy to use.
   D. Because the history of bike sharing is not long.

4. Which city uses blaze laserlights to make other travelers aware of approaching bicycles?
   A. Portland.

B. New York.

C. London.

D. Beijing.

5. What is "ofo"?

    A. It's a cycling startup.

    B. It's a docking station.

    C. It's a two-wheeled revolution.

    D. It's an accompanying app.

6. What is the author's attitude towards the prospect of bike sharing system?

    A. Negative.

    B. Positive.

    C. Neutral.

    D. Critical.

Language Practice

Fill in the blanks with words or phrases listed in the *Words and Phrases to Learn*.

1. The scheme's investors decided to _____ the project.
2. We can't take your advice. _____, thank you for putting it.
3. This is the government's latest plan to reduce traffic _____ in our city centers.
4. Play is an _____ part of a child's development.
5. He has exhibited symptoms of anxiety and _____ worry.
6. She really _____ in that orange coat.
7. She had a piece of metal _____ deep in her skull.
8. Color-blind people can't _____ between red and green.
9. The only way to clear this capacity is either to wait a very long time for the economy to catch up, or for prices to _____.
10. I _____ down three steps.
11. He suffered from hypertension and _____ heart problems.
12. Illness had _____ his progress.
13. The seats are _____ to the candidates who have won the most votes.
14. In recent years our university's enrollments have been going up by _____.
15. There is a chain of stores selling _____ parts.

Part II Listening

Section A

Directions: In this section you will hear five short conversations. At the end of each conversation a question will be asked about what was said. Both the conversation and the question will be spoken only once. Listen carefully and choose the best answer.

1. A. On weekends.
   B. On weekdays.
   C. In the evenings.
   D. During the day.
2. A. Neither the man nor the woman thinks Frank is humorous.
   B. The man appreciates Frank's sense of humor but the woman doesn't.
   C. The woman appreciates Frank's sense of humor but the man doesn't.
   D. Both the man and the woman think Frank has a good sense of humor.
3. A. The man is looking for a place to live in.
   B. The man is paying a visit to the woman.
   C. The two speakers are old friends.
   D. The woman is inviting the man to her house.
4. A. They have a lot in common.
   B. They have been eating a lot recently.
   C. They have been earning extra money.
   D. They are planning for their Christmas holiday.
5. A. Something went wrong with the bus.
   B. She took somebody to hospital.
   C. She missed the bus.
   D. She came on foot instead of taking a bus.

Section B

Directions: In this section you will hear a long conversation. At the end of the conversation you will hear some questions. Both the conversation and the questions will be spoken only once. After you hear a question, you must choose the best answer.

6. A. He wants her to apply for a job online for him.
   B. He wants her to recommend him to her company.

C. He wants her to write a resume for him.

D. He wants her to help him improve his computer skills.

7. A. She thinks his computer skills are amazing.

B. She thinks his computer skills need to be improved.

C. She doesn't think highly of his computer skills.

D. She really appreciates his computer skills.

8. A. He is good at writing resumes.

B. He is good at applying for jobs online.

C. He is good at surfing the Internet.

D. He is good at talking with people.

Section C

Directions: In this section you will hear a passage. At the end of the passage, you will hear some questions. The passage and the questions will be spoken only once. After you hear a question, you must choose the best answer.

9. A. It is a seaside resort near the River Rhine in Germany.

B. It can be a dangerous place to visit during winter.

C. Only in winter can you see a stunning view in St. Peter-Ording.

D. It's a place that is full of dangers all year round.

10. A. A man got lost in St. Peter-Ording when it was getting dark.

B. A man broke his leg when he was looking for his flashing light in St. Peter-Ording.

C. A man took photographs of the beautiful sunset in St. Peter-Ording.

D. A man visited St. Peter-Ording alone after breaking up with his girlfriend.

11. A. A woman in the Westerwald region went to St. Peter-Ording to save the man.

B. The flashing light caught the police's attention in St. Peter-Ording.

C. Other climbers in St. Peter-Ording immediately came to his rescue.

D. A woman 500 kilometers away spotted the man on the webcam and called the police.

12. A. The flashlight.

B. The freezing temperature.

C. The pictures taken by the man.

D. The live webcam.

Part III Speaking

Section A

Directions: Discuss the following questions in small groups.

1. What are the effects of the increased use of automobiles?
2. Describe the rush hour in your city.
3. What means of transportation should be the priority in an underdeveloped city?

Section B

Directions: Read aloud the following passage.

Edmunds: Your One-Stop Car Shop

For some people, car shopping can be overwhelming. You have to go to this site to find savings and incentives, then that site for buying and leasing guides, and even another site for a payment calculator. But Edmunds is your trusted advisor—we have everything you need to find your perfect new or used car in one place. No matter where you are in the car shopping process, we can help. Need detailed side-by-side comparisons of car features and specs? Detailed expert and user reviews of the latest makes and models? Informed buying and leasing guides? Connections to thousands of dealers in your area with available new and used cars? We've got it all. And after you find your perfect car, we can help you lock in upfront pricing and get exclusive extras. So no matter where you are, we can provide you with a simple, easy and efficient car shopping experience.

Part IV Writing

Directions: Write a composition on the topic "Are Cars Making our Life More Convenient or More Troublesome?" You should write at least 100 words, and base your composition on the outline given below.

1. Some people think that cars make our life convenient.
2. Others think that cars can make our life troublesome.
3. In my opinion ...

Unit 1

Dream & Pursuit

Vocabulary & Structure

I. Choose the answer that best completes each of the following sentences.

1. A rare smile _____ her stern features.
   A. lit up   B. outgrew   C. stunned   D. converted
2. It's stupid of you to lose your temper when you ought to _____ your argument.
   A. object to   B. list   C. apply   D. reinforce
3. The kitchen _____ freshly baked bread, which carried her back to her childhood.
   A. emerged   B. smelled of   C. displayed   D. pervaded
4. He declared it was his wife's handwriting, _____ his lawyer.
   A. as done
   C. as did
   B. so as to
   D. protesting against
5. We should try to _____ that he is wasting his life in his job.
   A. put him through
   C. enlighten him with
   B. get through to him
   D. come about
6. Reducing the gap between the rich and poor is one of the main _____ facing the government.
   A. confrontations
   C. challenges
   B. confrontation
   D. challenge
7. In his speech he _____ the importance of education by giving full details of the most serious problems caused by the educational system.
   A. talked   B. reported on   C. dealt with   D. dwelt on
8. Celina's parents are Spanish _____, but they have British citizenship.
   A. by birth   B. from birth   C. in origin   D. of origin
9. After the ex-manager resigned, Fred was _____ to the vacant post.
   A. obtained   B. accepted   C. appointed   D. employed

10. Make sure that the name on the envelope _____ with the name on the letter inside.
    A. amounts   B. equals   C. corresponds   D. echo

II. Spell out each word according to the Chinese given. The first letter is written for you.

1. 给……以荣誉；使增光   vt.   h_____
2. 签（名）   vt.   s_____
3. 价值   n.   v_____
4. 好奇心   n.   c_____
5. （大学）校园   n.   c_____
6. 使……变化   vt.   v_____
7. 迷人的   a.   f_____
8. 标签   n.   l_____
9. 捕获   vt.   c_____
10. 存款   n.   d_____
11. 雇员   n.   e_____
12. 以前的   a.   p_____
13. 拒绝；驳回   vt.   r_____
14. 替代，取代   vt.   r_____
15. 现在的，目前的   a.   c_____

Cloze

III. Fill in the gaps with the words you think fit.

I'm pretty sure none of this would have happened if I hadn't been fired __1__ Apple. It was awful-tasting medicine, but I guess the patient __2__ it. Sometimes life hits you in the head __3__ a brick. Don't lose faith. I'm convinced that the only thing that __4__ me going was that I loved what I did. You've got to find __5__ you love. And that is as true for your work as it is __6__ your lovers. Your work is going to fill a large __7__ of your life, and the only way to be truly satisfied is to do what you believe is great work. And the only __8__ to do great work is to love what you do. If you haven't found it yet, keep looking. Don't settle. As with all matters of the heart, you'll know __9__ you find it. And, like any great relationship, it just gets better and better as the years roll on. So keep looking __10__ you find it. Don't settle.

IV. In this part there is a passage with 20 blanks in it. For each blank there are four choices marked A, B, C and D. You are required to choose the one that best fits into the passage.

As the plane circled over the airport, everyone sensed that something was wrong. The plane was moving unsteadily through the air, and __1__ the passengers had fastened their seat belts, they were suddenly __2__ forward. At that moment, the air-hostess __3__ . She looked very pale, but was quite __4__. Speaking quickly but almost in a whisper, she __5__ everyone that the pilot had __6__ and asked if any of the passengers knew anything about machines or at __7__ how to drive a car. After a moment's __8__, a man got up and followed the hostess into the pilot's cabin. Moving the pilot __9__, the man took his seat and listened carefully to the __10__ instructions that were being sent by radio from the airport __11__. The plane was now dangerously close __12__ the ground, but to everyone's __13__, it soon began to climb. The man had to __14__ the airport several times in order to become __15__ with the controls of the plane. __16__ the danger had not yet passed. The terrible __17__ came when he had to land. Following __18__, the man guided the plane toward the airfield. It shook violently __19__ it touched the ground and then moved rapidly __20__ the runway and after a long run it stopped safely.

1. A. although   B. while   C. therefore   D. then
2. A. shifted   B. thrown   C. put   D. moved
3. A. showed   B. presented   C. exposed   D. appeared
4. A. well   B. still   C. calm   D. quiet
5. A. inquired   B. insured   C. informed   D. instructed
6. A. fallen   B. failed   C. faded   D. fainted
7. A. best   B. least   C. length   D. first
8. A. hesitation B. surprise   C. doubt   D. delay
9. A. back   B. aside   C. about   D. off
10. A. patient   B. anxious   C. urgent   D. nervous
11. A. beneath   B. under   C. down   D. below
12. A. to   B. by   C. near   D. on
13. A. horror   B. trust   C. pleasure   D. relief
14. A. surround   B. circle   C. observe   D. view
15. A. intimate   B. familiar   C. understood   D. close
16. A. Then   B. Therefore   C. But   D. Moreover
17. A. moment   B. movement   C. idea   D. affair
18. A. impression B. information C. inspections D. instructions
19. A. as   B. unless   C. while   D. so
20. A. around   B. over   C. along   D. above

Reading Comprehension

V. Read the following passage and do the multiple-choice exercises after it.

Psychologists take opposing views of how external rewards, from warm praise to old cash, affect motivation and creativity. Behaviorists, who study the relation between actions and rewards, argue that rewards can improve performance at work and school. Some other researchers who study various aspects of mental life, maintain those rewards often destroy creativity by encouraging dependence on approval and gifts from others. The latter view has gained many supporters, especially among educators. But the careful use of small monetary rewards sparks creativity in grade-school children, suggesting that properly presented inducements indeed aid inventiveness, according to a study in June from *Journal Personality and Social Psychology.*

"If they know they're working for a reward and can focus on a relatively challenging task, they show the most creativity," says Robert Esenberger of the University of Delaware in Newark. "But it's easy to kill creativity by giving rewards for poor performance or creating too much anticipation for rewards."

A teacher who continually draws attention to rewards or who hands out high grades for ordinary achievements ends up with uninspired students, Esenberger holds. As an example of the latter point, he notes growing efforts at major universities to tighten grading standards and restore failing grades.

1. Psychologists are divided with regard to their attitudes toward _____.
   A. the choice between spiritual encouragement and monetary rewards
   B. the appropriate quantity of external rewards
   C. the study of the relationship between actions and rewards
   D. the effects of external rewards on students' performance

2. What is the view held by many educators concerning external rewards for students?
   A. They approve of external rewards.
   B. They don't think that external rewards are useful.
   C. They have doubts about external rewards.
   D. They believe external rewards can motivate small children, but not college students.

3. According to the result of the study mentioned in the passage, what should educators do to stimulate motivation and creativity?
   A. Give rewards for achievements which deserve them.
   B. Always promise rewards.
   C. Assign tasks which are not very challenging.
   D. Be more lenient to students when mistakes are made.

4. "Uninspired" in the last paragraph is closest in meaning to _____.
   A. aimless   B. imaginative   C. average   D. diligent

5. It can be inferred from the passage that major universities are trying to tighten their grading standards because they believe _____.
   A. rewarding poor performance may kill the creativity of students
   B. punishment is more effective than rewarding
   C. failing uninspired students helps improve their overall academic standards
   D. discouraging students' anticipation for easy rewards is a matter of urgency

Unit Two

Maintaining a Healthy Lifestyle

Vocabulary & Structure

I. **Choose the answer that best completes each of the following sentences.**

1. —Jack, have you got that job yet?
   —Not yet. It's still _____. I haven't made up my mind yet.
   A. off balance B. in the balance
   C. on balance D. out of balance

2. _____ to the doctor right away, he might have been alive today.
   A. If he went B. Had he gone
   C. Were he gone D. Should he have gone

3. Careful planning and hard work will _____ our final success.
   A. enclose B. ensure C. discharge D. deny

4. When you fill in the application form, please use your _____ address so that we can contact you easily later.
   A. policy B. plain C. permanent D. principal

5. He _____ to study harder in the future so that he could have more opportunities to find a better job.
   A. resolved B. resorted C. requested D. reserved

6. When a spacecraft travels, one of the major problems is the reentry into the Earth's _____.
   A. surface B. atmosphere C. attitude D. bent

7. After working for twenty hours without any rest, the doctors were _____.
   A. exhausted B. mounted C. wrapped D. restored

8. This movie has a _____ ending. You can not imagine who will be killed finally.
   A. dramatic B. original C. considerable D. tempting

9. He always _____ to everything and never agrees with anybody.
   A. protests B. gives C. yields D. objects

10. These programs are designed for those young people who want to _____ a higher education but do not have enough time to go to university.
    A. persist B. purse C. purchase D. pursue

II. Spell out each word according to the Chinese given. The first letter is written for you.

1. 大气;大气层　　　　　　　　　n.　　　　　　a＿＿＿＿＿
2. 气候　　　　　　　　　　　　　n.　　　　　　c＿＿＿＿＿
3. 运送,运输　　　　　　　　　　vt.　　　　　 t＿＿＿＿＿
4. 集中;专心　　　　　　　　　　n.　　　　　　c＿＿＿＿＿
5. 自觉有罪的,内疚的　　　　　　a.　　　　　　g＿＿＿＿＿
6. 偶然地　　　　　　　　　　　　ad.　　　　　 o＿＿＿＿＿
7. 燃料　　　　　　　　　　　　　n.　　　　　　f＿＿＿＿＿
8. 援救,解救　　　　　　　　　　n.　　　　　　r＿＿＿＿＿
9. 压力,重压　　　　　　　　　　n.　　　　　　s＿＿＿＿＿
10. 反映　　　　　　　　　　　　vt.　　　　　 r＿＿＿＿＿
11. 关心;忧虑　　　　　　　　　　n.　　　　　　c＿＿＿＿＿
12. 洞察力;见识　　　　　　　　　n.　　　　　　i＿＿＿＿＿
13. 身体的　　　　　　　　　　　　a.　　　　　　p＿＿＿＿＿
14. 积极的;肯定的　　　　　　　　a.　　　　　　p＿＿＿＿＿
15. 回想起,回忆起　　　　　　　　vt.　　　　　 r＿＿＿＿＿

Cloze

III. Fill in the gaps with the words you think fit.

Eat wisely and healthily. Your food choices directly __1__ your health. Stop smoking. Or, __2__ you are a non-smoker, avoid __3__ who smoke and __4__ going to smoke-filled places. Having alcoholic drinks may be a social habit, __5__ too much drinking (more than two __6__ for men, more than one for women daily) could lead __7__ weight gain, __8__ blood sugar levels, wrinkles, eye bags. If you must __9__, have a full meal first.

Start a moderate, exercise plan, one suited __10__ your personality—walk, run, bike, swim, play badminton, dance.

IV. In this part there is a passage with 20 blanks in it. For each blank there are four choices marked A, B, C and D. You are required to choose the one that best fits into the passage.

One day a police officer managed to get some fresh mushrooms. He was so __1__ what he had bought that he offered to __2__ the mushrooms with his brother officers. When their breakfast arrived the next day, each officer found some mushrooms on his plate.

"Let the dog __3__ a piece first," suggested one __4__ officer who was afraid that the mushrooms might be poisonous. The dog seemed to __5__ his mushrooms, and the officers then began to eat their meal saying that the mushrooms had a very strange __6__ quite pleasant taste.

An hour __7__, however, they were all astonished when the gardener rushed in and said

___8___ the dog was dead. ___9___, the officers jumped into their cars and rushed into the nearest hospital. Pumps (泵) were used and the officers had a very ___10___ time getting rid of the mushrooms that ___11___ in their stomachs. When they ___12___ to the police station, they sat down and started to ___13___ the mushroom poisoning. Each man explained the pains that he had felt and they agreed that ___14___ had grown worse on their ___15___ to the hospital. The gardener was called to tell the way ___16___ the poor dog had died. "Did it ___17___ much before death?" asked one of the officers, ___18___ very pleased that he had escaped a ___19___ death himself. "No," answered the gardener looking rather ___20___, "It was killed the moment a car hit it."

1. A. sure of   B. careless about
   C. pleased with   D. disappointed at
2. A. share   B. grow   C. wash   D. cook
3. A. check   B. smell   C. try   D. examine
4. A. frightened   B. shy   C. cheerful   D. careful
5. A. refuse   B. hate   C. want   D. enjoy
6. A. besides   B. but   C. and   D. or
7. A. later   B. after   C. past   D. over
8. A. cruelly   B. curiously   C. seriously   D. finally
9. A. Immediately B. Carefully   C. Suddenly   D. Slowly
10. A. hard   B. busy   C. exciting   D. unforgettable
11. A. stopped   B. dropped   C. settled   D. remained
12. A. hurried   B. drove   C. went   D. returned
13. A. study   B. discuss   C. record   D. remember
14. A. this   B. these   C. it   D. they
15. A. road   B. street   C. way   D. direction
16. A. how   B. in that   C. which   D. in which
17. A. suffer   B. eat   C. harm   D. spit
18. A. to feel   B. feeling   C. felt   D. having felt
19. A. strange   B. painful   C. peaceful   D. natural
20. A. happy   B. interested   C. surprised   D. excited

Reading Comprehension

V. Read the following passage and do the multiple-choice exercises after it.

A lot of people don't like to give waiters money—a tip, but maybe those people don't understand about waitresses and waiters. You see, we get very low wages, most of the time less than the minimum wage. We count on the tips as part of our salary. If waiters and waitresses didn't get tips, they wouldn't get enough money to live.

People asked me, "What's a good tip?" I like to get 15% of the bill. So if a customer has to pay $20.00 for her dinner, I like to get about $3.00 for a tip. Sometimes I expect 20% if I did a lot of work for the customer. For example, if I got her a special kind of food or recipe from the chef. But do you know something? Very often it's the person for whom you work the most gives you the smallest tips.

But to tell the truth, I do pretty well with tips. I'm a friendly person, so people like me. They talk to me during their meal and leave me a good tip. Of course some people prefer a quiet waitress and every once in a while I get some pretty small tip or no tip at all.

Once I looked up "tipping" in a dictionary. It said that the letters in the word "tip" stand for "To Insure Promptness". In other words, to make sure that we do things right away. The dictionary said that no one knows if that is the real meaning of "tip", but it makes sense to me. If we know a regular customer is a good tipper, then we make sure he gets good service. But if someone gives small tips, we aren't in a hurry to bring him food or get his drinks. So remember, be nice to your waitress and she'll be nice to you.

1. What's the author's job?
  A. A dictionary complier. B. A restaurant manager.
  C. A regular customer. D. A server in the restaurant.

2. The phrase "count on" in Paragraph One probably means _____.
  A. rely on B. work out C. feel like D. take place

3. How much does the author expect from the customer if he does extra work for him?
  A. $3.00. B. 15%.
  C. 20%. D. As much as possible.

4. The author gets satisfying tips because _____.
  A. she has regular customers
  B. she manages to satisfy the customers
  C. she asks the customers for those
  D. the restaurant requires the customers to pay them

5. The dictionary defines "tip" as _____.
  A. to make sense B. to ensure promptness
  C. to get good service D. to give extra money

Unit 3

Leisure & Entertainment

Vocabulary & Structure

I. Choose the answer that best completes each of the following sentences.

1. Contrary _____ all our expectations, he's found a well-paid job and a nice girlfriend.
   A. with   B. for   C. in   D. to
2. Sir Williams, who is 80, has made it known that much of his collection _____ to the local museum.
   A. is left   B. had been left C. is being left D. is to be left
3. The records _____ to show an improvement in sales that didn't exist.
   A. were pretended   B. were pretending
   C. were faked   D. were lied
4. At such a young age, these innocent girls, who always take anything _____, get _____ easily.
   A. on trust; taken   B. on the trust; taken
   C. on trust; took   D. in trust; taken
5. I am quite _____ your opinion that we need a more harmonious society.
   A. in agree with   B. in agreement for
   C. in agreement with   D. in the agreement with
6. Learning languages is a long, _____ process with _____ and it is too easy just to give up.
   A. gradually; ups and downs B. gradually; up and down
   C. gradual; ups and downs   D. gradual; up and down
7. All _____ is a continuous supply of fuel oil, which is fundamental to the development of every country.
   A. what is needed   B. that is needed
   C. the thing needed   D. for their needs
8. I regret to inform you that your son has been _____ to the police for breaking the street lights.
   A. handed in   B. turned in   C. handed out   D. turned out
9. Only when your identity has been checked, _____.

A. you are allowed in B. you'll be allowed in
C. will you allow in D. will you be allowed in

10. Anne dreaded giving a speech before three hundred people; even thinking about it made her _____.

A. ambitious B. optimistic C. passionate D. anxious

II. Spell out each word according to the Chinese given. The first letter is written for you.

1. 神秘的   *a.*   m_____
2. 具体的；明确的   *a.*   s_____
3. 机会   *n.*   o_____
4. 例行公事；日常工作   *n.*   r_____
5. 拼命的，不顾一切的   *a.*   d_____
6. 片断；碎片   *n.*   f_____
7. 智慧，才智   *n.*   w_____
8. 现时的，当前的   *a.*   c_____
9. 目的地，终点   *n.*   d_____
10. 相当数量的；重要的   *a.*   s_____
11. 财富   *n.*   w_____
12. 对比，对照   *n.*   c_____
13. 特征，特点   *n.*   f_____
14. 给人印象，引人入胜   *v.*   i_____
15. 有力的；给人深刻印象的   *a.*   e_____

Cloze

III. Fill in the gaps with words you think fit.

Watching "Precious", I was reminded of another film about the sufferings of women in distress, "Dancer in the Dark". Both films are __1__ with care. Both films __2__ strong performances. Both films contain a story that is increasingly cruel to its central __3__. I can understand the __4__ for either film and I can understand the criticism __5__ either film. On an objective (客观的) level, I can understand it. But movies become __6__ experiences and that's __7__ I don't like "Dancer in the Dark" and will not defend it. I will surely __8__ "Precious". I walked out of Lars von Trier's movie in a __9__ of despair. I left "Precious" encouraged. There are two worlds here: one hopeless, one __10__. I choose to live in the latter.

IV. In this part there is a passage with 20 blanks in it. For each blank there are four choices marked A, B, C and D. You are required to choose the one that best fits into the passage.

From Monday until Friday, most people are busy working or studying, but in the evenings and on weekends they are free to relax and enjoy themselves. Some watch television __1__ go to the cinema, others take part in sports. It __2__ on individual interests. There are many different __3__ to spend our __4__ time.

Almost everyone has some kind of hobby. It may be __5__ from collecting stamps to __6__ model airplanes. Some hobbies are very expensive, but others are valuable __7__ to their owners.

I know a man who has a __8__ collection worth several thousand dollars. A short time ago, he bought a __9__ fifty-cent piece worth $250! He was very __10__ about his purchase and thought the price was __11__. On the other hand, my younger brother __12__ match boxes. He has almost 600 of them, but I doubt if they are worth __13__ money. However, to __14__ they are extremely valuable. Nothing makes him happier than to find a new __15__ for his collection.

That's what a hobby __16__, I guess. It is something we like to do __17__ our spare time simply for the __18__ of it. The __19__ in dollars is not important, but the pleasure it __20__ us is.

1. A. and   B. but   C. so   D. or
2. A. lies   B. works   C. depends   D. waits
3. A. ideas   B. ways   C. places   D. periods
4. A. full   B. work   C. spare   D. busy
5. A. nothing   B. everything   C. something   D. anything
6. A. making   B. buying   C. selling   D. inventing
7. A. only   B. especially   C. fully   D. simply
8. A. stamp   B. coin   C. money   D. ring
9. A. common   B. usual   C. rare   D. new
10. A. happy   B. careful   C. worried   D. anxious
11. A. high   B. low   C. reasonable   D. unbelievable
12. A. gathers   B. picks out   C. chooses   D. collects
13. A. some   B. any   C. no   D. much
14. A. me   B. others   C. my brother   D. my family
15. A. coin   B. match box   C. diamond   D. jewel
16. A. is   B. means   C. includes   D. remains
17. A. for   B. to   C. on   D. in
18. A. benefit   B. good   C. fun   D. money
19. A. value   B. cost   C. meaning   D. amount
20. A. has   B. gets   C. produces   D. gives

Reading Comprehension

V. Read the following passage and do the multiple-choice exercises after it.

The success of *Pickwick Papers* made Dickens very popular. He suddenly found himself at the age of twenty-four, the most famous novelist of his day. Busy as his social life was, he worked on two novels at the same time—*Oliver Twist* and *Pickwick Papers*. He was particularly proud of the latter as a comic (喜剧的) masterpiece. He once said, "If I were to live a hundred years and write three novels in each year, I should never be so proud of any of them as I am proud of *Pickwick Papers*."

It is said that Dickens grasped the imagination of his readers because his imagination grasped himself. The characters in his works were so real that they could make him laugh or cry. When writing *Oliver Twist*, he said that he could not rest at ease until Fagin, the wrong-doer, was hanged.

Dickens's marriage to Catherine Hogarth, with whom he had nine children, ended unhappily in 1858. He started to travel about, giving readings of his works. His interest in the theatre gave his novels the qualities that made them suitable for reading about on the stage. A tiring travel to the United States resulted in his death. He died on July 9, 1870, while working on a new novel and that was exactly what Dickens had always wanted—to die of working.

1. Which of the following is true according to the passage?

    A. Dickens was one of the 24 world-famous novelists of his day.

    B. It was *Oliver Twist* that made Dickens very popular.

    C. Dickens became the most famous novelist for *Pickwick Papers*.

    D. Dickens did not become famous at the age of 24.

2. From the passage we know that Dickens _____.

    A. wanted to live a long life and write three hundred novels

    B. didn't believe he could write a better one than *Pickwick Papers*

    C. was only interested in writing about his own social life

    D. did not like to work on two novels at the same time

3. As a novelist, Dickens _____.

    A. was often in deep thought

    B. liked to write about real people in his novels

    C. was often grasped by his readers

    D. was a man full of imagination

4. When writing the novel *Oliver Twist*, Dickens could not rest at ease because _____.

    A. Fagin had not been severely punished

    B. Fagin had done much wrong

    C. Fagin could not live without the evil

    D. Dickens was not able to finish the novel

5. According to the passage, Dickens did many things after 1858 EXCEPT _____.

    A. traveling around
    B. writing new novels
    C. acting on the stage
    D. giving readings of his works

Unit 4

Love

Vocabulary & Structure

I. Choose the answer that best completes each of the following sentences.

1. Some words, such as "sandwich" and "hamburger", were _____ the names of people or even towns.
   A. ideally　　　B. relatively　　　C. precisely　　　D. originally

2. I had to _____ Jack's invitation to the party because it conflicted with an important business meeting.
   A. decline　　　B. reject　　　C. deny　　　D. accept

3. Selling fried chicken at the night market doesn't seem to be a decent business, but it is actually quite _____.
   A. plentiful　　　B. precious　　　C. productive　　　D. profitable

4. Criticism and self-criticism is necessary _____ it helps us to find and correct our mistakes.
   A. by that　　　B. at that　　　C. in that　　　D. on that

5. People who live in small towns often seem more friendly than those living in _____ populated areas.
   A. intensely　　　B. abundantly　　　C. highly　　　D. densely

6. The mayor is a woman with great _____ and therefore deserves our political and financial support.
   A. instinct　　　B. integrity　　　C. intention　　　D. intensity

7. One of the requirements for a fire is that the material _____ to its burning temperature.
   A. is heated　　　B. will be heated　　　C. be heated　　　D. would be heated

8. The business of each day, _____ selling goods or shipping them, went quite smoothly.
   A. it being　　　B. be it　　　C. was it　　　D. it was

9. He doesn't _____ the usual stereotype of the city businessman with a dark suit and rolled umbrella.
   A. obey　　　B. conform to　　　C. abide by　　　D. agree to

10. The public health programs associated with Beijing's hosting the 2008 Olympic and

Paralympic Games should not be limited _____ six weeks during which the competitions take place.

A. to B. with C. for D. on

II. Spell out each word according to the Chinese given. The first letter is written for you.

1. 虚拟的   *a.*   v_____
2. 商业   *n.*   c_____
3. 展示,陈列   *vt.*   d_____
4. 行为,举止   *n.*   b_____
5. 可用的,可得到的   *a.*   a_____
6. 有形的;实物的   *a.*   p_____
7. 货币;流通   *n.*   c_____
8. 代替者;代用品   *n.*   s_____
9. 消费者   *n.*   c_____
10. 将……联系起来   *vt.*   a_____
11. 系,贴   *vt.*   a_____
12. 把……排除在外   *vt.*   e_____
13. 保持,维持   *vt.*   m_____
14. 认出,识别   *vt.*   i_____
15. 使困窘,使局促不安   *vt.*   e_____

Cloze

III. Fill in the gaps with the words you think fit.

My husband and I had been together for six years, and with him I had watched __1__ his young children became young teenagers. __2__ they lived primarily with their mother, they __3__ a lot of time with us as well. Over the years, we all learned to adjust, to become more comfortable __4__ each other, and to adapt __5__ our new family arrangement. We enjoyed vacations together, __6__ family meals, worked on homework, played baseball, rented videos. However, I continued to feel somewhat __7__ an outsider, infringing upon foreign territory. There was a definite boundary line __8__ could not be crossed, an inner family circle which excluded me. Since I had no children of my __9__, my experience of parenting was limited to my husband's four, and often I lamented that I would never know the special bond that exists __10__ a parent and a child.

IV. In this part there is a passage with 20 blanks in it. For each blank there are four choices marked A, B, C and D. You are required to choose the one that best fits into the passage.

The dictionary tells us an absent-minded person is so busy with his thought that he does not notice other things that are happening, __1__ the thing that he is doing. Professor Egghead is one of the absent-minded ones.

__2__ his glasses on his nose, he often asks himself, "Where __3__ I put my glasses?"

One afternoon when he came back home, he said with __4__ to his wife, "Look! I haven't __5__ to bring my umbrella home with me today." But his wife, bursting into __6__, said, "You __7__ take your own umbrella with you __8__ morning."

Last Sunday, Professor Egghead was __9__ at the railway station with his two friends. They were deep in __10__. The train had just moved, but they didn't notice it. Then the guard shouted, "Take your __11__, please!"

The __12__ heard the guard and __13__ for the train. Two of them got on the train __14__ it moved. The third one was __15__ behind. It was Professor Egghead. He looked __16__.

One of the professor's students __17__ to be at the station. He tried to __18__ the professor. "It wasn't really bad, sir," said the student. "Two __19__ three caught the train. That's quite good, you know."

"I know," the professor said. "But it was my __20__. My friends only came to see me off."

1. A. and   B. but   C. so   D. or
2. A. Wearing   B. Putting on   C. Hanging   D. Dressed
3. A. would   B. shall   C. did   D. can
4. A. respect   B. care   C. pride   D. satisfaction
5. A. thought   B. remembered   C. expected   D. forgotten
6. A. tears   B. anger   C. quarrel   D. laughter
7. A. didn't   B. hadn't   C. shouldn't   D. couldn't
8. A. that   B. this   C. next   D. last
9. A. walking   B. sitting   C. studying   D. reading
10. A. trouble   B. mind   C. silence   D. conversation
11. A. possessions B. luggage   C. tickets   D. seats
12. A. two   B. three   C. one   D. professor
13. A. rushed   B. waited   C. struggled   D. searched
14. A. until   B. before   C. while   D. since
15. A. pushed   B. lost   C. left   D. thrown
16. A. sad   B. pleased   C. astonished   D. frightened
17. A. appeared B. seemed   C. turned   D. happened
18. A. comfort   B. persuade   C. blame   D. praise
19. A. of   B. between   C. out of   D. from
20. A. fault   B. mistake   C. train   D. ticket

Reading Comprehension

V. Read the following passage and do the multiple-choice exercises after it.

When a consumer finds that an item she or he bought is faulty or in some other way does not live up to the manufacturer's claims, the first step is to present the warranty, or any other records which might help, at the store of purchase. In most cases, this action will produce results. However, if it does not, there are various means the consumer may use to gain satisfaction. A simple and common method used by many consumers is to complain directly to the store manager. In general, the "higher up" his or her complaint, the faster he or she can expect it to be settled. In such a case, it is usually settled in the consumer's favor, assuming he or she has a just claim.

Consumers should complain in person whenever possible, but if they cannot get to the place of purchase, it is acceptable to phone or write the complaint in a letter.

Complaining is usually most effective when it is done politely but firmly, and especially when the consumer can demonstrate what is wrong with the item in question. If this cannot be done, the consumer will succeed best by presenting specific information as to what is wrong, rather than by making general statements. For example, "The left speaker does not work at all and the sound coming out of the right one is unclear" is better than "This stereo does not work". The store manager may advice the consumer to write to the manufacturer. If so, the consumer should do this, stating the complaint as politely and firmly as possible. If a polite complaint does not achieve the desired result, the consumer can go a step further. He or she can threaten to take the seller to court or report the seller to a private or public organization responsible for protecting the consumer's rights.

1. When a consumer finds the item he or she bought faulty, the first thing he or she should do is to _____.

    A. complain personally to the manager

    B. threaten to take the matter to court

    C. write a firm letter of complaint to the store of purchase

    D. show some written proof of the purchase to the store

2. How can a consumer make his or her complaint more effective, according to the passage?

    A. Explain exactly what is wrong with the item.

    B. Threaten to take the seller to court.

    C. Make polite and general statements about the problem.

    D. Avoid having direct contact with the store manager.

3. According to the passage, which of the following is suggested as the last alternative that consumers may turn to?

    A. Complain to the store manager in person.

    B. Complain to the manufacturer.

    C. Write a complaint letter to the manager.

    D. Turn to the Consumers' Rights Protection Organization for help.

4. The phrase "live up to" in this context means _____.
   A. meet the standard of   B. realize the purpose of
   C. fulfill the demands of   D. keep the promise of
5. The passage tells us _____.
   A. how to settle a consumer's complaint about a faulty item
   B. how to make an effective complaint about a faulty item
   C. how to avoid buying a faulty item
   D. how to deal with complaints from customers

Unit 5

Fashion

Vocabulary & Structure

I. Choose the answer that best completes each of the following sentences.

1. He wasn't asked to take on the chairmanship of the society, _____ insufficiently popular with all members.
   A. being considered   B. considering
   C. to be considered   D. having considered

2. _____ for the timely investment from the general public, our company would not be so thriving as it is.
   A. Had it not been   B. Were it not
   C. Be it not   D. Should it not be

3. The 20th century witnessed an enormous worldwide political, economic and cultural _____.
   A. transformation   B. transportation
   C. transmission   D. transition

4. I am not very familiar _____ botanical names, which are beyond the scope of my study.
   A. to   B. on   C. upon   D. with

5. It is necessary for a qualified teacher to have good manners and _____ knowledge.
   A. intense   B. tense   C. intensive   D. extensive

6. It has been reported that some officials _____ their authority and position to get illegal profits for themselves.
   A. exploit   B. abuse   C. overlook   D. employ

7. Something unexpected happened in my company when I was on vacation, and the situation required that I _____ there, so I had to end my vacation.
   A. am   B. be   C. being   D. been

8. Since I was not interested in the topic, it was _____ a boring speech for me _____ I fell asleep.
   A. so; that   B. such; as   C. such; that   D. so; as

9. Most of the news on the front pages of those newspapers _____ the progress of the conference.
   A. concerns   B. is concerning
   C. concern   D. are concerned
10. The weeks of training _____ for sport writers as it is for basketball players and coaches.
    A. are often as tense   B. are as often tense
    C. is often as tense   D. is tense as often

II. Spell out each word according to the Chinese given. The first letter is written for you.

1. 属性,特性	*n.*	a_____
2. 有吸引力的,引起注意的	*a.*	a_____
3. 财富,命运	*n.*	f_____
4. 出现;浮现	*v.*	e_____
5. 有效的,效率高的	*a.*	e_____
6. 倾向,趋势	*n.*	t_____
7. 宣传;推销(商品等)	*v.*	p_____
8. 样子;外表	*n.*	a_____
9. 使卷入,连累	*v.*	i_____
10. 消费;花费	*v.*	c_____
11. 有关的,有重大关系的	*a.*	r_____
12. 细节,详情	*n.*	d_____
13. 表达,陈述	*n.*	e_____
14. 企业,公司	*n.*	e_____
15. 经历,经受	*v.*	u_____

Cloze

III. Fill in the gaps with words you think fit.

Be it music, food or cars, all trends have a life cycle and none more so than __1__ trends. One of the first people to try and explain our __2__ attitude to what's hot and what's __3__ was the highly-respected fashion historian James Laver. In 1937 he __4__ a timeline of how a style was __5__ over the years, __6__ became known as Laver's Law. This states that a trend does not start to look attractive __7__ 50 years after its time. If you __8__ something 10 years after it was in fashion, you look "ugly", 20 years after you __9__ "ridiculous" and so on. __10__ after 50 years do things start turning towards the positive and you look "attractively odd".

IV. In this part there is a passage with 20 blanks in it. For each blank there are four choices marked A, B, C and D. You are required to choose the one that best fits into the passage.

Playing organized sports is such a common experience in the United States that many children and teenagers take them for granted. This is especially true __1__ children from families and communities that have the resources needed to organize and __2__ sports programs and make sure that there is easy __3__ to participation opportunities. Children in low-income families and poor communities are __4__ likely to take organized youth sports for granted because they often __5__ the resources needed to pay for participation __6__, equipment, and transportation to practices and games __7__ their communities do not have resources to build and __8__ sports fields and facilities.

Organized youth sports __9__ appeared during the early 20th century in the United States and other wealthy nations. They were originally developed __10__ some educators and developmental experts __11__ that the behavior and character of children were __12__ influenced by their social surrounding and everyday experiences. This __13__ many people to believe that if you could organize the experiences of children in __14__ ways, you could influence the kinds of adults that those children would become.

This belief that the social __15__ influenced a person's overall development was very __16__ to people interested in progress and reform in the United States __17__ the beginning of the 20th century. It caused them to think about __18__ they might control the experiences of children to __19__ responsible and productive adults. They believed strongly that democracy depended on responsibility and that a __20__ capitalist economy depended on the productivity of workers.

1. A. among   B. within   C. on   D. towards
2. A. spread   B. speed   C. spur   D. sponsor
3. A. access   B. entrance   C. chance   D. route
4. A. little   B. less   C. more   D. much
5. A. shrink   B. tighten   C. limit   D. lack
6. A. bill   B. accounts   C. fees   D. fare
7. A. so   B. as   C. and   D. but
8. A. maintain   B. sustain   C. contain   D. entertain
9. A. last   B. first   C. later   D. finally
10. A. before   B. while   C. until   D. when
11. A. realized   B. recalled   C. expected   D. exhibited
12. A. specifically B. excessively   C. strongly   D. exactly
13. A. moved   B. conducted   C. put   D. led
14. A. precise   B. precious   C. particular   D. peculiar
15. A. engagement   B. environment   C. state   D. status
16. A. encouraging   B. disappointing   C. upsetting   D. surprising

17. A. for   B. with   C. over   D. at
18. A. what   B. how   C. whatever   D. however
19. A. multiply   B. manufacture   C. produce   D. provide
20. A. growing   B. breeding   C. raising   D. flying

Reading Comprehension

V. Read the following passage and do the multiple-choice exercises after it.

Relationships in general have gone downhill because of two factors: technology and our demanding drive for excitement.

Body language, especially eye contact, is very important to a relationship. With one glance we can tell the mood of a close friend, if they are happy or sad. Thus, visual contact has a major impact on the amount of understanding we have with another person and the amount of connection that can be achieved. However, when the telephone, e-mail and message come into play, all of that human interaction is lost. We have increasingly less human contact and start lacking social skills because of a lack of communication.

Technology greatly influences our standpoint on how fast we think everything needs to be done. If you put a dollar in the soda machine, you expect the bottle to move forward and fall down to the bottom. You can't count how many times you've smacked the machine if it went too slow for your expectations. You wanted instant results, immediate fulfillment.

Another shot against healthy relationships is everyone's demanding need for excitement. Society in general has increased its expectations for excitement. Little kids spending time playing outside together now replace that with hours of playing video games alone at home. On the weekends we seize every minute with "exciting" activities, rushing from one to the next. The effect on relationships from all these activities is that they take on more concern and that we have no patience for each other. Gradually we distance ourselves from our loved ones.

1. According to the author, good relationships mainly rely on communicating _____.
   A. voice-to-voice   B. face-to-face
   C. letter-to-letter   D. signal-to-signal

2. Which of the following is NOT true about the relationship going downhill?
   A. Visual contact is no longer commonly used in social connection.
   B. Technology makes us have less contact and lack social skills.
   C. We now pay much time and concern to "exciting" activities.
   D. The distance between us is gradually farther than before.

3. The underlined word "smacked" in the 3rd paragraph probably means _____.
   A. clapped   B. hit   C. kicked   D. pushed

4. What are the two factors contributing to the downhill relationships in current society?

   A. Video games and technology.

   B. Soda machines and exciting activities.

   C. Exciting activities and our demanding drive for excitement.

   D. Technology and our demanding drive for excitement.

5. What can be the best title of the passage?

   A. Relationships and Technology.

   B. Technology and Excitement.

   C. What Distances Our Relationships?

   D. Gestures Affect Relationships.

Unit 6

Shopping

Vocabulary & Structure

I. Choose the answer that best completes each of the following sentences.

1. My journey back to my hometown seemed slow because the train stopped _____ at different villages.
   A. gradually   B. continually   C. continuously   D. unceasingly
2. These two cities are similar _____ they both have a high rainfall in June.
   A. to that   B. except that   C. besides that   D. in that
3. Physics is _____ to the science which was called natural philosophy in history.
   A. uniform   B. alike   C. equivalent   D. likely
4. Race and sex are not relevant _____ whether a person is qualified for the job.
   A. to   B. for   C. on   D. with
5. First published in 1927, the chart remains an _____ source for researchers.
   A. identical   B. inevitable   C. intelligent   D. indispensable
6. What a fantastic journey! It's worth _____ all my life.
   A. remembering   B. being remembered
   C. to remember   D. to be remembered
7. I went along thinking of nothing _____, only looking at things around me.
   A. in brief   B. in doubt   C. in harmony   D. in particular
8. This decent and _____ teacher was once misunderstood by some students and experienced a tough time, but in the end he won all his students' respect.
   A. respectful   B. grateful   C. honored   D. honorable
9. She _____ with delight when she learned the news that she won the first prize in the dubbing contest.
   A. choked   B. beamed   C. groaned   D. recalled
10. They hung back in the _____ of a big rock so that the monster couldn't find them.
    A. place   B. gap   C. dent   D. shelter

II. Spell out each word according to the Chinese given. The first letter is written for you.

1. 两者挑一;取舍   n.   a _____
2. 爱好,兴趣   n.   t _____
3. 过多的;过分的   a.   e _____
4. 较少的;较次要的   a.   m _____
5. 知识分子   n.   i _____
6. 惯例的;常规的   a.   c _____
7. 地方(性)的;当地的   a.   l _____
8. 个人   n.   i _____
9. 相对地;比较而言   ad.   r _____
10. 适中的;适度的   a.   m _____
11. 潜在的;可能的   a.   p _____
12. 移民   n.   i _____
13. 取得,获得   v.   a _____
14. 使确信,使放心   v.   a _____
15. 抵制,抗拒   v.   r _____

Cloze

III. Fill in the gaps with words you think fit.

The girls' night adventure usually begins with a simple trip to the shopping mall. I usually __1__ shopping. I do not wander and __2__ around in stores. My mode of operation is __3__ forward movement—I snatch what I need, check out, and escape.

__4__ this particular weekend, however, we were __5__ relatives in Ohio over the holidays. We had __6__ a relaxing day wandering around and playing games. After supper, I __7__ that I needed a new jacket. My niece said she __8__ of a department store in the mall having a great sale.

"Let's go," I said suddenly without thinking, __9__ the surprise of everyone around me. My plan for this trip was to walk into the store, select a great jacket at an irresistible price, check out, and __10__. It would take a half hour at the most.

IV. In this part there is a passage with 20 blanks in it. For each blank there are four choices marked A, B, C and D. You are required to choose the one that best fits into the passage.

Wise buying is a positive way in which you can make your money go further. The __1__ you go about purchasing an article or a service can actually __2__ your money or can add __3__ the cost.

Take the __4__ example of a hairdryer. If you are buying a hairdryer, you might __5__ that you are making the __6__ buy if you choose one __7__ look you like and which is also the cheapest __8__ price. But when you get it home you may find that it __9__ twice as long as a more expensive __10__ to dry your hair. The cost of the electricity plus the cost of your time could well __11__ your hairdryer the most expensive one of all.

So what principles should you __12__ when you go out shopping?

If you __13__ your home, your car or any valuable __14__ in excellent condition, you'll be saving money in the long __15__.

Before you buy a new __16__, talk to someone who owns one. If you can, use it or borrow it to check if it suits your particular __17__.

Before you buy an expensive __18__, or a service, do check the price and __19__ is on offer. If possible, choose __20__ three items.

1. A. form   B. fashion   C. way   D. method
2. A. save   B. preserve   C. raise   D. retain
3. A. up   B. to   C. in   D. on
4. A. easy   B. single   C. simple   D. similar
5. A. convince   B. accept   C. examine   D. think
6. A. proper   B. best   C. reasonable   D. most
7. A. its   B. which   C. whose   D. what
8. A. for   B. with   C. in   D. on
9. A. spends   B. takes   C. lasts   D. consumes
10. A. model   B. copy   C. sample   D. model
11. A. cause   B. make   C. leave   D. prove
12. A. adopt   B. lay   C. stick   D. adapt
13. A. reserve   B. decorate   C. store   D. keep
14. A. products   B. possession   C. material   D. ownership
15. A. run   B. interval   C. period   D. time
16. A. appliance   B. equipment   C. utility   D. facility
17. A. function   B. purpose   C. goal   D. task
18. A. component   B. element   C. item   D. particle
19. A. what   B. which   C. that   D. this
20. A. of   B. in   C. by   D. from

Reading Comprehension

V. Read the following passage and do the multiple-choice exercises after it.

Today, there are many avenues open to those who wish to continue their education. However, nearly all require some break in one's career in order to attend school full-time.

Part-time education, that is, attending school at night or for one weekend a month, tends to drag the process out over time and puts the completion of a degree program out of reach of many people. Additionally, such programs require a fixed time commitment which can also impact negatively on one's career and family time.

Of the many approaches to teaching and learning, however, perhaps the most flexible and accommodating is that called distance learning. Distance learning is an educational method which allows the students the flexibility to study at his or her own pace to achieve the academic goals which are so necessary in today's world. The time required to study may be set aside at the student's convenience with due regard to all life's other requirements. Additionally, the student may enroll in distance learning courses from virtually any place in the world, while continuing to pursue their chosen career. Tutorial assistance may be available via regular airmail, telephone, facsimile machine(传真机), teleconferencing(电信会议) and over the Internet.

Good distance learning programs are characterized by the inclusion of a subject evaluation tool with every subject. This precludes(排除，使避免) the requirement for a student to travel away from home to take a test. Another characteristic of a good distance learning program is the equivalence(同等，等价) of the distance learning course with the same subject materials as those for students taking the course on the home campus. The resultant diploma or degree should also be the same whether distance learning or on-campus study is employed. The individuality(个性) of the professor/student relationship is another characteristic of a good distance learning program. In the final analysis, a good distance learning program has a place not only for the individual student but also the corporation or business that wants to work in partnership with their employees for the educational benefit, professional development, and business growth of the organization. Sponsoring(发起，赞助) distance learning programs for their employees gives the business the advantage of retaining career-minded people while contributing to their personal and professional growth through education.

1. According to the passage, which of the following is NOT a disadvantage of part-time education?
    A. It requires some break in one's career.
    B. It tends to last too long for many people to complete a degree program.
    C. It affects one's career.
    D. It gives the student less time to share with the family.

2. Which of the following is NOT an advantage of distance learning?
    A. The student may choose his or her own pace.
    B. The student may study at any time to his or her convenience.
    C. They can pursue their chosen career while studying.
    D. Their tutorial assistance comes through regular airmail, telephone, facsimile machine, etc.

3. What benefit will distance learning programs bring to a business?
    A. Recruitment of more talented people.
    B. Good image of the business.
    C. Better cooperation with universities.

D. Further training of employees and business growth.
4. A good distance learning program has the following characteristics EXCEPT _____ .
   A. the distance learning course is the same as what students take on campus
   B. the resultant diploma or degree should be same as that from on-campus study
   C. the professor-student relationship is strictly one to one all through the course
   D. it includes a subject evaluation tool
5. What benefit will distance learning bring to an employee of a business?
   A. Professional growth.
   B. Good relationship with the employer.
   C. Good impression on the employer.
   D. Higher salary.

Unit 7

Job & Occupation

Vocabulary & Structure

I. Choose the answer that best completes each of the following sentences.

1. The country used to be rich and prosperous, but right now it is _____ a period of economic instability.
   A. going on   B. going around   C. going through   D. going down
2. He earns 5,000 dollars a year _____ his wife earns at least 20,000 dollars a year.
   A. whereas   B. wherever   C. whenever   D. whether
3. Anthony and Martha have been _____ together for two years and they plan to get married in October.
   A. enrolling in   B. falling in love
   C. settling into   D. going out
4. When I realized I was being mugged, I tried to _____ him, but he was holding me too tight.
   A. break into   B. break down
   C. break away from   D. break through
5. The newly-elected President _____ his speech with an amusing anecdote, which immediately shortened the distance between the citizens and him.
   A. preceded   B. processed   C. proceeded   D. produced
6. It is reported that those infected with SARS _____ from the masses for fear that this highly infectious disease would sweep the whole country.
   A. are isolating   B. have isolated
   C. have been isolating   D. have been isolated
7. A three-month investigation has _____ him to be the murderer of his ex-wife, who was killed in her flat on Valentine's Day this year.
   A. revised   B. returned   C. revealed   D. reminded
8. What he has done is always in _____ with what he has said, so nobody wants to make friends with him.
   A. competition   B. compensation   C. conflict   D. comfort

9. The living standards of people in rural areas have been greatly _____ since the 1980s.
   A. approved   B. proved   C. improved   D. disapproved
10. I heard the giggling of the kids chasing each other in the room and then something fell on the floor with a _____.
    A. crash   B. crush   C. flash   D. dash

II. Spell out each word according to the Chinese given. The first letter is written for you.

1. 政策;方针   n.   p _____
2. 时常;经常地   ad.   f _____
3. 职业的   a.   v _____
4. 集中;集结   n.   c _____
5. 不足;缺乏   n.   s _____
6. 保险   n.   i _____
7. 满足的;满意的   a.   c _____
8. 复审;再检查   vt.   r _____
9. 设立;建立   vt.   e _____
10. 投资;投资的对象   n.   i _____
11. 挑战   n.   c _____
12. 最低的,最小的   a.   m _____
13. 感激;欣赏   vt.   a _____
14. 安全;保证   n.   s _____
15. 奇特的   a.   o _____

Cloze

III. Fill in the gaps with the words you think fit.

If your area has no hospital or nursing homes nearby, never fear. The __1__ of alternative jobs is great. Schools frequently need a __2__ nurse for the students, and local knowledge is always a __3__. Local doctors will need help in their offices. Home care services __4__ nursing care to patients who need it but can not stay in the hospital indefinitely. These services offer perhaps the greatest __5__, with you choosing your patient __6__ and arranging visit times around your __7__.

Local and State government employ rural Public Health Nurses __8__ help educate, track, and treat disease, and serve __9__ local resources to the community. Many businesses __10__ nurses to treat their staff. Insurance companies use nurses to review cases, often at home over the Internet.

IV. In this part there is a passage with 20 blanks in it. For each blank there are four choices marked A, B, C and D. You are required to choose the one that best fits into the passage.

When Phillip was on his way to the airport one afternoon, he asked the driver to wait outside the bank while he collected some traveler's check.

The plane was to __1__ at 5:30. From the bank there was still a __2__ journey to the airport. Phillip __3__ watched the scene along the way. Shortly before arriving, he began __4__ the things he would need for the __5__. Tickets, money, the address of his hotel, traveler's checks just a moment. How about his passport? Phillip went through his pocket. He suddenly __6__ that he must have left his passport __7__.

What could he do? It was now five past four and there would be too little __8__ to return to the bank. This was the __9__ time he was representing his firm for an important __10__ with the manager of a French firm in Paris the following morning. Without a passport he would be __11__ to board the plane. At the moment, the taxi __12__ outside the air terminal. Phillip got out, took his suitcase and __13__ the driver. He then __14__ a good deal of confusion in the building. A __15__ could be heard over the loudspeaker.

"We very much __16__ that owing to a twenty-four-hour strike of airport staff, all flights for the rest of today have had to be called off. Passengers are __17__ to get in touch with their travel agents or with this terminal for __18__ on tomorrow's flights. Phillip gave __19__. He would let his firm know about this situation and, thank goodness, he would have the opportunity of calling at his bank the following morning to __20__ his passport.

  1. A. leave   B. arrive   C. check in   D. fly
  2. A. pleasant   B. short   C. long   D. rough
  3. A. carefully   B. merely   C. excitedly   D. slightly
  4. A. counting   B. looking for   C. thinking about   D. checking
  5. A. trip   B. plane   C. meeting   D. flight
  6. A. remembered   B. realized   C. noticed   D. learned
  7. A. at home   B. at the office   C. at the bank   D. in the taxi
  8. A. time   B. chance   C. possibility   D. use
  9. A. golden   B. last   C. only   D. first
10. A. journey   B. meeting   C. business   D. visit
11. A. sad   B. unable   C. impossible   D. difficult
12. A. stopped   B. was driven   C. arrived   D. was parked
13. A. left   B. sent away
     C. paid   D. said bye-bye to
14. A. started   B. noticed   C. caught   D. found
15. A. voice   B. noise   C. call   D. speech
16. A. apologize   B. announce   C. worry   D. regret

17. A. advised   B. forced   C. told   D. persuaded
18. A. ideas   B. information   C. plans   D. time
19. A. a loud laugh   B. a deep sigh   C. a big smile   D. a sharp cry
20. A. return   B. find   C. recover   D. gather

Reading Comprehension

V. Read the following passage and do the multiple-choice exercises after it.

Becket not only traveled light, but also lived light. He owned just the clothes he stood up in, a full suitcase and a bank account. Arriving anywhere with these possessions, he might just as easily put up for a month or a year as for a single night. For long stays not less than a month, he might take a furnished flat, sometimes even a house. But whatever the case was, he rarely needed anything he did not have with him.

Becket had one occasional anxiety: he suspected that he owned more than would fit comfortably into the suitcase. Having no use for choice or variety, he kept just a raincoat, a suit, a pair of shoes, a few shirts and some socks; no more in the clothing line. He bought many books and left them wherever he happened to be sitting when he finished them.

Becket was a professional traveler, interested and interesting. He was not the type to "do" a country in a week or a city in three days. He liked to get the feel of a place by living in it, reading its newspapers, watching its TV and discussing its affairs. He always tried to make a few friends—if necessary even by stopping a suitable-looking person in the street and talking to him. It worked well in about one case out of ten. Though Becket's health gave him no cause for alarm, he made a point of seeing a doctor as soon as he arrived anywhere. "A doctor knows a place and its people better than anyone," he used to say.

Becket was an artist as well. He painted pictures of the places he visited and, when he had gathered enough information, he wrote about them. He sold his works to newspapers and magazines. It was an agreeable sort of life for a good social mixer, and as Becket never stayed anywhere for long, he enjoyed the satisfying advantage of paying very little in taxes.

1. What do we know about Becket's possessions?

   A. He carried all of them with him.

   B. He wanted to have more clothes.

   C. He left all his belongings at home.

   D. He carried some of them with him.

2. Becket would rent a flat when he _____.

   A. was to stay over a month

   B. could not find a suitable hotel

   C. was to put up for several nights

   D. planned to stay at least for a year

3. When Becket tried to make friends with strangers in the street, _____.

A. most people felt very pleased

B. his attempts failed in most cases

C. he preferred good-looking people

D. many people stopped to talk with him

4. According to the passage, Becket made a living by _____.

   A. travelling   B. social work

   C. painting and writing   D. collecting information

5. As far as taxes were concerned, Becket probably _____.

   A. hated to pay any taxes   B. enjoyed paying very little

   C. traveled abroad and paid more D. felt ashamed of not paying any

Unit 8

Science & Technology

Vocabulary & Structure

I. Choose the answer that best completes each of the following sentences.

1. The theatre said that they would _____ the ticket for me until next Monday.
   A. reserve B. deserve C. conserve D. preserve

2. People have never stopped arguing over who on earth should _____ the elderly in the United States today.
   A. take after B. look after C. look for D. take care

3. In the past, the reason for many Chinese couples being eager to have a son was fear _____ no one being able to care for them when they were old.
   A. with B. in C. for D. of

4. All applicants thought they were the best for the job, _____ different reasons.
   A. in B. with C. under D. for

5. Though she was pretty, _____ I especially remember was her eloquence.
   A. that B. which C. what D. whatever

6. As an ancient Chinese proverb puts it, "_____ seeks revenge should dig two graves."
   A. Who B. Whom C. Whoever D. Whomever

7. Nobody invited Miss Honey to sit down, but she sat down _____.
   A. at all B. anyway C. too D. sometime

8. _____ has broken the window, I'll take him to his parents.
   A. Who B. Which one C. Whatever D. Whoever

9. At the beginning people knew very little about him, but soon he admitted _____ something of a leader.
   A. to be B. have been C. be D. to being

10. I didn't have a chance to apologize; she was very angry and immediately _____ up on me.
    A. made B. picked C. hung D. put

II. Spell out each word according to the Chinese given. The first letter is written for you.

1. 宣布;宣告   v.   a_____

2. 奇怪的;特有的　　　　　　　a.　　　　　p _____
3. 最初的,开始的　　　　　　　a.　　　　　i _____
4. 信号;标志　　　　　　　　　n.　　　　　s _____
5. 偶尔的,间或发生的　　　　　a.　　　　　o _____
6. 乘客,旅客　　　　　　　　　n.　　　　　p _____
7. 讨厌的,恼人的　　　　　　　a.　　　　　a _____
8. 犹豫,踌躇　　　　　　　　　v.　　　　　h _____
9. 更喜欢,宁愿　　　　　　　　v.　　　　　p _____
10. 模糊的;微弱的　　　　　　a.　　　　　f _____
11. 有希望的,有前途的　　　　a.　　　　　p _____
12. 不可避免的　　　　　　　　a.　　　　　i _____
13. 安装,安置　　　　　　　　v.　　　　　i _____
14. 预言,预测,预告　　　　　　v.　　　　　p _____
15. 紧急情况,突然事件　　　　n.　　　　　e _____

Cloze

III. Fill in the gaps with words you think fit.

I spend 12~14 hours a day being completely __1__ via either phone __2__ my computer. There's email, Twitter, Facebook, Instant Messenger, my mum, etc. I constantly get __3__ by something. The only time I am myself and with my own thought is __4__ I am running errands or traveling from one distraction to the __5__. But not when I am __6__ my cell phone. __7__ taking away my cell phone, I now have at least 1~2 hours a day where __8__ can get a hold of me and my brain can __9__ without interruption. I can __10__ again.

IV. In this part there is a passage with 20 blanks in it. For each blank there are four choices marked A, B, C and D. You are required to choose the one that best fits into the passage.

In a telephone survey of more than 2,000 adults, 21% said they believed the sun revolved (旋转) around the earth. An __1__ 7% did not know which revolved around __2__. I have no doubt that __3__ all of these people were __4__ in school that the earth revolves around the sun; __5__ may even have written it __6__ a test. But they never __7__ their incorrect mental models of planetary (行星的) __8__ because their everyday observations didn't support __9__ their teachers told them: People see the sun "moving" __10__ the sky as morning turns to night, and the earth seems stationary (静止的) __11__ that is happening.

Students can learn the right answers __12__ heart in class, and yet never combined them __13__ their working models of the world. The objectively correct answer the professor accepts and the __14__ personal understanding of the world can __15__ side by side, each unaffected by the other.

Outside of class, the student continues to use the __16__ model because it has always worked well __17__ that circumstance. Unless professors address __18__ errors in students' personal models of the world, students are not __19__ to replace them with the __20__ one.

1. A. excessive   B. extra   C. additional   D. added
2. A. what   B. which   C. that   D. other
3. A. virtually   B. remarkably   C. ideally   D. preferably
4. A. learned   B. suggested   C. taught   D. advised
5. A. those   B. these   C. who   D. they
6. A. on   B. with   C. under   D. for
7. A. formed   B. altered   C. believed   D. thought
8. A. operation   B. position   C. motion   D. location
9. A. how   B. which   C. that   D. what
10. A. around   B. across   C. on   D. above
11. A. since   B. so   C. while   D. for
12. A. to   B. by   C. in   D. with
13. A. with   B. into   C. to   D. along
14. A. adult's   B. teacher's   C. scientist's D. student's
15. A. exist   B. occur   C. survive   D. maintain
16. A. private   B. individual   C. personal   D. for
17. A. in   B. on   C. to   D. for
18. A. general   B. natural   C. similar   D. specific
19. A. obliged   B. likely   C. probable   D. partial
20. A. perfect   B. better   C. reasonable   D. correct

Reading Comprehension

V. Read the following passage and do the multiple-choice exercises after it.

Culture is one of the most challenging elements of the international marketplace. This system of learned behavior patterns characteristic of the members of a given society is constantly shaped by a set of dynamic variables (动态的变量): language, religion, values and attitudes, manners and customs, aesthetics(美学), technology, education, and social institutions. To cope with this system, an international manager needs both factual and interpretive (解释的) knowledge of culture. To some extent, the factual knowledge can be learned; its interpretation comes only through experience.

The most complicated problems in dealing with the cultural environment stem from the fact that one cannot learn culture—one has to live it. Two schools of thought exist in the business world on how to deal with cultural diversity. One is that business is business the world around, following the model of Pepsi and McDonald's. In some cases, globalization is a fact of life; however, cultural differences are still far from converging.

The other school proposes that companies must tailor business approaches to individual cultures. Setting up policies and procedures in each country has been compared to an organ transplant (移植); the critical question centers around acceptance or rejection. The major challenge to the international manager is to make sure that rejection is not a result of cultural myopia (近视) or even blindness.

Fortune examined the international performance of a dozen large companies that earn 20 percent or more of their revenue overseas. The internationally successful companies all share an important quality: patience. They have not rushed into situations but rather built their operations carefully by following the most basic business principles. These principles are to know your adversary (对手), know your audience, and know your customer.

1. According to the passage, which of the following is true?
    A. All international managers can learn culture.
    B. Business diversity is not necessary.
    C. Views differ on how to treat culture in business world.
    D. Most people do not know foreign culture well.

2. According to the author, the model of Pepsi _____.
    A. is in line with the theories of the school advocating business is business the world around
    B. is different from the model of McDonald's
    C. shows the reverse of globalization
    D. has converged cultural differences

3. The two schools of thought _____.
    A. both propose that companies should tailor business approaches to individual cultures
    B. both advocate that different policies be set up in different countries
    C. admit the existence of cultural diversity in business world
    D. both A and B

4. This article is supposed to be most useful for those _____.
    A. who are interested in researching the topic of cultural diversity
    B. who have connections to more than one type of culture
    C. who want to travel abroad
    D. who want to run business on the international scale

5. According to *Fortune*, successful international companies _____.
    A. earn 20 percent or more of their revenue overseas
    B. all have the quality of patience
    C. will follow the overseas local cultures
    D. adopt the policy of internationalization

Unit 9

Health

Vocabulary & Structure

I. Choose the answer that best completes each of the following sentences.

1. The question his son asked took David _____ surprise while he was concentrating on his work.
    A. in   B. on   C. at   D. by
2. She turned the top floor _____ a temporary bedroom because she found it was a quiet place.
    A. of   B. out   C. in   D. into
3. Cyril had a lot of azaleas（杜鹃花）in pots. I picked _____ a big red one just coming into bloom.
    A. up   B. out   C. of   D. into
4. He _____ a lot lately. He ought to give up smoking.
    A. coughed   B. was coughing
    C. coughs   D. has been coughing
5. After their grandma passed away, the children were left _____ feelings of loss.
    A. to   B. with   C. for   D. of
6. He's got a big nose and it _____ up slightly, which makes him look funny.
    A. holds   B. brings   C. turns   D. gives
7. In addition to his intelligence, he works very hard, so he is well _____ to becoming a fine mechanic.
    A. in the way   B. on his way   C. all the way D. by the way
8. _____ I managed to get the work done, though it is difficult.
    A. Somehow   B. Just as   C. As long as   D. However
9. People of different classes _____ different kinds of newspapers.
    A. tend to read   B. tend to reading
    C. attend to reading   D. pretend to read
10. I'm sorry you have resorted _____ deception. I used to think you were an honest boy.

A. of   B. at   C. to   D. in

II. Spell out the word according to the Chinese given. The first letter is written for you.

1. 期刊,杂志   *n.*   j_____
2. 古典的;古典主义的   *a.*   c_____
3. 东西;物质   *n.*   s_____
4. 因此;从而   *ad.*   t_____
5. 邪恶的   *a.*   e_____
6. 使……降低   *vt.*   l_____
7. 表达的,表示的   *a.*   e_____
8. 节奏;旋律   *n.*   r_____
9. 压制;抑制   *vt.*   s_____
10. 神经   *n.*   n_____
11. 十年   *n.*   d_____
12. 富有成就的   *a.*   p_____
13. 相同的   *a.*   i_____
14. 分开;隔开   *vt.*   s_____
15. 监督;监视   *vt.*   m_____

Cloze

III. Fill in the gaps with the words you think fit.

Like many if not most __1__ centenarians, according to the findings of the New England Centenarian Study at Boston University, Mrs. Tuttle has many friends, healthy self-esteem and strong relations __2__ family and community. She continues to enjoy her __3__ love for the theater and opera.

A study of centenarians in Sardinia found that they __4__ to be physically active, have large social networks and keep strong relations with family and friends. They are also less __5__ to be depressed than the ordinary 60-year-olds.

Tuttle could be a __6__ for that study's findings. Each morning, she does an hour of yoga and other floor __7__, then dresses and goes out on the street or to the top of her Manhattan apartment building for a half-hour walk __8__ breakfast. Her usual __9__: orange juice, oatmeal, a banana and black coffee. Then she works at her desk, mostly __10__ with her 11 grandchildren, 21 great grandchildren and 1 great-great-grandchild, now 3.

IV. In this part there is a passage with 20 blanks in it. For each blank there are four choices marked A, B, C and D. You are required to choose the one that best fits into the passage.

One summer night, on my way home from work I decided to see a movie. I knew the theatre would be air-conditioned and I couldn't face my __1__ apartment.

Sitting in the theatre I had to look through the __2__ between the two tall heads in front of me. I had to keep changing the __3__ every time she leaned over to talk to him, __4__ he leaned over to kiss her. Why do Americans display such __5__ in a public place?

I thought the movie would be good for my English, but __6__ it turned out, it was an Italian movie. __7__ about an hour I decided to give up the movie and __8__ on my popcorn. I've never understood why they give me so much popcorn! It tasted pretty good, __9__ . After a while I heard __10__ more of the romantic-sounding Italians. I just heard the __11__ of the popcorn crunching（咀嚼）between my teeth. My thought started to __12__ . I remembered when I was in South Korean, I __13__ to watch Kojak on TV frequently. He spoke perfect Korean—I was really amazed. He seemed like a good friend to me __14__ I saw him again in New York speaking __15__ English instead of perfect Korean. He didn't even have a Korean accent and I __16__ like I had been betrayed. When our family moved to the United States six years ago, none of us spoke any English. __17__ we had began to learn a few words, my mother suggested that we all should speak English at home. Everyone agreed, but our house became very __18__ and we all seemed to avoid each other. We sat at the dinner table in silence, preferring that to __19__ a difficult language. Mother tried to say something in English but it __20__ out all wrong and we all burst into laughter and decided to forget it! We've been speaking Korean at home ever since.

1. A. warm   B. hot   C. heated   D. cool
2. A. opening   B. blank   C. break   D. middle
3. A. side   B. view   C. space   D. angle
4. A. while   B. whenever   C. or   D. and
5. A. attraction B. attention   C. feeling   D. motion
6. A. since   B. when   C. what   D. as
7. A. Within   B. After   C. For   D. Over
8. A. concentrate B. swallow   C. fix   D. taste
9. A. too   B. still   C. though   D. certainly
10. A. much   B. any   C. no   D. few
11. A. voice   B. sound   C. noise   D. smell
12. A. wonder   B. wander   C. imagine   D. depart
13. A. tied   B. happened   C. turned   D. used
14. A. until   B. because   C. then   D. therefore
15. A. broken   B. informal   C. perfect   D. practical
16. A. felt   B. looked   C. seemed   D. appeared
17. A. While   B. If   C. Before   D. Once
18. A. empty   B. quiet   C. happy   D. calm
19. A. telling   B. giving   C. saying   D. speaking
20. A. worked   B. got   C. came   D. made

Reading Comprehension

V. Read the following passage and do the multiple-choice exercises after it.

The U.S. Department of Labor statistics show that there is an oversupply of college-trained workers and that this oversupply is increasing. Already there is an oversupply of teachers, engineers, physicists, aerospace experts, and other specialists. Yet college and graduate schools continue every year to turn out highly trained people to compete for jobs that aren't there. The result is that graduates can't enter the positions for which they were trained and must take jobs which do not require a college degree.

On the other hand, there is a great need for skilled workers of all kinds—carpenters, electricians, mechanics, plumbers and TV repairmen.

These people have more work than they can deal with and their incomes every year are higher than those of college graduates. The opinion that white-collar workers make a better living than blue-collar workers no longer holds true. The law of supply and demand now favors the skilled workmen.

The reason for this situation is the traditional <u>myth</u> that a college degree is a passport to a bright future. A large number of people in American society connect success in life with a college degree. Parents begin forcing their children to believe this myth before they are out of grade school. Higher school teachers play their parts by acting as if a high-school education were a preparation for college rather than for life. Under this pressure the kids fall in line. Whether they want to go to college or not doesn't matter. Everybody should go to college, so of course they must go. And every year college enrollments go up and up, and more and more graduates are over-graduated for the kinds of job suited to them.

One result of this importance on a college education is that many people go to college who do not belong there. Of the sixty percent of high school graduates who enter college, half of them do not graduate with their class. Many of them drop out within the first year. Some struggle on foot for two or three years and then give up.

1. What do we know about college graduates in terms of employment prospect?
    A. It's easy for them to find a well-paid job.
    B. It's impossible for them to find a job.
    C. It's difficult for them to find a job related to their major.
    D. It's difficult for them to become a skilled worker.

2. From the passage we can infer that in the past _____.
    A. white-collar workers made a better living than blue-collar workers
    B. blue-collar workers made a better living than white-collar workers
    C. blue-collar workers were looked down upon
    D. white-collar workers were looked up to

3. The underlined word "myth" in the fourth paragraph means _____.
    A. a false belief   B. a strong argument

C. an unbelievable story　　　　　D. an opinion

4. By saying that "many people go to college who do not belong there", the writer means _____.

　　A. many people who do not have enough money go to college

　　B. many people who go to college drop out within the first year

　　C. many people who go to college have their hopes destroyed

　　D. many people who are not fit for a college education go to college

5. What can we infer from the passage?

　　A. The writer believes that a college education is not a help in getting a job.

　　B. The writer believes that people with a college education should receive higher pay.

　　C. The writer believes that fewer people should go to college while more should be trained for skilled jobs.

　　D. The writer believes that every young man and woman should go to college.

Unit 10

Transportation

Vocabulary & Structure

I. **Choose the answer that best completes each of the following sentences.**

1. A fighter must _____ his own strengths and weaknesses, as well as his opponent's.
   A. count down   B. count on
   C. account for   D. take into account

2. It is taken _____ granted that everyone is equal before the law, regardless of skin color.
   A. for   B. into   C. as   D. by

3. The little boy is clever and loves to study. _____, he is careless and always makes mistakes.
   A. In addition   B. On the other hand
   C. What is worse   D. What's more

4. I enjoy my job in research because I can _____ all the latest developments.
   A. keep in with   B. keep up
   C. keep on   D. keep pace with

5. I will take any job that _____, within reason. I need terribly to earn money to support my family.
   A. comes round   B. comes out   C. comes along   D. comes in

6. This practice would offend against the _____ of fairness, since it only allows a few people to have the right to vote.
   A. principal   B. principle   C. prime   D. privacy

7. _____ is a good way to avoid wasting energy on meaningless pursuits.
   A. Set priorities   B. Set properties
   C. Setting priorities   D. Setting properties

8. His incredible _____ of foreign words and phrases serves him well, especially when traveling.
   A. retention   B. intention   C. mention   D. tension

9. They owed their boss a large amount of money and it took them three years to _____

the debt.

   A. take back   B. take off   C. pay out   D. pay off

10. In China, students majoring _____ medicine must study for five years before receiving a diploma.

   A. /   B. at   C. on   D. in

II. **Spell out each word according to the Chinese given. The first letter is written for you.**

1. 现象　　　　　　　　　　n.　　　　　　p _____
2. 消灭,消除　　　　　　　vt.　　　　　　e _____
3. 愿望,欲望　　　　　　　n.　　　　　　d _____
4. 州与州之间的　　　　　　a.　　　　　　i _____
5. 转移;迁移　　　　　　　vt.　　　　　　t _____
6. 体现　　　　　　　　　　vt.　　　　　　e _____
7. 男性的;男子气概的　　　a.　　　　　　m _____
8. 娱乐,消遣　　　　　　　n.　　　　　　r _____
9. 成熟;长成　　　　　　　vi.　　　　　　m _____
10. 惊人的,了不起的　　　　a.　　　　　　m _____
11. 自由选择　　　　　　　　n.　　　　　　o _____
12. 守时,准时　　　　　　　n.　　　　　　p _____
13. 同意,准予　　　　　　　vt.　　　　　　g _____
14. 个人主义(行为)　　　　　vt.　　　　　　i _____
15. 容量;容积　　　　　　　n.　　　　　　c _____

Cloze

III. **Fill in the gaps with the words you think fit.**

　　Our intense love affair with cars began as soon as they __1__ invented. Since its first __2__ in the 1890s, the automobile has embodied deep-seated cultural and emotional __3__ that have become an integral part of the American Dream. All of the romantic mythology associated __4__ the frontier experience has been transferred to the car culture.

　　Americans have always __5__ personal freedom and mobility, individualism and masculine force. The __6__ of the horseless carriage combined all these qualities and more. The automobile traveled __7__ than the speed of reason; it promised to make everyone a pathfinder to a better life. It was the vehicle of personal democracy, acting __8__ a social leveling force, granting more and more people a wide __9__ of personal choice—where to travel, where to work and live, where to __10__ personal pleasure and social recreation.

IV. In this part there is a passage with 20 blanks in it. For each blank there are four choices marked A, B, C and D. You are required to choose the one that best fits into the passage.

I left my friend's house after seven. It was still too early for me to have my dinner, __1__ I walked along the sea-front for about an hour __2__ I began to feel hungry. By that time I was not far from a favorite restaurant of mine, __3__ I often went to eat. I went into the restaurant and __4__ my meal. While I was waiting for the soup __5__ I looked around to see if I knew anyone in the restaurant. It was then __6__ I noticed that a man sitting at a corner table kept glancing __7__ my direction, as if he knew me. The man had a newspaper in front of him, which he was __8__ to read. When the waiter __9__ me my soup, the man was clearly puzzled by the __10__ way in which the waiter and I addressed each other. He became more __11__ as time went on and it grew more and more __12__ that I was well known in the restaurant. Eventually, he stood up and went into the __13__. After a few minutes he came out again, __14__ the bill and left. Then I called the owner of the restaurant and asked him __15__ the man had wanted. At first the owner did not want to tell me, but I __16__. "Well," he said, "That man was from the police." "Really?" I said, considerably surprised. "He was very __17__ me. But why?" "He __18__ you here because he thought you were the man he was __19__," the owner said, "When he came into the kitchen, he showed me a photograph of the __20__. Of course, since we know you, we told him that he made a mistake."

1. A. and   B. but   C. so   D. yet
2. A. until   B. since   C. before   D. after
3. A. where   B. what   C. which   D. that
4. A. took   B. ordered   C. had   D. got
5. A. arrive   B. to arrive   C. to be ready   D. ready
6. A. that   B. when   C. who   D. which
7. A. at   B. in   C. on   D. to
8. A. trying   B. pretending   C. holding   D. going
9. A. brought   B. fetched   C. carried   D. took
10. A. familiar   B. strange   C. interesting   D. easy
11. A. puzzled   B. interested   C. funny   D. impatient
12. A. obvious   B. known   C. difficult   D. possible
13. A. room   B. restaurant   C. kitchen   D. house
14. A. gave   B. sent   C. paid   D. ordered
15. A. how   B. that   C. which   D. what
16. A. thought   B. said   C. explained   D. insisted
17. A. excited at B. worried about C. satisfied with D. interested in
18. A. searched   B. followed   C. persuaded   D. advised

19. A. finding   B. looking for   C. talking to   D. proud of
20. A. wanted man   B. owner   C. policeman   D. waiter

Reading Comprehension

V. Read the following passage and do the multiple-choice exercises after it.

You've no doubt heard people say how much they "need" a holiday, when what they really mean is that they want one. Certainly, people working under pressure feel a very strong desire to escape from work and become less tight during their holidays, and experience a changed environment. For this reason, holidays away from home are now seen by most people as necessary to their quality life.

However, work for many people today is mental, rather than physical. These people may seek much more energy-taking activities while on holiday, rather than simply lying on a beach.

Once people become used to going on holiday, taking holidays becomes a habit. Even in a recession, for many people the holiday is one of the last things to be given up, and indeed many workers have chosen to spend some of their last pay when being laid off on a holiday, perhaps to give themselves a "lift" before facing a gloomy future.

Perhaps we don't like to admit it, but most of us also enjoy showing off about the places we have been to, and the lovely tans—dark skins we have got. The idea of tanning, however, is becoming less attractive than it was. So many tourists are now able to afford holidays in the sun that tans have become quite common; and although we join a tan together with health (and it is true that a certain amount of sunshine gives us a feeling of being healthy), it has been fully shown that sunshine, especially when received over a short, focused period of time, results in high danger of skin problems, as well as drying out one's skin and leading to more lines on your face later in life.

1. More and more people choose to have holidays because they _____.
   A. hate working indoors all the time
   B. want to get away from work
   C. love enjoying the beauties of nature
   D. become rich and want a better life

2. What do office people often do when they have holidays?
   A. They lie on the beach and enjoy sunshine.
   B. They spend more than they can afford.
   C. They think about their work on the beach.
   D. They choose to do more physical exercise.

3. A holiday may _____ when one has to face some difficulties in life.
   A. cheer someone up
   B. help someone find a job
   C. be the last thing to give up

D. bring good luck to someone

4. What does the writer try to tell the reader at the end of the passage?

   A. The importance of getting sunshine.

   B. The bad effect of being on holiday.

   C. The result of getting suntanned.

   D. The healthy look of being tanned.

5. From the passage we learned that some people can not live without _____.

   A. a tan   B. a job   C. a pay   D. a holiday

全国英语等级考试第三级

历年真题(一)

SECTION I　Listening (25 minutes)

Directions:

This section is designed to test your ability to understand spoken English. You will hear a section of recorded materials and you must answer the questions that accompany them. There are two parts in this section, Part A and Part B.

Remember, while you are doing the test, you should first put down your test booklet. At the end of the listening section, you will have 3 minutes to transfer all your answers from your test booklet to ANSWER SHEET.

If you have any questions, you may raise your hand **now** as you will not be allowed to speak once the test has started.

Now look at Part A in your test booklet.

Part A

Directions:

You will hear 10 short dialogues. For each dialogue, there is one question and four possible answers. Choose the correct answer—A, B, C or D, and mark it in your test booklet. You will have 15 seconds to answer the question and you will hear each dialogue **only once**.

1. What will the woman do tomorrow?
   A. Hold a party.　　　　　　　　B. See Mr. Smith.
   C. Work overtime.　　　　　　　D. Attend a wedding.

2. Who is Mr. Johnson according to the speakers?
   A. Their former colleague.　　　　B. Their former neighbor.
   C. Their former teacher.　　　　　D. Their former client.

3. What are the speakers talking about?
   A. A job interview.　　　　　　　B. A reporter's work.
   C. How to impress people.　　　　D. How to handle an interview.

4. How many flights to Sydney will there be next Tuesday afternoon?
   A. One.　　　B. Two.　　　C. Four.　　　D. Five.

5. What did the man's teacher tell him to do?

   A. Polish his essay.　　　　　　　B. Hand in his essay.

   C. Rewrite his essay.　　　　　　 D. Write a shorter essay.

6. What can we learn about the woman's son?

   A. He often talks with his mother.　　　B. He often drives in a careless way.

   C. He is willing to listen to his mother.　D. He is worried about his driving skills.

7. What do we know about Jack?

   A. He is a company manager.　　　　B. He makes emergency calls.

   C. He records emergency calls.　　　D. He is a company technician.

8. What can we learn from this conversation?

   A. The woman is paying the bill.

   B. Bill's phone number is 510 −1520 −20.

   C. The man pays 20 dollars to the woman.

   D. The woman has a 20-dollar bill changed.

9. What does the woman mean?

   A. The dentist's is at a convenient place.

   B. The dentist's is close to Times Square.

   C. It was comfortable to sit at the dentist's.

   D. It was not so terrible a visit to the dentist's.

10. What do we know about the woman?

    A. She is going to deliver a lecture.

    B. She spent a year in the rain forest.

    C. She is looking forward to the lecture.

    D. She will finish her report this weekend.

Part B

Directions:

You will hear four dialogues or monologues. Before listening to each one, you will have 5 seconds to read each of the questions which accompany it. While listening, answer each question by choosing A, B, C or D. After listening, you will have 10 seconds to check your answer to each question. You will hear the recording only once.

Questions 11 − 13 are based on the following conversation between a reporter and a female writer.

11. What do we know about the woman's family?

    A. They kept a lot of birds.　　　　B. They lived in a big house.

    C. They owned a small farm.　　　 D. They suffered from poverty.

12. What did the woman's mother impress her with?

    A. Her love.　　　　　　　　　　B. Her success.

    C. Her ambition.　　　　　　　　 D. Her knowledge.

13. What did the woman's mother wish her to do?
    A. Go to college.   B. Become a writer.
    C. Have a better life.   D. Support her family.

Questions 14 – 17 are based on the following conversation.

14. Whom is the man probably complaining to?
    A. A receptionist.   B. A travel agent.
    C. A coach driver.   D. A hotel staff member.

15. Why did the man wait in the heat for two hours?
    A. The coach had to be replaced.   B. The coach driver felt sick.
    C. The hotel rooms were full.   D. The hotel had to be cleaned.

16. What did the man mention in his complaint?
    A. Impolite hotel cleaners.   B. Dark light and dirty rooms.
    C. Rude people living downstairs.   D. Disturbing noise and poor food.

17. How did the man feel about the woman's apology?
    A. Amusing.   B. Annoying.   C. Desirable.   D. Reasonable.

Questions 18 – 21 are based on the following interview with John Smith, chairman of National Weight and Health Association (NWHA).

18. What did the NWHA survey aim to explore?
    A. The incidences of obesity.   B. Popular views on obesity.
    C. Ways to fight obesity.   D. The causes of obesity.

19. How many people in the world are rated as being overweight?
    A. 16 million.   B. 18 million.   C. 1.6 billion.   D. 1.8 billion.

20. In which country do people feel the most pressure to be thin?
    A. Brazil.   B. India.   C. France.   D. America.

21. Who are most likely to blame their parents for obesity?
    A. The French.   B. The Swiss.   C. Germans.   D. Russians.

Questions 22 – 25 are based on the following interview with Emily Galash, a high school student who works part-time as a trendspotter.

22. What do trendspotters do?
    A. Take pictures of youth culture.   B. Write reports on youth culture.
    C. Sell products to young people.   D. Create websites for young people.

23. What does Look-Look concentrate on?
    A. Recruiting trendspotters for its clients.
    B. Providing advice to young trendspotters.
    C. Organizing sales networks for its clients.
    D. Dealing in information about youth trends.

24. Why do some companies use Look-Look's images on their websites?

   A. To promote visits to Look-Look.com.

   B. To attract young people to their new products.

   C. To learn about what makes young people buy.

   D. To encourage young people to be photographed.

25. Why is it difficult for trendspotters to catch original styles?

   A. Many young people like to show off.

   B. Many young people stick to the rules.

   C. Many young people try to copy trends.

   D. Many young people refuse to take pictures.

You now have 3 minutes to transfer all your answers from your test booklet to your ANSWER SHEET.

That is the end of listening section.

SECTION II   Reading (50 minutes)

Part A

Directions:

Read the following two texts. Answer the questions on each text by choosing A, B, C or D. Mark your answers on your ANSWER SHEET.

Text 1

In 1997, 25 Japanese citizens, all older than 60, launched Jeeba (the name means "old man and old woman") to make senior-friendly products. They knew they were making history when they coined their company motto: "Of the elderly, by the elderly and for the elderly." They do not hire young people, and the oldest of their workers is 75.

Firms run by senior citizens are still a rarity, in Japan and worldwide. But the elderly have numbers on their side. Healthier and longer-living seniors, born immediately after World War II, are reaching retirement age in huge numbers all over the developed world. Extremely low birthrates in those same countries mean there are far fewer young workers to take their place. One likely consequence is now clear: shrinking work forces.

While the streamlining effects of international competition are focusing attention on the need to create and keep good jobs, those fears will eventually give way to worries about the growing shortage of young workers. One unavoidable solution: putting older people back to work, whether they like it or not. Indeed, advanced economies like those of Finland and Denmark have already raised their retirement ages. Others are under severe pressure to follow suit, as both the European Commission and the Organization for Economic Cooperation and Development have recently warned their members that their future prosperity depends on a growing contribution from the elderly.

Whether these changes are good or bad news to workers depends on whether they anticipate retirement with eagerness or dread. In the United States, half of working-age Americans now expect to work into their 70s, whether by financial necessity or by lifestyle choice, according to a new study by Putnam Investments.

Contrary to still widespread assumptions, there is very little hard evidence to suggest that companies cannot stay competitive with a rising share of older workers. At British hardware chain B&Q, its "elder worker" stores in Manchester and Exmouth were 18 percent more profitable than its regular outlets—due in part, the company says, to six times less employee turnover and 60 percent less shoplifting and breakage.

26. Jeeba's difference from a conventional company mainly lies in _____.
    A. the age of its employees   B. the number of its owners
    C. the quality of its products   D. the scope of its operations

27. In the developed world, compared with young people, the elderly _____.
    A. are better at business   B. are greater in number
    C. have healthier lifestyles   D. have more job opportunities

28. According to the writer, in the current situation companies are faced with the tough task of _____.
    A. creating good positions   B. employing retired workers
    C. filling vacant positions   D. replacing unskilled workers

29. For future prosperity, many European countries will have to _____.
    A. increase the number of young workers
    B. offer many senior-friendly jobs
    C. improve services for seniors
    D. raise their retirement ages

30. B&Q's "elder worker" stores are mentioned to show that the employment of older workers _____.
    A. does not reduce a company's competitiveness
    B. does not affect older workers' lifestyle choices
    C. is not a usual practice among competitive firms
    D. is not good news to those who are eager to retire

Text 2

One important thing during the pre-Christmas rush at our house was the arrival of my daughter's kindergarten report card. She got high praise for her reading, vocabulary and overall enthusiasm. On the other hand, we learnt that she has work to do on her numbers and facility with the computer, though the detailed handwritten report her teachers prepared is absent of any words that might be interpreted as negative in describing her efforts. A number system indicates how she's measuring up in each area without any mention of passing or failing.

All of that seems to make my daughter's school neither fish nor fowl when it comes to the debate over the merits of giving formal grades to kids. At one level, the advantages and disadvantages are obvious. A grade system provides a straightforward standard by which to measure how your child is progressing at school, and how he or she is getting on compared to other children. But as the writer Sue Ferguson notes, "Grades can deceive." The aim should be "to measure learning, not simply what a student can recall on a test." The two aren't the same—and if you doubt that as an adult, ask yourself whether you could sit down without any preparation and still pass those high-school-level examinations.

If you're old enough, you've lived through this debate before. At one time, it was considered unfair to put children in direct competition with one another if it could be avoided. The intention behind that may have been good, but it ignored the fact that competition, and what will to come out on top, are essential components of the human condition.

This time around, educators working with a no-grades approach are emphasizing different reasons. The thing is, that approach is much more commonplace in the adult workplace than is the traditional pass-fail system we place on our children. Many workplaces conduct regular employee evaluations. There are usually fairly strict limits to what an employer can tell an employee in those evaluations, and even then, negative evaluations can be challenged by the employee. No matter where you sit in the debate over the grade system, then, the real question is this: if it's so good for kids, why isn't that also true for adults?

31. The school report indicates that the writer's daughter_____.

   A. lacks interest in her school work

   B. ranks among the best at language

   C. has some trouble with her handwriting

   D. needs to improve in math and computer skills

32. We can learn that the girl's school tries to deliver the report _____.

   A. in a positive way   B. in a scientific way

   C. in an attractive way   D. in an enthusiastic way

33. Sue Ferguson seems dissatisfied with the grade system for its focus on _____.

   A. the process of getting the knowledge

   B. the capability of memorizing for the test

   C. the procedure of measuring learning

   D. the standard of comparing schools

34. The writer would agree that cutting children off from competition is _____.

   A. fit for human development

   B. fit for their age and experience

   C. against a key part of human nature

   D. out of consideration for children

35. It can be learned that today's educators supporting the no-grades approach insist that _____.

   A. kids be allowed to challenge the negative evaluations
   B. the traditional teacher-student relationship be changed
   C. the evaluation system for kids be similar to that for adults
   D. strict rules be set up in evaluating school children

Part B

Directions:

Read the texts from a magazine in which five people voice their different opinions in response to an article on the issue of praising. For questions 36 – 40, match the name of each person to one of the statements (A – G) given below. Mark your answers on ANSWER SHEET.

Mike:

Praise often and sincerely—it's as simple as that. Employees want to feel needed and appreciated. By offering sincere praise with examples about what they did right, you'll go far in creating an energetic team. Meanwhile, I don't agree with the assertion that "to focus on what needs improving isn't good management". In fact, it's the balance of praise along with constructive criticism that drives employees to work smarter and reach higher.

Frank:

This article makes a valid point that needs to be understood, especially for the new generation of workers, my generation. We don't see ourselves as parts in the machine to be put in the dark to work. My generation needs respect in return from our employer. We need to feel appreciated beyond just a pay check. It's the difference between being fulfilled at our career and being sad at our job.

Joyce:

One skill missing in today's workplace is the ability to build effective business relationships. At the core of that relationship is the need for consistent feedback. "How am I doing?" is a question that should be answered consistently. When you tell an employee once a year what is needed to improve, you have not done your job as a leader—build skills, provide feedback and help the employee grow and develop.

Ellen:

I don't see a problem with praising employees when it's truly deserved (insincere praise is entirely different story). It's a cost-free "benefit", if you will, in that it allows employees to see that their efforts are both noticed and valued. In the work world there are always people available to tell that you are doing something wrong and far too few occasions when employees are told that they've done something right!

Diana:

Praise what the employee did. Be specific about why it was helpful. An employee who continually earns your praise also deserves your attention as to how else to reward their behavior. Meaningful praise encourages people beyond anything else. Written comments are available for later review. They give them confidence that they can "do it again". I never regretted praising an employee who deserved it but often kicked myself for missing an opportunity.

Now match the name of each person (36 – 40) to the appropriate statement.

Note: there are two extra statements.

Statements

36. Mike _____
37. Frank _____
38. Joyce _____
39. Ellen _____
40. Diana _____

A. Praise combined with criticism is helpful.
B. Praise can bring about many kinds of desired behavior.
C. Employees may feel it hard to accept insincere praise.
D. Let employees know exactly for what they are praised.
E. In my opinion, we are not generous enough to give praise.
F. Employees need helpful advice on a regular basis.
G. Money alone cannot guarantee a sense of career fulfillment for me.

Part C

Directions:

Read the following text from which five sentences have been removed. Choose from the sentences A – G the most suitable one to fill each numbered gap in the text (41 – 45). There are TWO extra sentences that you do not need to use. Mark your answers on your ANSWER SHEET.

At 21, Ricardo Semler became boss of his father's business in Brazil, Semco, which sold parts for ships. Semler Junior worked like a madman, from 7:30 a.m., until midnight every day. One afternoon, while touring a factory in New York, he collapsed. The doctor who treated him said, "There's nothing wrong with you. But if you continue like this, you'll find a new home in our hospital." Semler got the message. He changed the way he worked. In fact, he changed the ways his employees worked too.

He let his workers take more responsibility so that they would be the ones worrying when things went wrong. He allowed them to set their own salaries, and he cut all the jobs he thought were unnecessary, like receptionists and secretaries. ___41___ "Everyone at Semco, even top managers, meets guests in reception, does the photocopying, sends faxes, types letters and dials the phone."

He completely reorganized the office: instead of walls, they have plants at Semco, so bosses can't shut themselves away from everyone else. ___42___ as for uniforms, some people wear suits and others wear T-shirts.

Semler says, "We have a sales manager named Rubin Agater who sits there reading the newspaper hour after hour. He doesn't even pretend to be busy. But when a Semco pump on the other side of the world fails millions of gallons of oil are about to spill into the sea. Rubin springs into action. ___43___ That's when he earns his salary. No one cares if he doesn't look busy the rest of the time."

Semco has flexible working hours: the employees decide when they need to arrive at work. ___44___

It sounds perfect, but does it work? The answer is in the numbers: in the last six years, Semco's revenues have gone from $35 million to $212 million. The company has grown from eight hundred employees to 3,000. Why?

Semler says it's because of "peer pressure". Peer pressure makes employees work hard for everyone else. ___45___ In other words, Ricardo Semler treats his workers like adults and expects them to act like adults. And they do.

A. This saved money and brought more equality to the company.
B. He knows everything there is to know about our pumps and how to fix them.
C. And the workers are free to decorate their workspace as they want.
D. Most managers spend their time making it difficult for workers to work.
E. If someone isn't doing his job well, the other workers will not allow the situation to continue.
F. Also, Semco lets its workers use the company's machines for their own projects, and makes them take holidays for at least thirty days a year.
G. After years of hard-working, he was tired.

Part D

Directions:

Read the following text from which 10 words have been removed. Choose from the words A – O the most suitable one to fill each numbered gap in the text (46 – 55). There are FIVE extra words that you do not need to use. Mark your answers on your ANSWER SHEET.

America's Internet is faster than ever before, but people still complain about their Internet being too slow.

New York's Attorney General's office ___46___ an investigation in the fall into whether or not Verizon, Cablevision and Time Warner are delivering broadband that's as fast as the providers ___47___ it is. Earlier this month, the office asked for the public's help to measure their speed results, saying consumers ___48___ to get the speeds they were promised. "Too many of us may be paying for one thing, and getting another," the Attorney General said.

If the investigation uncovers anything, it wouldn't be the first time a telecom provider got into ___49___ over the broadband speeds it promised and delivered to customers. Back in June, the Federal Communications Commission fined AT&T $100 million over ___50___ that the carrier secretly reduced wireless speeds after customers consumed a certain amount of _____51_____.

Even when they stay on the right side of the law, Internet providers arouse customers' anger over bandwidth speed and cost. Just this week, an investigation found that media and telecom giant Comcast is the most _____52_____ provider. Over 10 months, Comcast received nearly 12,000 customer complaints, many _____53_____ to its monthly data cap and overage charges.

Some Americans are getting so _____54_____ with Internet providers they're just giving up. A recent study found that the number of Americans with high-speed Internet at home today _____55_____ fell during the last two years, and 15% of people now consider themselves to be "cord-cutters".

A. accusations	B. actually	C. claim
D. communicating	E. complain	F. data
G. deserved	H. frustrated	I. hated
J. launched	K. relating	L. times
M. trouble	N. usually	O. worried

SECTION III Writing (45 minutes)

Directions:

You should write your responses to both Part A and Part B of this section on your ANSWER SHEET.

Part A

56. Write a letter to Andy and tell her about your situation. The letter must include:

1) your family;

2) your school or work;

3) Your hobby.

You should write about 100 words. Do not sign your own name at the end of the letter. Use "Wang Lin" instead.

Part B

57

Directions:

Read the text below. Write an essay in about 120 words, in which you should summarize the key points of the text and make comments on them. Try to use you own words.

Computer is playing vital role in modem life. Computer education has great importance because use of computer has reached almost all spheres of life.

The modern life of today includes information and contacts with people all over the world. Computer has helped considerably to achieve this. This is possible through computer education when a person knows the use of computer, he can employ in his business, for planning and chalking out programmed calculations and statistical works. The Internet helps to have contact with any one in any part of the world. Today, by the help of Internet, business has progressed very much. This is also possible with the knowledge of computer.

Today computer education is must for the job of even an ordinary clerk in the office. The knowledge and use of computer is essential for him. In modern countries the running of trains, machines, the flight of planes, the work in the bank and progress of business, all these are controlled by computer. This is possible only by the knowledge and use of computer. Computer education enables the artist in creating the realistic images. In the field of entertainment too, musicians, having computer education, create multiple voice composition and the play back music with hundreds of variations.

Not only this, the knowledge of computer helps in domestic work likes making the home budget doing calculations, and playing with confidence.

听力原文：

Part A

1. W: Oh, I'm sorry, Mr. Smith.
   M: What's up, Mary?
   W: I'm afraid I can't work overtime tomorrow. John and I are holding a party for the 5th anniversary of our wedding.
   M: That's all right. Enjoy yourselves.

2. W: Guess who I met at the grocery store this morning?
   M: Well, I can't imagine.
   W: Do you remember Mr. Johnson? He used to live in the building next to ours.
   M: Oh, yes, now I remember. He had dark hair and wore glasses.

3. M: I've just been interviewed for a reporter's job on the evening paper.
   W: What's your overall feeling about how it went?
   M: Well, I think I made a good impression. It seems that they were interested in me because I've worked as a reporter before.

4. W: Northwest Airways, good morning. Can I help you?
   M: Yes, do you have any flights to Sydney next Tuesday afternoon?
   W: Yes, there is a flight at 6:45 and one at 18:00.
   M: That's fine. Could you tell me how much return flight costs?
   W: That would be 418 dollars.

5. W: You look tired, John. What have you been doing?
   M: My teacher wasn't happy with my mid-term essay. She told me to do it all over again.
   W: At least, she gave you a second chance.

M: Yeah, I have to admit that.

6. W: I'm worried about my son at driving, but he won't listen to me.

   M: Well, teenagers always think they won't get hurt, but the fact is just the opposite.

   W: What should I do?

   M: Keep talking with him and lead by an example. Parents always matter.

7. W: Where is Jack? His manager is trying to catch him several times but has always just missed him.

   M: That's because he is being in and out all day.

   W: What's been going on?

   M: There has been many emergency calls and he is the only technician available to go out and deal with them.

8. W: Can you change the bill for me, please?

   M: Sure, 5,10,15,20. OK, 20.

   W: Can I have some coins? I need them for a phone call.

   M: Here you are.

9. W: I went to the dentist's to get my teeth polished this morning.

   M: How terrible!

   W: Well, the chair was so cleverly placed. I got a terrific view of Times Square down below. He finished the job before I knew it.

10. M: I hear the guy who is going to deliver the lecture this weekend spend a year living in the rainforest.

    W: Great. I'm doing a report on the rainforest. Maybe I can get some new information to add to it

Part B

Questions 11–13

M: Your readers are interested in your childhood. What was it like?

W: I grew up in a small town. We lived in very poor housing but we lived always in very beautiful settings, so I have favorite trees and I have contacted with birds. My parents were farm workers. Though we were poor for most of part, I think I was often happy.

M: It would not have been expected from that background that you'll become a literary figure. Was your mother ambitious with you?

W: Well, my mother wasn't especially ambitious with me in the sense of going to college when I grew up. I think her greatest contribution was simply that she loved me very much. No matter what happened, I had my mother with me.

M: She gave you confidence.

W: Oh, she did. She earned very little money, offering about $10 a week and never more than $20 a week. And in spite of that, she managed to buy a typewriter for me. She managed to buy me my first toothpaste when I left home. She just wanted me to be able to do things that she couldn't do even she didn't know what they were.

Questions 14–17

W: Good morning. Can I help you?

M: I'd like to make a complaint about my holiday in Paris last week.

W: I'm sorry to hear that. What exactly was the problem?

M: First of all, the coach taking us to the hotel broke down and we had to wait for over 2 hours in the terrible heat before our replacement arrived. Then when we got to the hotel, we found our room hadn't been cleaned.

W: Oh, dear. Did you complain to the hotel staff?

M: Of course, but we were told all the cleaners were off duty. Anyway, that's not all. The people in room above sounded like they were having all night parties every night. I demanded another room but the receptionist told me the hotel was full.

W: Oh, I see.

M: And the worst thing was the food in the restaurant was awful. It was so bud we had to eat out all the time despite having paid for meals in the price of our holiday.

W: I do apologize. I'd like to offer you a 20% discount on the price of one of our autumn breaks as a gesture of good will.

M: A 20% discount? You must be joking. I want to see the manager.

Questions 18–21

W: Good evening. Welcome back to Miss Know It All. For today's program, Mr. John Smith, chairman of National Weight and Heath Association, has come with findings from our recent NWHA survey on obesity. Now, Mr. Smith, what is the purpose of your survey?

M: We wanted to explore how people around the world view obesity or being overweight. Actually, obesity has gone global.

W: How did you do it?

M: We interviewed 16,000 people in 16 countries.

W: How large is the overweight population of the world according to your estimates?

M: 1.6 billion including 18 million children under age 5.

W: Really surprising, isn't it? And what are your findings about people's attitudes regarding obesity?

M: Our survey found that people in Brazil feel the most pressure to be thin, 83% of Brazilians think there is too much emphasis placed on weight. French are most likely to blame Americans. They use American's fast food as an excuse for their overweight problem. Russians are most likely to blame their parents for obesity. They are followed by Germans and Indians. When asked who encouraged them to try to lose weight, the Swiss tend to exclude their doctor.

W: Stay tuned for more about the NWHA survey. We will be back soon after the break.

Questions 22 – 25

M: Emily, what do you do as a trendspotter?

W: Very simple, Take digital photos of youth culture and send them to my company. It's called Look-Look.

M: What kind of company is it?

W: It's a youth culture marketing and trend forecasting film in Hollywood, I'm one of Look Look's 65,000 trendspotters worldwide.

M: Look-Look gets a lot of information about the ever-shifting tastes of the youth market by these images.

W: Yes, its clients are mostly companies. They get information about trends from Look-Look and develop their products. They also use their images of Look-Look on their websites to impress young people and promote their newly designed products.

M: But are there any people who don't like their pictures to be used on the website?

W: I always have my subjects' permission before I take their pictures and put up their images onto Look-Look. com.

M: Where do you find your best subjects?

W: At school, in the park, at local supermarkets and near many music clubs.

M: What is difficult about this job?

W: To catch our original styles many young people try hard to stand out. You have to be able to find the difference between someone who is copying trends and someone who is truly inventing a new look.

M: Thank you for talking with us, Emily.

参考答案

SECTION I   Listening (25 minutes)

1 – 5 ABAAC   6 – 10 BDDBC   16 – 20 DBBCA   21 – 25 DADBC

SECTION II   Reading (50 minutes)

Part A   Text 1   26 – 30 ABBDA
         Text 2   31 – 35 DABCB

Part B   36 – 40   AGFED

Part C   41 – 45   ACBFE

Part D   46 – 55   JCGMAFIKHB

全国英语等级考试第三级

历年真题(二)

SECTION I　Listening (25 minutes)

Directions:

This section is designed to test your ability to understand spoken English. You will hear a section of recorded materials and you must answer the questions that accompany them. There are two parts in this section, Part A and Part B.

Remember, while you are doing the test, you should first put down your test booklet. At the end of the listening section, you will have 3 minutes to transfer all your answers from your test booklet to ANSWER SHEET.

If you have any questions, you may raise your hand now as you will not be allowed to speak once the test has started.

Now look at Part A in your test booklet.

Part A

Directions:

You will hear 10 short dialogues. For each dialogue, there is one question and four possible answers. Choose the correct answer—A, B, C or D, and mark it in your test booklet. You will have 15 seconds to answer the question and you will hear each dialogue only once.

1. Where are the speakers?
   A. At a party.　　　　　　　　　B. At a cinema.
   C. At a restaurant.　　　　　　　D. At a bus station.
2. What do we learn about the man?
   A. He wants to rent an apartment.　B. He plans to leave his company.
   C. He has found a job in London.　D. He will inquire for the woman.
3. What is the man going to do?
   A. Go out with Nick.　　　　　　B. Eat out with Linda.
   C. Meet with a client.　　　　　　D. Discuss work with Mary.
4. What are the speakers talking about?
   A. How to manage people.　　　　B. Their departmental work.

C. How to avoid getting fired.   D. Their incompetent manager.
5. What do we learn about Mary?
   A. She is not interested in shopping.   B. She is not free for housework.
   C. She is too busy to go shopping.   D. She is interested in office work.
6. What is the man?
   A. He is a judge.   B. He is a lawyer.
   C. He is a teacher.   D. He is a researcher.
7. Why does the woman eat out at noon?
   A. To keep fit.   B. To save time.
   C. To save money.   D. To make friends.
8. What do we learn about David?
   A. He lost his job last week.   B. He is working with Mary.
   C. He has been ill for a year.   D. He earns less than before.
9. What does the woman think of the texts?
   A. They are too long.   B. They read poorly.
   C. They suit beginners.   D. They are interesting.
10. What do we learn about the man?
    A. He prefers fact-based reports.   B. He spends a lot of time online.
    C. He enjoys exciting things in life.   D. He puts much blame on technology.

Part B

Directions:

You will hear four dialogues or monologues. Before listening to each one, you will have 5 seconds to read each of the questions which accompany it. While listening, answer each question by choosing A, B, C or D. After listening, you will have 10 seconds to check your answer to each question. You will hear the recording only once.

Questions 11 – 13 are based on the following conversation between a reporter and a female writer.
11. Where did the woman take her first job after college?
    A. In a film studio.   B. In a talent agency.
    C. In a publishing firm.   D. In a television station.
12. Why did the woman's mother put her in acting classes?
    A. To enrich her after-school life.   B. To develop her talent in acting.
    C. To make her know more people.   D. To help her get over her shyness.
13. What is the woman's favorite sport?
    A. Table tennis.   B. Swimming.   C. Baseball.   D. Skating.

Questions 14 – 17 are based on the following dialogue.

14. What do we know about the woman?
    A. She dislikes a challenging job.　　B. She is tired of her present job.
    C. She works in a big company.　　D. She is eager to get a pay rise.
15. What does the woman want the man to do?
    A. Give her some advice.　　B. Give her an interview.
    C. Help her write a resume.　　D. Help her find a good job.
16. What is the good start for an interview according to the man?
    A. Being confident.　　B. Being well-prepared.
    C. Showing proper manners.　　D. Doing a good self-introduction.
17. What should the woman avoid according to the man?
    A. Using the interviewer's words.　　B. Anticipating possible questions.
    C. Talking too much about herself.　　D. Memorizing answers beforehand.

Questions 18 – 21 are based on the following dialogue about a visit to Athens, the capital of Greece.

18. Why does the woman ask the man for advice?
    A. He has a business in Athens.　　B. He spent a night in Athens.
    C. He is familiar with Athens.　　D. He used to study in Athens.
19. What does the man advise the woman to do?
    A. Take part in a bus tour.　　B. See as much as possible.
    C. Go to the Phaliron coast.　　D. Stay in central Athens.
20. What does the man think the woman can enjoy at the Paralia?
    A. A peaceful walk.　　B. Historical sites.
    C. Greek food.　　D. Local music.
21. Which of the following impressed the man most?
    A. A harbor.　　B. A stadium.　　C. A nightclub.　　D. A performance.

Questions 22 – 25 are based on the following interview with John Smith, CEO of a shoe-making company.

22. Why did the man start the shoe-making company?
    A. To build his own shoe brand.　　B. To help children without shoes.
    C. To sell shoes to poor countries.　　D. To broaden his business scope.
23. What had the man done before he started the shoe-making company?
    A. He had started five companies.　　B. He had worked as a technician.
    C. He had worked in South America.　　D. He had taught five media courses.
24. When did the man come up with this new business model?
    A. Three years ago.　　B. Five years ago.
    C. Six years ago.　　D. Eight years ago.

25. What is the man's biggest focus in giving shoes to poor children?
   A. Giving them access to school.
   B. Cultivating their sense of wealth.
   C. Raising their sense of self-worth.
   D. Preventing horrible foot diseases.

You now have 3 minutes to transfer all your answers from your test booklet to your ANSWER SHEET.

This is the end of listening section.

SECTION Ⅱ Reading (50 minutes)

Part A

Directions:

Read the following two texts. Answer the questions on each text by choosing A, B, C or D. Mark your answers on your ANSWER SHEET.

Text 1

Passwords are everywhere in computer security. All too often, they are also ineffective. A good password has to be both easy to remember and hard to guess, but in practice people seem to pay attention to the former. Names of wives, husbands and children are popular. "123456" or "12345" are also common choices.

That predictability lets security researchers (and hackers) create dictionaries which list common passwords, useful to those seeking to break in. But although researchers know that passwords are insecure, working out just how insecure has been difficult. Many studies have only small samples to work on.

However, with the co-operation of Yahoo!, Joseph Bonneau of Cambridge University obtained the biggest sample to date—70 million passwords that came with useful data about their owners.

Mr. Bonneau found some interesting variations. Older users had better passwords than young ones. People whose preferred language was Korean or German chose the most secure passwords; those who spoke Indonesian the least. Passwords designed to hide sensitive information such as credit-card numbers were only slightly more secure than those protecting less important things, like access to games. "Nag screens" that told users they had chosen a weak password made virtually no difference. And users whose accounts had been hacked in the past did not make more secure choices than those who had never been hacked.

But it is the broader analysis of the sample that is of most interest to security researchers. For, despite their differences, the 70 million users were still predictable enough that a generic password dictionary was effective against both the entire sample and any slice of it. Mr. Bonneau is blunt:

"An attacker who can manage ten guesses per account will compromise around 1% of accounts." And that is a worthwhile outcome for a hacker.

One obvious solution would be for sites to limit the number of guesses that can be made before access is blocked. Yet whereas the biggest sites, such as Google and Microsoft, do take such measures, many do not. The reasons of their not doing so are various. So it's time for users to consider the alternatives to traditional passwords.

26. People tend to use passwords that are _____.
    A. easy to remember   B. hard to figure out
    C. random numbers   D. popular names
27. Researchers find it difficult to know how unsafe passwords are due to _____.
    A. lack of research tools   B. lack of research funds
    C. limited time of studies   D. limited size of samples
28. It is indicated in the text that _____.
    A. Indonesians are sensitive to password security
    B. young people tend to have secure passwords
    C. nag screens help little in password security
    D. passwords for credit cards are usually safe
29. The underlined word "compromise" in Para. 5 most probably means _____.
    A. comprise   B. compensate   C. endanger   D. encounter
30. The last paragraph of the text suggests that _____.
    A. net users regulate their online behaviors
    B. net users rely on themselves for security
    C. big websites limit the number of guesses
    D. big websites offer users convenient access

Text 2

John Lubbock, a British member of the Parliament, led to the first law to safeguard Britain's heritage—the Ancient Monuments Bill. How did it happen?

By the late 1800s more and more people were visiting Stonehenge for a day out. Now a World Heritage Site owned by the Crown, it was, at the time, privately owned and neglected.

But the visitors left behind rubbish and leftover food. It encouraged rats that made holes at the stones' foundations, weakening them. One of the upright stones had already fallen over and one had broken in two. They also chipped pieces off the stones for souvenirs and carved pictures into them, says architectural critic Jonathan Glancey.

It was the same for other pre-historic remains, which were disappearing fast. Threats also included farmers and landowners as the ancient stones got in the way of working on the fields and were a free source of building materials.

Shocked and angry, Lubbock took up the fight. When he heard Britain's largest ancient stone circle at Avebury in Wiltshire was up for sale in 1871 he persuaded its owners to sell it to him and the stone circle was saved.

"Lubbock aroused national attention for ancient monuments," says Glancey. "At the time places like Stonehenge were just seen as a collection of stones, ancient sites to get building materials."

"Lubbock knew they were the roots of British identity. He did for heritage what Darwin did for natural history."

But Lubbock couldn't buy every threatened site. He knew laws were needed and tabled the ancient Monuments Bill. It proposed government powers to take any pre-historic site under threat away from uncaring owners, a radical idea at the time.

For eight years he tried and failed to get the bill through parliament. Finally, in 1882, it was voted into law. It had, however, been watered down; people had to willingly give their ancient monuments to the government. But what it did do was plant the idea that the state could preserve Britain's heritage better than private owners.

Pressure started to be put on the owners of sites like Stonehenge to take better care of them.

31. According to the text, Stonehenge in the late 1800s was _____.
    A. a royal property   B. utterly neglected
    C. legally protected   D. a public property
32. One stone in Stonehenge fell over because _____.
    A. rats weakened its foundation   B. farmers cut it to build houses
    C. visitors carved pictures into it   D. visitors chipped pieces off it
33. Lubbock proposed a bill to _____.
    A. push people to learn history   B. ensure government function
    C. enforce ancient site protection   D. push visitors to behave properly
34. When the bill was voted into law in 1882, it had been made less _____.
    A. severe   B. biased   C. implicit   D. complex
35. This text is mainly about _____.
    A. a famous British Parliament member
    B. the value of ancient heritages in the UK
    C. the history and protection of Stonehenge
    D. the origin of the Ancient Monuments Bill

Part B

Directions:

Read the texts from a magazine in which five people voice their different opinions in response to an article on the issue of praising. For questions 36 – 40, match the name of each person to one of the statements (A – G) given below. Mark your answers on ANSWER SHEET.

Lucy:

As the mother of two girls, I was moved to tears by your article, because it echoed so many of my own feelings. I don't think I should feel ashamed or that I am failing my child in any way because I feel like this. I think it's really normal and I love the way you have put into words what so many mums feel at this stage in their lives.

Anna:

My husband and I both read this article and we think it is moving, thoughtful, and the ending is wonderful. People cannot deny that jealousy is a natural emotion between children and parents. It is wonderful to see someone emotionally mature enough to be so aware of their own feelings, and celebrate them. You have written what I am sure most mothers feel, but are too scared to admit.

Beth:

There is some form of jealousy between mother and daughter. I remember suspecting that my mother was jealous of me but kept it under wraps. I understood that my mother was not happy with my father and the good relationship between myself and him. The strange thing is years later my own daughter and her father have a good relationship with each other and I can feel jealousy creeping in.

Clare:

When I realized my daughter had become a young woman, I was not jealous. At first I felt sad that I had lost my little girl, then I accepted this and rejoiced in her loveliness. I feel protective towards her because it is too natural for young girls to meet men. Offer your child advice on things like wearing fancy clothes which men do see as charming, and hope that she enjoys her life.

Ruth:

I think that a mature person judges herself based on her own qualities. A loving mother does not compare herself to her children and advertise her unhealthy thoughts to the world in a newspaper. I am surrounded all day at work by hot, smart young undergraduates, many of whom are hotter and smarter than I was at their age. When they succeed socially and academically, I feel happy for them.

Now match the name of each person (36 – 40) to the appropriate statement.

Note: there are two extra statements.

Statements

36. Lucy   A. You have spoken out the true feelings of mothers like me.

37. Anna   B. It is helpful for mothers to reveal their hidden feelings.

38. Beth   C. Emotionally mature mothers understand their daughters.

39. Clare   D. I understand my mother now, being a mother myself.

40. Ruth   E. You have expressed what most mothers feel but dare not say.

                F. Do your duty as a mother and hope for the best for your daughter.

                G. A mother should not envy her children and make public her improper feelings.

Part C

Directions:

Read the following text from which five sentences have been removed. Choose from the sentences A – G the most suitable one to fill each numbered gap in the text (41 – 45). There are TWO extra sentences that you do not need to use. Mark your answers on your ANSWER SHEET.

Whenever I hear a recording of John Denver singing "Sunshine on My Shoulders", I find myself smiling, drawn to a love of the sun and outdoors I've had for decades as a Michigan native. Walking barefoot to the lake, playing shirtless in the sunlight, and breathing fresh air feel good. ___41___

Studies have found higher rates of high blood pressure among people with the lowest sun exposure. One reason may be due to nitric oxide, a gas whose production is stimulated when your skin is exposed to the sun's rays. ___42___ Vitamin D, which sunlight helps your body produce, is also linked to better heart health. So walk outdoors for 15 to 30 minutes daily.

___43___ Research on 280 volunteers there found that people had a reduced heart rate, and lower blood pressure when they walked through a forest than when they spent time in an urban area.

One of the consequences of modern society is that rarely is our body in direct contact with the ground. The earth has an electrical current. ___44___ Although "earthing" or "grounding" is considered alternative by mainstream medicine, research shows that the practice seems to be able to reduce heart disease risk. So, walk around barefoot whenever possible, let your backyard grass tickle your feet, and dig your toes into sandy beaches.

___45___ A 2011 British review of 11 studies found that people who exercised outside generally reported more energy and less anger, tension, and depression—all factors contributing to heart attack—than those who worked out indoors.

A. Exercising indoors is another option.
B. It reduces both heart attack and stroke risks.
C. Exercising outdoors may be more beneficial than working out indoors.
D. In Japan, walking through forests for healing has become a popular practice.
E. Direct contact with it may be a stabilizing force for good health.
F. As a doctor, I can tell you they are also very good for your hear.
G. You'll get greater health benefits exercising where it's green.

Part D

Directions:

Read the following text from which 10 words have been removed. Choose from the words A – O the most suitable one to fill each numbered gap in the text (46 – 55). There are FIVE extra words that you do not need to use. Mark your answers on your ANSWER SHEET.

Some of the greatest successes you can think of began with failure. What a big ___46___ a little continued effort and determination can make.

Workplace expert Nan Russell, author of "The Titleless Leader: How to Get Things Done When You're Not in Charge", offers a number of ___47___ of people who were deemed failures—and then turned successful.

Albert Einstein was ___48___ to be mentally challenged as a child and told he would never amount to anything. Need we say how that one turned out?

Walt Disney was fired from the Kansas City Star because the editor thought he lacked ___49___.

Chester Carlson's early Xerox machines were ___50___ by 20 companies before he finally found a business partner.

Thomas Edison failed thousands of times before inventing the light bulb. There are many quotes from the great inventor that are worth ___51___ to memory. Here's just one: "Many of life's failures are people who did not realize how ___52___ they were to success when they gave up."

So, while failure may not feel good, it's often an essential part of success, the trial-and-error that can lead to greater things. If you spend all your time ___53___ about past mistakes, you might not notice when real opportunity arrives, so by all ___54___, learn from your mistakes—then put them behind you, roll up your sleeves and get back to work.

Here's one more quote from Edison for us to think about: "If we all did the things we are ___55___ of, we would astound ourselves."

A. capable   B. close   C. combination
D. committing   E. contributing   F. creativity
G. difference   H. encouraged   I. examples
J. judged   K. means   L. rejected
M. typical   N. ways   O. worrying

SECTION III Writing (45 minutes)

Directions:

You should write your responses to both Part A and Part B of this section on your ANSWER SHEET.

Part A

56

You have just had a terrible trip to a foreign country. Post a message to an English online forum:

1) telling other travelers some of your bad experiences

2) giving them some suggestions about taking a trip

You should write about 100 words. Do not sign your own name at the end of your message. Use "Li Ming" instead.

Part B

57

Directions:

Read the text below. Write an essay in about 20 words, in which you should summarize the key points of the text and make comments on them. Try to use your own words.

Dear Sally,

It was amazing to see your dance performance last weekend. I felt so proud of you when your schoolmates congratulated you upon your completion of the performance.

While you continue to enjoy the moment, I'd like to share with you a small quote from Abraham Lincoln, "This, too, shall pass away." I want these words to be your guide at every turning point in your life.

When you're feeling very proud of yourself at an achievement, knowing no bounds at that moment, remember that "This, too, shall pass away."

When you're at a difficult moment in your life and don't know what to do, find comfort in the same words—"This, too, shall pass away."

I'm not saying that the ache of some losses and setbacks will completely go away from you.

In fact, often the memories of painful events will hit you unexpectedly like tons of bricks and take your breath away years after they happen.

But, like all humans, you have an almost infinite capacity to adapt to life's changes and a great ability to bounce back from trying times. This understanding should give you a spark of hope when you're in a season of despair; it should also build up your confidence for taking risks in the future.

Sally, our lives are made up of several peaks and several valleys. That's the nature of life. Live each moment as it comes. And always remember "This, too, shall pass away."

Love,
Papa

听力原文：

Part A

1. M: Hey, Shelly, I am going to get some chips and water, what can I get for you?
   W: Well, I don't really need anything, maybe just a coke, but hurry up, the movie will start soon.
   M: Dont worry, I'll be right back.

2. M: Is your next door neighbor moving out?

W: Yes, she's found a job in London.

M: Do you know if her apartment has been rented yet? I am thinking of moving. My apartment is too far away from the company.

W: I will inquire for you then.

3. M: Hey, Mary, can you do something for me, please?

   W: Sure, Nick. What do you need?

   M: Could you tell Linda that I won't be able to have lunch with her today. I have to meet with a client.

   W: OK, no problem.

4. M: We are all so frustrated because our department manager is just hopeless.

   W: What do you mean exactly?

   M: Well, he doesn't know how to manage people, he just upsets everybody. We are all hoping he'll get fired.

   W: You'd better shut up. He is heading straight for us.

5. M: I went to the supermarket yesterday. I mean shopping alone is indeed a challenge.

   W: Didn't Mary go with you?

   M: No way. Even though she didn't have a lot of work in the office, she would prefer staying home.

6. W: As an attorney, you have practiced law over twenty years, and dealt with all types of cases. It seems that you enjoy your work so much.

   M: Yeah, but you know, my childhood dream was to be a judge.

7. M: I love eating in the restaurants, but it is so expensive now.

   W: I know. That's why I have stopped going out for dinner. I now meet my friends at noon, because lunch is a bargain at many places.

   M: That's a good idea.

8. M: David finally found a new job last week. He has been unemployed for a year.

   W: But Mary told me he is now paid only 1/3 as much as before.

   M: It is still much better than being out of work.

9. M: Do you like our textbook? I think the texts are too long.

   W: For me, long texts are easy to read.

   M: That's an interesting point. But long texts are not suitable for the beginners, don't you think?

   W: Well, you have your viewpoint, I have mine.

10. W: Listen! John, the report says the adults spend an average of five hours online at home every day, and miss many exciting things.

    M: So what? No evidence of how bad modern technology is!

    W: Come on, at least it fits you well.

Part B

Questions 11–13

M: What prompted you to pursue a career as a TV host?

W: Well, I had no idea. I was going to be a TV host. I was actually thinking of going to work in film production or for a talented agency. After college, I first worked for a publishing firm for two years. But I never looked for this job, it found me. So I must surprise, does anyone?

M: You said you were shy growing up. Is it still hard for you to be in front of the camera?

W: Since I was very shy, my mom put me in acting classes to help me get over my shyness. I tried it and then realized that I have no talent for acting. Well, I say I am still shy. I don't tend to go up and introduce myself to others. But at work I'm not shy at all, because I know everyone there.

M: What do you like to do when you are free?

W: I like watching sports games. Actually, I am a great sportswoman. I do a lot of skiing and skating during the winter and I play baseball in spring. I also play table tennis. But I think swimming is my favorite sport.

Questions 14–17

W: Bob, I've been doing the same job for six years, it pays well. But I'd like to do a more challenging job. I am worried about going for an interview. Any advice?

M: Yes, I guess the first thing is to try to make a good impression.

W: Sure, a good start is very important. But how do I make a good first impression?

M: To begin with, you should formally shake the interviewer's hand while greeting him or her with a smile. Be sure to keep eye contact, especially when listening to the interviewer.

W: I see. Body language is important, isn't it?

M: Yes, it is. The second thing is to have confidence. You get confidence from being prepared. You should learn a little bit about the company before the interview. You should also anticipate possible questions and think about how you will answer.

W: Should I memorize my answers beforehand?

M: Definitely not. That sounds very mechanical. You should be natural when you speak. Just think about how you want to answer and you can use the interviewer's words in your answer which shows you've been listening. Then you are sure to make a good impression.

W: I've never thought about that before. That really helps, Bob.

Questions 18–21

W: Tom, you have a good knowledge of Athens, don't you?

M: Well, I've been there a few times. Why do you ask?

W: I'm going to Paris on business next month. They told me I can spend one night in Athens on my way home. I've long been fascinated by the central city and want to make the best out of this coming night, you know, what's your advice?

M: Your stay is short, but it still can be an unforgettable experience. From my experience, you can take the new street car from the center of Athens to the Phaliron coast. It's slow but delightful. There must be a lot to see on the way.

M: Sure, when you get to the Phaliron coast, you have two choices. You can turn left for the paralia.

W: What can I see there?

M: A strip of seaside nightclubs and famous Bazokiya.

W: Bazokiya?

M: Yes, there're clubs with light Greek music, but I can't tell you more about them. Because I turned right for the Peace and Friendship stadium. From there, walk half a mile. And you can see the greatest charming small harbor. Meiconomano. If you feel hungry, you can visit the Duringbay restaurant for the dinner of fresh fish and luxurious salad.

W: Thank you, Tom.

M: My pleasure.

Questions 22 – 25

W: So, John, what's different about Toms?

M: Well, Toms is really simple. For every pair of shoes that we sell, we also give a pair of way to a child somewhere in the world that doesn't have shoes.

W: How did you come up with this idea?

M: I've set up five more businesses in the last eight years, mainly in media and technology. I was just a kind of worn out. I went to South America looking for some time to relax. When I went to a village, I knew that most of children didn't have shoes. It just shocked me. I wanted to help them, but I didn't just want to give them shoes once. So I decided to create this business marvel that was an idea three years ago and it hasn't changed one bit since.

W: What does having shoes mean to those kids?

M: Firstly, it gives them self-worth. It's a sense of wealth in this communities. It's a passport into important things. A lot of kids cannot go to school unless they have a proper uniform. And a proper uniform includes shoes. Thirdly, some horrible foot diseases are completely preventable with shoes. It is actually my biggest focus.

参考答案

SECTION Ⅰ   Listening(25 minutes)

1-5 BACDA   6-10 BCDCB   11-15 CDBBA   16-20 CDCCD

21-25 ABAAD

SECTION Ⅱ   Reading(50 minutes)

Part A   Text 1   26-30   ADCCB

　　　　　Text 2   31-35   BACAD

Part B   36-40   AEDFG

Part C   41-45   FBDEC

Part D   46-55   GIJFLEBOKA

如需以上真题录音,请联系汤定军老师(550434105@qq.com)或徐萍老师(2278527262@qq.com)。

Appendix I
Transcripts for Listening

Unit 1

Section A

Directions: In this section you will hear five short conversations. At the end of each conversation a question will be asked about what was said. Both the conversation and the question will be spoken only once. Listen carefully and choose the best answer.

1. M: Hello, I'd like to rent a car please. I am going to Las Vegas so I need a nice car.
   W: I see ... well, would you like a car with a sunroof or a convertible for an extra 40 dollars per day?
   Q: Where does the conversation take place?
2. W: What's your impression of New York, Alan?
   M: Well, it is crowded, the streets, the stores ... The museums do attract me, though.
   Q: What does the man like about New York?
3. W: This ivory box costs 750 dollars? It's too much. What's your best price?
   M: Well, the best price is 700.
   Q: How much will the man pay if he buys the ivory box?
4. W: Janet is quite interested in camping, isn't she?
   M: Yes, she often goes for weeks at a time.
   Q: What does the man say about Janet?
5. W: Do you know Professor Johnson's brother?
   M: I've never met him, but I've heard that he is as well-known as Johnson herself.
   Q: What do we learn from the man's reply?

Section B

Directions: In this section you will hear a long conversation. At the end of the conversation you will hear some questions. Both the conversation and the questions will be spoken only once. After you hear a question, you must choose the best answer.

M: Patty, are you planning on living on campus or are you going to look for an apartment?
W: Well, housing is included in my scholarship, so I have to live on campus.

M: What are the good things about living in a college dorm?
W: There are lots of advantages. For example, I like studying and hanging out with my roommates.
M: Wow, it sounds like the people in your dorm are pretty close.
W: Yeah, we really are. How about you, Eric? Are you living on campus?
M: Right now I live in an apartment off campus. I didn't like living on campus.
W: Why?
M: Because the people in my dorm always had their doors closed and were studying.
W: That's too bad. It sounds like the people in your dorm weren't as close as the people in my dorm.
M: No, you're right. Living off campus is OK, but I feel like I miss out on all of the fun stuff that happens on campus.

Questions:

6. Why is the woman living in a dorm on campus?
7. What does the woman think are the advantages of living in a college dorm?
8. What can we infer about the man from the conversation?

Section C

Directions: In this section you will hear a passage. At the end of the passage, you will hear some questions. The passage and the questions will be spoken only once. After you hear a question, you must choose the best answer.

The British education system is very flexible in order to provide for the needs of a modern, complex society. Degree courses are usually 3 years long. This is shorter and more intensive than in other countries. There are lots of scholarships.

You normally need 3 A-levels. These are the exams taken by people leaving school at 18, in order to enter an undergraduate degree course. You also need an IELTS score of at least 5.5, but many universities offer foundation courses to prepare students for their studies.

British universities emphasize on creative and independent thinking, which helps develop the skills you will need to compete in the global job market. Teachers not only teach but also provide support and guidance. As a result, international students have a very low drop out rate and very high pass rates.

It is very simple to become an international student in the UK. The British Council offers a free and fair service to anyone who is interested in studying in the UK, and an organization called UCAS helps you find a course and making an effective application.

Questions:

9. What is implied in the passage?
10. What requirements must you meet if you want to enter a British university?

11. Why do British universities lay emphasis on creative and independent thinking?
12. Whom can you turn to if you want to apply for a British university?

Unit 2

Section A

Directions: In this section you will hear five short conversations. At the end of each conversation a question will be asked about what was said. Both the conversation and the question will be spoken only once. Listen carefully and choose the best answer.

1. M: I like watching comedies because I love to laugh. Do you like watching comedies too?
   W: Not really. I like to be scared so I like watching horror movies, like "The Unborn".
   Q: What kind of movie does the man like to watch?
2. W: Why didn't you call me last night, Tom?
   M: I did. But your line was always busy.
   Q: What does the man mean?
3. W: Hello, what can I do for you today?
   M: Well, I've got a terrible stomach-ache and I keep needing to use the toilet.
   Q: What is the possible relationship between the two speakers?
4. W: You look upset. Anything wrong?
   M: I failed in the physics exam again in spite of all the efforts I made.
   Q: What do we know about the man from the conversation?
5. W: Did Henry paint the whole house himself?
   M: He had it painted, because he doesn't like climbing ladders.
   Q: What do we learn from the conversation?

Section B

Directions: In this section you will hear a long conversation. At the end of the conversation you will hear some questions. Both the conversation and the questions will be spoken only once. After you hear a question, you must choose the best answer.

W: Good afternoon, sir. May I help you?
M: Yes, I need to buy a ticket from Los Angeles to the capital of Alaska.
W: Alright, when would you like to leave?
M: I would like to leave December 24th and return January 3rd.
W: Do you want a direct flight?
M: Yes, I want to fly non-stop.

W: Alright. Where would you like to sit?
M: Is there an aisle seat available?
W: No, there is only a window seat.
M: Alright, I'll take the window seat. What if I need to cancel my trip for some reason?
W: You can get a refund if you cancel your trip one day before you leave.

Questions:

6. When will the man start his trip to Alaska?
7. Where does the man prefer to sit?
8. What will the man get if he cancels his trip one day before he leaves?

Section C

Directions: In this section you will hear a passage. At the end of the passage, you will hear some questions. The passage and the questions will be spoken only once. After you hear a question, you must choose the best answer.

If you're a T-shirts and jeans kind of a person, then here's some statistics worth knowing.

According to a recent poll, you should go to Hungary for a job, given that only twelve percent of people there dress smartly for work. The situation in India on the other hand might be much tougher, with nearly six in ten Indians wearing formal clothes in the office.

As a rule it seems Europeans don't care too much about what they wear, while workers in South Korea, China, Turkey and Saudi Arabia all tend to make more effort. If you want to wear a pair of shorts in the office, then nearly half of all Australians asked think that's fine. However a mere tenth of Brazilians would agree. Russians too would disapprove, although they are experiencing a heat wave now.

And what happens if you want to get promoted to the top in the office? Around two thirds of people believe senior managers should be dressed more properly than others. In Sweden you're less likely to be judged on what you wear on your way to the top. But in France you might find the door of power closed to you if you intend to wear whatever you could find that morning.

Questions:

9. According to the passage, why is Hungary the best country to go to for a job?
10. In which country will it be considered fine if you wear just a pair of shorts in the office?
11. Which of the following is true?
12. What can we conclude from the passage?

Unit 3

Section A

Directions: In this section you will hear five short conversations. At the end of each conversation a question will be asked about what was said. Both the conversation and the question will be spoken only once. Listen carefully and choose the best answer.

1. M: Did you download a movie or rent it at the store?
   W: I downloaded it so that I didn't have to remember to return it.
   Q: What are the two ways to watch movies that the speakers talked about?
2. W: It's 9:15 already and I'll miss my 10 o'clock bus.
   M: Don't worry. The clock is half an hour fast.
   Q: When does the conversation take place?
3. M: Vicki, can you tell me something about the London Eye?
   W: Well, it's the 6th tallest structure in London. And you can get a great view of the Thames River from the top of it.
   Q: What do you learn about the London Eye?
4. W: John, do you want to go swimming with me today?
   M: Sure. But I can't leave now. I have an appointment with my professor at three o'clock.
   Q: What is John going to do?
5. W: How long will it take you to fix my watch?
   M: I'll call you when it's ready, but it shouldn't take longer than a week.
   Q: What is the probable relationship between the speakers?

Section B

Directions: In this section you will hear a long conversation. At the end of the conversation you will hear some questions. Both the conversation and the questions will be spoken only once. After you hear a question, you must choose the best answer.

W: Hi, Kevin, I heard you are dating someone. How did you meet your girlfriend?
M: I met Amanda through a friend a year ago.
W: That's great. Did you start dating right after you met, or did you become friends first?
M: We started dating right away.
W: So you said you and Amanda met through a mutual friend. How did it happen?
M: Well, my roommate was friend with Amanda, so he introduced us.
W: Did he tell you what she was like first?
M: Yes, he described her to me, and she sounded like my type. I like girls who are not too serious.

W: How did you first meet?

M: My roommate invited both of us to dinner.

Questions:

6. How long has the man been dating his girlfriend?

7. What do you know about the man's roommate?

8. What kind of girl does the man like?

Section C

Directions: In this section you will hear a passage. At the end of the passage, you will hear some questions. The passage and the questions will be spoken only once. After you hear a question, you must choose the best answer.

The past 20 years have seen great changes in the lives and structure of families in Britain. The biggest change has been caused by divorce. As many as 2 out of 3 marriages now end in divorce. As a result, many children live with one parent and only see the other at weekends or holidays. There has also been a huge rise in the number of working women with children. The large rise in divorces has meant many women need to work to support themselves and their children. Even where there is no divorce, many families need both parents to work in order to survive. This has caused an increase in childcare facilities, though it is very expensive and can be difficult to find in many areas.

In addition, women are no longer happy to stay at home raising children, and many have careers earning as much or even more than men. Although it is difficult to be a working mother, it has become normal and is no longer seen as a bad thing for the children. Modern children grow up more independent and mature than in the past. From an early age they have to go to nurseries, and so are used to dealing with strangers and mixing with other children.

Questions:

9. What is the main cause of the changes in the lives and family structure in Britain?

10. What is the result of a huge rise in the number of working mothers?

11. What can be inferred about the role of British women in the past?

12. Why are modern children more independent and mature than in the past?

Unit 4

Section A

Directions: In this section you will hear five short conversations. At the end of each conversation a question will be asked about what was said. Both the conversation and the question will be spoken only once. Listen carefully and choose the best answer.

Appendix | Transcripts for Listening

1. M: I'm really into video games. All my friends are on the Internet. In fact I've never met any of them in the real world.
   W: Oh, really ... well you must be very popular on the Internet.
   Q: What can you infer from the conversation?
2. W: Do you like Professor Brown's lecture?
   M: I never miss her class, you know.
   Q: What does the man mean?
3. W: The Museum of London is one of the biggest social history museums in the world.
   M: Yes, it is. There are over 2 million objects in their collection. But not all the objects are on display.
   Q: What do you know about the Museum of London from the dialogue?
4. W: We do need another bookshelf in this room, but the problem is the space for it.
   M: How about moving the old dining table to the kitchen?
   Q: What does the man suggest they should do?
5. W: Excuse me, sir, but have you seen a young gentleman looking for his watch?
   M: A young man, Madam?
   Q: What's the woman doing?

Section B

Directions: In this section you will hear a long conversation. At the end of the conversation you will hear some questions. Both the conversation and the questions will be spoken only once. After you hear a question, you must choose the best answer.

W: Good afternoon, sir! Can I help you find something?
M: Sure, I'm looking for something special for my girlfriend.
W: Sure, do you know what size she is?
M: Uh ... I'm not really sure. She's about your size.
W: You don't know your girlfriend's size? Uh ... OK. Alright ... well, what is her style like?
M: Well, she works in an office so she always dresses really professionally. But for her birthday I want to get her something really trendy.
W: We have some really nice skirts. Well, do you want something inexpensive, or is money no object?
M: I want to get her something reasonably priced, but nice. I think my budget is closer to $20.
W: Umm ... I don't think we have any outfits for $20 here. You could probably find some really cheap clothes in Bargain Basement.
M: Wow, that sounds perfect for my budget. I'll go try to find her a present there. Thanks!

Questions:

6. What is the man doing in the store?
7. What does his girlfriend normally wear?
8. Why will the man go and shop at Bargain Basement?

Section C

Directions: In this section you will hear a passage. Listen to the passage three times and fill in the missing information.

With only two weeks to go before Christmas, buying presents is a high priority for a lot of people. However, these days lots of people can do their shopping in the comfort of their own home with the help of the Internet.

Online shopping is becoming more and more popular for a number of reasons; prices are often lower online, you don't have to queue up in busy shops and you can buy almost any product imaginable with just a few clicks of your mouse.

Computer trends are often male-dominated but this year women are expected to do more shopping on the Internet than men. It seems women are now more attracted to the convenience of online shopping than they used to be.

In the past a lot of people were reluctant to shop online. Many were worried about the security of entering their card details on the Internet and the reliability of the Internet. But as shopping online has become more widespread, these worries have begun to disappear.

However, many companies are concerned that not enough shoppers are coming through their doors. As a result, there are lots of special offers in the shops. Most shops traditionally have sales after Christmas but this year the bargains have come early in an attempt to attract consumers to spend.

Unit 5

Section A

Directions: In this section you will hear five short conversations. At the end of each conversation a question will be asked about what was said. Both the conversation and the question will be spoken only once. Listen carefully and choose the best answer.

1. W: Why did Margaret call yesterday?
   M: She wanted to pick up some magazines she lent me.
   Q: What do you learn from the dialogue?

2. W: Did you go out and do anything fun last weekend?
   M: I was very tired after working all week. I didn't want to go out so I stayed home and watched a movie.

Q: What did the man do last weekend?
3. W: We're planning a trip to Florida this summer vacation. Want to join us?
   M: I'd love to, but I'll be working part-time at the local Wal-mart.
   Q: What will the man do during the summer holidays?
4. M: Hello, I'd like to check in, please.
   W: Certainly. Can I have your name, please?
   Q: Where does the conversation take place?
5. W: Is that course as hard as everybody says?
   M: It's even worse, believe it or not.
   Q: What did the man say about the course?

Section B

Directions: In this section you will hear a long conversation. At the end of the conversation you will hear some questions. Both the conversation and the questions will be spoken only once. After you hear a question, you must choose the best answer.

W: Hey, Patrick, you really look fit, masculine, strong ...
M: Well, that goes without saying. I'm just awesome.
W: You know what? I think you look like Arnold Schwarzenegger. What do you do to keep fit?
M: Well, actually I lift weights and do cardiovascular exercises.
W: What are cardiovascular exercises?
M: It is exercise that helps burn calories by working the heart, such as running, biking, and hiking.
W: I don't go to the gym every day like you do.
M: Why not?
W: I can't afford the membership fee. But I do exercise.
M: How?
W: Shopping.

Questions:
6. What does the man think of himself?
7. What exercises does the man usually do?
8. Why doesn't the woman go to the gym every day?

Section C

Directions: In this section you will hear a passage. Listen to the passage three times and fill in the missing information.

Here are four basic steps to staying warm. Think of COLD—C. O. L. D.

The C stands for cover. Wear a hat and scarf to keep heat from escaping through the head, neck and ears. And wear mittens instead of gloves. In gloves, the fingers are separated, so the hands may not stay as warm.

The O stands for overexertion. Avoid activities that will make you sweaty. Wet clothes and cold weather are a bad mix.

L is for layers. Wearing loose, lightweight clothes, one layer on top of another, is better than wearing a single heavy layer of clothing. Also, make sure outerwear is made of material that is water resistant and tightly knit.

Can you guess what the D in COLD stands for? D is for dry. In other words, stay as dry as possible. Pay attention to the places snow can enter, like the tops of boots, the necks of coats and the wrist areas of mittens.

And here are two other things to keep in mind, one for children and the other for adults. Eating snow might be fun but it lowers the body's temperature. And drinking alcohol might make a person feel warm. But what it really does is weaken the body's ability to hold heat.

Unit 6

Section A

Directions: In this section you will hear five short conversations. At the end of each conversation a question will be asked about what was said. Both the conversation and the question will be spoken only once. Listen carefully and choose the best answer.

1. W: I like "Titanic". It's romantic. When it first came out, I saw it in the theaters five times in one week.
   M: Really? Well, the special effects might have been good in 1997, but when you watch it today, they make the film seem not that great.
   Q: What does the man think of the special effect of "Titanic"?
2. M: I'm fond of playing basketball, football and tennis.
   W: Football is the last kind of thing for me to play and swimming is my favorite sport.
   Q: Which sport does the woman not like?
3. W: Harrods is the second biggest department store in the world and is well known for its luxury products. But I'm not rich.
   M: We have sales periods, and we have discounts too. We encourage everybody to come.
   Q: What does the man mean?
4. W: Were you hurt in the accident?
   M: I was shocked at the time, but wasn't hurt at all. My bike was totally damaged

though.

Q: What do we know about the man?

5. M: It's seven o'clock already. Mary should be home by now.

    W: Oh, I forgot to tell you that she was going to a party at her classmate's house and wouldn't be home until 10.

    Q: What was Mary going to do?

Section B

Directions: In this section you will hear a long conversation. At the end of the conversation you will hear some questions. Both the conversation and the questions will be spoken only once. After you hear a question, you must choose the best answer.

W: So, Mark, what kind of music do you listen to?

M: I listen to a lot of hip hop. What about you?

W: I mostly listen to pop music, but I like a lot of different stuff.

M: Yes, me too. I mostly listen to hip hop, but there are many genres of music I like.

W: How did you get into hip hop?

M: Well, all my friends listen to it, so I became a big fan too. How did you get into pop music?

W: Well, I always hear it on the radio, so I started to get into it.

M: What are the pop groups that you like?

W: Oh, there are so many good ones! I loved the Spice Girls. They were so cool!

M: I agree! I was upset for a week when they broke up.

W: I was really sad too, but at least I can still listen to their CDs.

M: It seems we both like the same artists.

Questions:

6. What do you know about the man?
7. How did the woman get into pop music?
8. What do the two speakers say about the Spice Girls?

Section C

Directions: In this section you will hear a passage. Listen to the passage three times and fill in the missing information.

The world's most famous footballer, David Beckham, is leaving his club, Real Madrid, to sign for the American side, LA Galaxy.

Why has the former England captain decided to leave the most high-profile club in the world to play in a country where football isn't popular? Beckham says he likes the challenge of playing football in the USA and wants to build a bridge between America and the rest of the sporting world by making football a major sport. He's already set up a soccer academy for children in Los Angeles to help promote the game.

Some people think that David Beckham decided to move because he's been unhappy at Real Madrid. He hasn't won any major trophies during his four-year service there and he seems to have fallen out of favor with the manager, Fabio Capello: Beckham has spent most of the season on the bench.

But Beckham has no regrets about his time in Madrid. He said that playing with people like Zinedine Zidane, from France, and Ronaldo, from Brazil, has been the biggest honor in his career.

David Beckham's already played for two of the biggest clubs in the world: Manchester United and Real Madrid. He's been the captain of England and now he could become one of the richest athletes in history. If he manages to conquer America then, some say, he'll be the most popular British export since the Beatles.

Unit 7

Section A

Directions: In this section you will hear five short conversations. At the end of each conversation a question will be asked about what was said. Both the conversation and the question will be spoken only once. Listen carefully and choose the best answer.

1. W: Well, hello, Phil. This is certainly a surprise. What are you doing at my apartment? You never come by unless you want a favor.
   M: What? Of course not! I came by just because I wanted to say hello! Well ... alright. I want to drive to Las Vegas this weekend. Would it be possible for me to borrow your car?
   Q: Why did the man come to see the woman?

2. W: The sports meet will be held on Thursday, Nov. 20th.
   M: You are right. That's the day after tomorrow.
   Q: What day is today?

3. W: Good evening, I have a reservation under the name of Tomlinson.
   M: OK, I've found it. Also, you'd like a non-smoking room. Here's your key. Room 781.
   Q: What is the man doing?

4. M: Well, the holiday will soon be here.
   W: Yes, isn't it exciting? By this time next week, we'll be on the plane.
   Q: What do we learn from the dialogue?

5. W: Dear, I feel hungry now. How about you?

M: So do I. Let me call Room Service. Hello, Room Service? Please send a menu to 320 right away.
Q: Where are the two speakers?

Section B

Directions: In this section you will hear a long conversation. At the end of the conversation you will hear some questions. Both the conversation and the questions will be spoken only once. After you hear a question, you must choose the best answer.

M: Excuse me, madam! Please make sure to take off your shoes, jacket and belt and put them through the x-ray machine.
W: OK, just a moment ... Alright, there you go.
M: Hmm ... the X-ray machine is showing some strange things in your bag. I'll have to search it.
W: Sure, go ahead. I don't have any dangerous items on me.
M: Madam! Have these bags been in your possession at all times?
W: Yes, I've had them in my sight since I packed them.
M: I see ... And what is this? You didn't think you could get on the plane with such a dangerous item, did you?
W: It's just a bottle of water.
M: Don't you know people can make bombs out of liquid? You can't take it on the plane.
W: Well, alright ... I didn't realize liquids aren't allowed on planes.
M: Alright, I'm finished searching your belongings. You can go now.

Questions:

6. What is the woman doing?
7. Why is the man going to search the woman's bag?
8. Why is water considered to be a dangerous item on the plane?

Section C

Directions: In this section you will hear a passage. At the end of the passage, you will hear some questions. The passage and the questions will be spoken only once. After you hear a question, you must choose the best answer.

There are different types of transport in London. The London Underground is often the fastest way to get around London because it avoids the heavy traffic above ground.

London streets are full of buses. They are another very common way to get around in London. Traditionally, London buses are red double-deckers. The most famous London bus is the Routemaster. It was first used in 1957 and taken out of service in 2005. These days there are still double-decker buses in London, but they are modern ones, which are more suitable for disabled passengers. But there are also long joined buses which can fit a lot of people without needing two floors.

There were also trams in London for nearly a hundred years, from Victorian times until the 1950s. Later they were replaced with buses. But in the year 2000 a new tram system was built in South London with modern electric trams. There are now plans to build new tram systems in other parts of London too.

To get around London, it is best for a tourist to buy a one-day travel card. This allows passengers to travel on all the different types of public transport as much as they like for one day.

Questions:

9. How many types of public transport are mentioned in the passage?
10. What is the difference between the traditional double-decker buses and the modern ones?
11. What happened in the year 2000?
12. What is a tourist advised to do if he wants to get around London within a day?

Unit 8

Section A

Directions: In this section you will hear five short conversations. At the end of each conversation a question will be asked about what was said. Both the conversation and the question will be spoken only once. Listen carefully and choose the best answer.

1. W: Do you know that John is quitting his job?
   M: Yes. But he is really walking on thin ice, because he hadn't found a new job yet.
   Q: What does the man think of John's quitting his job?
2. W: The train is leaving in half an hour.
   M: Yes. It's a quarter to ten now.
   Q: When will the train leave?
3. W: So, Neil, which of the parks is the most famous in Britain?
   M: The Royal Parks. There are eight of them in total, but the two most famous are probably Regent's Park and Hyde Park in central London.
   Q: Where are the two most famous parks in Britain located?
4. M: Can you stay for dinner?
   W: I'd love to, but I have to go and send some letters before picking up the children from school.
   Q: Where will the woman go first?
5. W: The speech the blind girl gave this evening was extremely moving.

M: I think everyone felt the same.
Q: How did the man feel about the girl's speech?

Section B

Directions: In this section you will hear a long conversation. At the end of the conversation you will hear some questions. Both the conversation and the questions will be spoken only once. After you hear a question, you must choose the best answer.

W: Hi, Matt, thanks for coming over to help me fix my computer.
M: No problem. I know everything about computers. What's the problem?
W: I can't surf the Internet. What do you think the problem is?
M: Well, it could be a software problem, or it could be a hardware problem. Hmm ... have you tried re-starting your computer?
W: Matt, of course I tried re-starting my computer. That was the first thing I did!
M: Really? Well, if that didn't work, I don't know what to do.
W: That's your only idea? You said you know everything about computers. I should have just called technical support.
M: Well, re-starting the computer always works for me. Wait! I know how to fix the problem!
W: Great! What should we do?
M: We should contact the Internet company to see if their service is down. Let's log on to their website to find their phone number.
W: Uh, Matt? The Internet isn't working. How can we log on to the website?
M: Oh, yeah.

Questions:
6. What do you know about the man from the conversation?
7. Why does the man suggest that the woman re-start her computer?
8. What can you infer from the conversation?

Section C

Directions: In this section you will hear a passage. At the end of the passage, you will hear some questions. The passage and the questions will be spoken only once. After you hear a question, you must choose the best answer.

Every four years, the year has 366 days in it instead of 365—but why does this happen? Well, it actually takes the planet Earth 365 days and six hours to revolve completely around the sun. After four years extra 24 hours have accumulated, so an extra day is added to the calendar.

It is called a leap year because hundreds of years ago in England, the extra day wasn't legally recognized. The British just leapt over that day. Therefore, a year with 29 days in February is consequently called a leap year and that 29th day is sometimes called Leap Day.

There is a well-known tradition in the UK associated with 29th February. Women are allowed to break with tradition and propose to their boyfriends this day, which was even written in law in the 13th century. Scotland passed a law allowing women to propose to men in a leap year. It was said that if the men refused, they had to pay a fine!

Now there are demands for 29th February to become a public holiday. Some people believe that it should be an official day off, because no one gets paid extra for working an extra day in a leap year. For the moment though, the British still have to go to work on this day.

Questions:

9. What will happen when the earth moves round the sun four times?
10. What is the tradition associated with February 29th in the UK?
11. In Scotland, what is the consequence if a man refuses his girlfriend's proposal on Feb. 29th?
12. What are some people calling for in Britain?

Unit 9

Section A

Directions: In this section you will hear five short conversations. At the end of each conversation a question will be asked about what was said. Both the conversation and the question will be spoken only once. Listen carefully and choose the best answer.

1. W: My university is very diverse. It tries to find students from all over the world.
   M: Oh, yeah, my university has lots of minority students too. I've really enjoyed learning about lots of different cultures from them.
   Q: What's the advantage of studying in a diverse university according to the dialogue?
2. W: Shall we make another pot of tea?
   M: Why not?
   Q: What does the man mean?
3. M: Have you been to the British Library in London, Carol?
   W: Not yet. But I know it is one of the three largest libraries in the world. They have over 150 million items in the library.
   Q: What do you know about the British Library?
4. M: Boating and skating are my favorite sports.
   W: I like swimming but not boating or skating.
   Q: Which sport does the woman like?

5. M: Mary, would you like to go to the movies with me after dinner?
   W: Well, I'll go if you really want me to, but I'm rather tired.
   Q: What can we conclude from this conversation?

Section B

Directions: In this section you will hear a long conversation. At the end of the conversation you will hear some questions. Both the conversation and the questions will be spoken only once. After you hear a question, you must choose the best answer.

W: Good afternoon. Merrybest International Company. May I help you?
M: Please connect me to the export Manager, Mr. David Lee.
W: May I ask who's calling, please?
M: This is Tim Smith from ABC Company.
W: I am sorry, Mr. Lee is not in right now.
M: Do you know when he'll be back?
W: He went to meet some clients and won't be back today. Would you like to leave a message?
M: Yes. Would you have him return my call, please?
W: OK. Please tell me your hotel name and room number.
M: You can reach me at the Ambassador Hotel. I am staying in Room 1225.
W: What's the best time to call you?
M: Tomorrow morning before 10 o'clock would be fine as I will go out after 10 o'clock.
W: I'll pass your message onto him when he comes to work tomorrow morning.
M: Thank you very much.
W: You are welcome.

Questions:
6. What message has Tim Smith left?
7. What is David Lee probably doing now?
8. What is the best time for David Lee to call back?

Section C

Directions: In this section you will hear a passage. At the end of the passage, you will hear some questions. The passage and the questions will be spoken only once. After you hear a question, you must choose the best answer.

Chess must be one of the oldest games in the world. An Arab traveler in India in the year 900 wrote that it was played "long, long ago". Chess was probably invented in India, and it has been played everywhere from Japan to Europe since 1400. The name "chess" is interesting. When one player is attacking the other's king, he says, in English, "Check". When the king has been caught and cannot move anywhere, he says "Check mate". These words are Persian. "Check mate" means "the king is dead". In this case, one player has won, and the game is over.

Such an old game changes very slowly. The rules have not always been the same as they are now. For example, at one time the queen could only move one square at a time. Now she is the strongest piece on the board. It would be interesting to know why this has happened!

Chess takes time and thought, but it is a game for all kinds of people. You don't have to be a champion in order to enjoy it. It is not always played by two people sitting at the same table. The first time the Americans beat the Russians was in a match played by radio. Some of the chess masters are able to play many people at the same time. The record was when one man played 400 games! It is said that some people play chess by post. This must make chess the slowest game in the world.

Questions:

9. When was chess invented?
10. From what culture are the words "check" and "check mate"?
11. Which of the following might be the slowest match?
12. What shows the game is over?

Unit 10

Section A

Directions: In this section you will hear five short conversations. At the end of each conversation a question will be asked about what was said. Both the conversation and the question will be spoken only once. Listen carefully and choose the best answer.

1. M: I usually go to the movies in my free time on the weekends. How about you?
   W: The movie theater is always so crowded on the weekends. I like to go to the movies during the weekdays. Besides, sometimes the tickets are cheaper during the weekdays as well.
   Q: When does the woman prefer to go to the movies?
2. W: Frank is very humorous, isn't he?
   M: I couldn't agree more.
   Q: What can you learn from the conversation?
3. M: I believe you have a room to rent?
   W: That's true. Yes, won't you come in?
   Q: What can we learn from the conversation?
4. W: I have really enjoyed my roast dinners and wines for the past few weeks.

M: Me too. So it was a bit depressing to learn that I am 5 pounds heavier after Christmas.

Q: What do you learn about the two speakers from the dialogue?

5. M: What happened to you? You are so late.

W: The bus I took broke down in front of the hospital, and I had to walk from there.

Q: Why was the woman so late?

Section B

Directions: In this section you will hear a long conversation. At the end of the conversation you will hear some questions. Both the conversation and the questions will be spoken only once. After you hear a question, you must choose the best answer.

M: Hey, Jane, it's great to see you again. How is your new job?

W: Hi, Toby, it's really interesting. The salary is good, and the company has great benefits.

M: Wow! You know, I would really love to work at such a great company.

W: Well, I guess you can apply online if we have any positions open.

M: Actually, I was hoping you could recommend me directly. Here is my resume.

W: Well, let me look at your resume. Your resume says you have great computer skills. Is that true?

M: Of course! I have extensive experience surfing the Internet.

W: I see. But I'm not sure that is a real qualification.

M: Oh, come on, Jane. I would really appreciate it if you could do this for me.

W: Hmm ... alright Toby. I'll give your resume to our human resources department. If they want to hire you, it's their decision.

M: Thanks, Jane, I really appreciate your help.

Questions:

6. What does the man want the woman to do for him?
7. What does the woman think of the man's computer skills?
8. What is the man good at?

Section C

Directions: In this section you will hear a passage. At the end of the passage, you will hear some questions. The passage and the questions will be spoken only once. After you hear a question, you must choose the best answer.

St. Peter-Ording is one of the most popular seaside resorts in Germany. Even in deepest winter you'll find people braving the snow and the ice and the freezing temperatures to experience the stunning beauty of the North Sea coast. But it's not without its dangers and its dramas.

German police have revealed that last week a man got lost on the ice. He'd been taking photographs of the beautiful sunset but, as it became dark, he lost his directions and was left in a very dangerous situation. In a desperate effort to attract assistance, the man had no other choice but flash a light.

He was spotted by a woman, 500 kilometers away in the Westerwald region, on the River Rhine. Luckily for him, at that moment she was at her computer, online and watching a live webcam of St. Peter-Ording, and in that little video box she noticed the figure in distress.

She called the local police and the trapped man was saved at once. All thanks to an Internet search and rescue.

Questions:

9. What can we learn about St. Peter-Ording?
10. What happened last week according to German police?
11. How was the man saved later?
12. What played the most important role in the rescue of the man?

Appendix II

Glossary

- 黑体表示重点词汇和短语,白体表示一般词汇和短语。
- 词条末尾处所标的"数字+A/B"符号中,数字表示单元,A 表示 Text A, B 表示 Text B。

A

abundant /ə'bʌndənt/ *a.* 大量的,充足的,丰富的 3A
academic /ˌækə'demɪk/ *a.* 传统的,拘泥刻板的;学术的 6A
accelerator /ək'seləreɪtə/ *n.* (汽车等的)加速装置;油门踏板 10A
access /'ækses/ *n.* 通道,入口;接近,进入 8A
accomplish /ə'kɒmplɪʃ/ *vt.* 完成(任务等);达到(目的) 6A
according to 根据,依照 5B
accredited /ə'kredɪtɪd/ *a.* 官方认可的;公认的 7A
accumulate /ə'kjuːmjəleɪt/ *vt.* 堆积;积累 3A
acquire /ə'kwaɪə/ *vt.* 取得,获得 6A
acre /'eɪkə/ *n.* 英亩 8A
act as 扮演;担当 10A
adapt /ə'dæpt/ *vi.* 适应(新环境等) 4B
addict /'ædɪkt/ *n.* 有瘾的人;对某事物有强烈兴趣的人 4A
addiction /ə'dɪkʃn/ *n.* 瘾;入迷 10A
address /ə'dres/ *vt.* 写信给;向……讲话(或发表演说) 4B
adjust /ə'dʒʌst/ *vi.* 适应 4B
admire /əd'maɪə/ *vt.* 赞美;钦佩;喜欢,爱慕 7A
admirer /əd'maɪərə/ *n.* 赞赏者;(女人的)爱慕者,情人 4A
admit to 承认;供认(事实、错误等) 6A
adopt /ə'dɒpt/ *vt.* 采用,采纳 6A
　　　　　　　　 vt. 收养 1A
adoption /ə'dɒpʃn/ *n.* 收养 1A
adrenalin /ə'drenəlɪn/ *n.* 〈生化〉肾上腺素 9A
advent /'ædvənt/ *n.* 出现,到来 10A
adventure /əd'ventʃə/ *n.* 冒险;冒险活动 10B
affection /ə'fekʃn/ *n.* 喜爱;爱 4A
Africa /'æfrɪkə/ *n.* 非洲 2A

after all　毕竟　7A

aggressively /əˈgresɪvli/ *ad.*　活跃有为地；积极进取地　5A

agree on　商定；达成　8A

all set　〈口〉作好(充分)准备的　1A

allow for　考虑到；顾及　7A

alternative /ɔːlˈtɜːnətɪv/ *a.*　可供选择的　7A

　　　　　　n.　两者挑一；取舍　6B

analyst /ˈænəlɪst/ *n.*　分析者，分析家　4A

announce /əˈnaʊns/ *vt.*　宣布；宣告　8A

annoying /əˈnɔɪɪŋ/ *a.*　讨厌的，恼人的　8A

anonymously /əˈnɒnɪməsli/ *ad.*　匿名地；不具名地　4A

apartment /əˈpɑːtmənt/ *n.*　公寓房　3A

appeal /əˈpiːl/ *n.*　吸引力；感染力；号召力　4A

appeal to　吸引　6A

application /ˌæplɪˈkeɪʃn/ *n.*　应用，实施　1A

apply /əˈplaɪ/ *vt.*　适用；应用　4B

appreciate /əˈpriːʃieɪt/ *vt.*　感激；欣赏　7A

approach /əˈprəʊtʃ/ *n.*　途径；方式，方法　1A

arcade /ɑːˈkeɪd/ *n.*　有拱顶的走道(两旁常设商店)　6A

arrange /əˈreɪndʒ/ *vt.*　安排　7A

artificial /ˌɑːtɪˈfɪʃl/ *a.*　人工的；假的　9B

as a result　作为(……的)结果　3A

as it turned out　结果　8A

aspect /ˈæspekt/ *n.*　样子；外表　5A

aspire to　渴望，追求　3A

assist /əˈsɪst/ *vt.*　援助，帮助　7A

associate /əˈsəʊʃieɪt/ *vt.*　将……联系起来　4A

associate ... with　(在思想上)把……和……联系在一起　6A

association /əˌsəʊʃiˈeɪʃn/ *n.*　联想；联系　3A

assume /əˈsjuːm/ *vt.*　假定，设想　3A

assure /əˈʃʊə/ *vt.*　使确信，使放心　6B

at present　目前，现在　5B

at the moment　此刻，现在，目前　2A

at worst　在最坏的情况下　8A

Atlantic /ətˈlæntɪk/ *n.*　大西洋　2A

atmosphere /ˈætməsfɪə/ *n.*　大气，大气层(包围地球的气体)；气氛　2A；8A

attach /əˈtætʃ/ *vt.*　系；贴；装，连接　4B

attract /əˈtrækt/ *vt.*　吸引，引起……的注意　6B

attractive /əˈtræktɪv/ *a.*　有吸引力的，引起注意的　5A

attribute /ˈætrɪbjuːt/ *n.* 属性,特性 5A
available /əˈveɪləbl/ *a.* 可用的;可得到的 4A
await /əˈweɪt/ *vt.* 等候,等待 10B

B

back and forth 来回,往返 2A
ban /bæn/ *n.* 禁止;禁令 6A
bargain /ˈbɑːɡɪn/ *n.* 廉价货 6B
be content to 对……满意,愿意 5A
be decorated with 用……装饰 5A
be deeply rooted in 深深地根植于 3A
be done with 结束 6A
be exposed to 暴露于;遭受 9A
be known as 被称为 7A
be responsible for 是……的原因;对……负责 9A
be traced back to 追溯到 5A
beat /biːt/ *n.* (音乐的)拍子;节拍 9A
behave /bɪˈheɪv/ *vi.* 举止,行为;表现 7B
behavior /bɪˈheɪvjə/ *n.* 行为;举止;表现 4A
behold /bɪˈhəʊld/ (beheld) *vt.* 〈书〉看,瞧(多用于祈使句,用以唤起注意) 5A
being /ˈbiːɪŋ/ *n.* 身心 9A
benefit /ˈbenɪfɪt/ *vi.* 得益;得到好处 9A
best of all 最好的 7A
billion /ˈbɪljən/ *n. & a.* 〈美〉十亿(的) 4A
biological /ˌbaɪəˈlɒdʒɪkl/ *a.* 生物的;与生命过程有关的 1A
birth /bɜːθ/ *n.* 出生 1A
blanket /ˈblæŋkɪt/ *n.* 毯子;覆盖物 2A
block /blɒk/ *n.* 街区;一排房屋 3A
blouse /blaʊz/ *n.* 女衬衫;宽大短外套 6A
blur /blɜː/ *vt.* 使……变得模糊不清 4A
bond /bɒnd/ *n.* 联结,联系 4B
boundary /ˈbaʊndəri/ *n.* 分界线,边界 4B
bourgeois /ˈbʊəʒwɑː/ *n.* 资产阶级 5A
　　　　　　　　　　a. 资产阶级的 6A
breather /ˈbriːðə/ *n.* 喘息时间,短暂的休息 3A
bring up 提出 8A
broadcast /ˈbrɔːdkɑːst/ (broadcast 或 broadcasted) *vt.* (用电台或电视)广播,播出 7B
buggy /ˈbʌɡi/ *n.* 四轮单马轻便马车 10A
burst with 充满 3B

C

calculate /ˈkælkjuleɪt/ vt. 计算；估计　2A
calligraph /ˈkælɪɡrɑːf/ vt. 用美术体书写　1A
calligraphy /kəˈlɪɡrəfi/ n. 书法；美术字(体)　1A
campus /ˈkæmpəs/ n. （大学）校园　1A
candidate /ˈkændɪdeɪt/ n. 候选人　3B
canvas /ˈkænvəs/ n. 帆布　5A
capacity /kəˈpæsəti/ n. 容量；容积　10B
capitalistic /ˌkæpɪtəˈlɪstɪk/ a. 资本主义的；资本家的　5A
capture /ˈkæptʃə/ vt. 捕获；引起（注意）　1A
car pool 〈美〉合伙用车　10A
carbon /ˈkɑːbən/ n. 碳　2A
cardiologist /ˌkɑːdɪˈɒlədʒɪst/ n. 心脏病专科医生　9A
cash in on 从……中获得利益或利润　4A
category /ˈkætɪɡəri/ n. 种；类　10B
cell service 手机服务　8A
certification /ˌsɜːtɪfɪˈkeɪʃn/ n. 证书；证明　7A
challenge /ˈtʃælɪndʒ/ n. 挑战　7B
challenging /ˈtʃælɪndʒɪŋ/ a. 挑战性的　3A
champagne /ʃæmˈpeɪn/ n. 香槟酒　4A
character /ˈkærɪktə/ n. 人物，角色　6A
charming /ˈtʃɑːmɪŋ/ a. 迷人的；可爱的　6A
checkup /ˈtʃekʌp/ n. 健康检查　9A
cheerful /ˈtʃɪəfl/ a. 快活的，高兴的　9B
cherish /ˈtʃerɪʃ/ vt. 珍惜，珍爱　10A
cholesterol /kəˈlestərɒl/ n. 〈生化〉胆固醇　9A
chore /tʃɔː/ n. 家庭杂务　3A
Christmas /ˈkrɪsməs/ n. 圣诞节　2A
circle /ˈsɜːkl/ n. （具有共同兴趣、利益的人们形成的）圈子　6A
clan /klæn/ n. 〈口〉家族　3A
clarify /ˈklærɪfaɪ/ vt. 澄清　4B
classical /ˈklæsɪkl/ a. 古典的；古典主义的　9A
click /klɪk/ vi. 咔哒一声地敲击　8A
climate /ˈklaɪmɪt/ n. 气候　2A
clip /klɪp/ (clipped; clipping) vt. 从报刊上剪取　3A
CO_2 /ˈkɑːbəndaɪˈɒksaɪd/ n. 二氧化碳　2A
coin /kɔɪn/ vt. 创造；杜撰（新词语等）　6A
collection /kəˈlekʃn/ n. 收集（物）　4A

column /ˈkɒləm/ n. 专栏(文章) 8A
combine ... with 使……与……结合(联合、混合、组合) 4B
come into being 形成,产生 5A
come up 产生 8A
commencement /kəˈmensmənt/ n. 〈美〉学位授予典礼(日);毕业典礼(日) 1A
commerce /ˈkɒmɜːs/ n. 商业 4A
committed /kəˈmɪtɪd/ a. 坚定的 10A
commonly /ˈkɒmənli/ ad. 通常地 7A
commonplace /ˈkɒmənpleɪs/ a. 平常的;平凡的 4A
community /kəˈmjuːnəti/ n. 社区;社区居民 7A
commuter /kəˈmjuːtə/ n. (市郊间)乘公交车辆上下班者;经常乘车往返者 10A
concentrate /ˈkɒnsəntreɪt/ vt. 集中;集结 7A
concentration /ˌkɒnsənˈtreɪʃn/ n. 集中;专心 2A
concern /kənˈsɜːn/ n. 关心;忧虑 2B
concerto /kənˈtʃɜːtəʊ/ n. 〈音〉协奏曲 9A
conclude /kənˈkluːd/ vt. 断定;决定;推断出 7B
concrete /ˈkɒnkriːt/ a. 具体的;有形的 6A
confess /kənˈfes/ vt. 承认;坦白,供认 5A
confirm /kənˈfɜːm/ vt. 证实,肯定 6B
connect /kəˈnekt/ vt. 连接;连结 1A
conspicuous /kənˈspɪkjuəs/ a. 明显的,显著的 6A
consume /kənˈsjuːm/ vt. 消费;花费 5B
consumer /kənˈsjuːmə/ n. 消费者;用户 4A
consumption /kənˈsʌmpʃn/ n. 消费 6A
contact /ˈkɒntækt/ n. 接触;联络 7A
contain /kənˈteɪn/ vt. 包含;容纳 3B
content /kənˈtent/ a. 满足的;满意的 7A
contract /ˈkɒntrækt/ n. 合同 8A
contradiction /ˌkɒntrəˈdɪkʃn/ n. 矛盾 6A
contrast /ˈkɒntræst/ n. 对比,对照;悬殊差别 3A
contributing /ˌkɒntrɪˈbjuːtɪŋ/ a. 贡献的;起作用的 7A
conventional /kənˈvenʃənl/ a. 惯例的;常规的 6A
convince /kənˈvɪns/ vt. 使确信,使信服 1B
correspond with 和……通信 9B
cortisol /ˈkɔːtɪsɒl/ n. 〈生化〉皮质(甾)醇 9A
counter /ˈkaʊntə/ a. 相反的;对立的 5A
couple /ˈkʌpl/ n. 一对;数个 7A
cracking /ˈkrækɪŋ/ a. 〈口〉精彩的;棒的 2A
crazy /ˈkreɪzi/ a. 发疯的;发狂的;着迷的 4A

creature /ˈkriːtʃə/ n. 人;动物;生物　7A
credit card　信用卡　6A
critical /ˈkrɪtɪkl/ a. 关键的　9B
crocodile /ˈkrɒkədaɪl/ n. 鳄鱼　5A
cross /krɒs/ vt. 穿过,越过　4B
cruise /kruːz/ vt. 航游于,巡航于　8A
cuddle /ˈkʌdl/ vt. 拥抱　4A
cupcake /ˈkʌpˌkeɪk/ n. 杯形蛋糕　3A
curiosity /ˌkjʊərɪˈɒsəti/ n. 好奇心　1A
currency /ˈkʌrənsi/ n. 货币;流通　4A
current /ˈkʌrənt/ a. 现在的;目前的　1B
currently /ˈkʌrəntli/ ad. 当前;时下　4A
custom-made /ˌkʌstəmˈmeɪd/ a. 定制的　5A
cut /kʌt/ vt. 削减　2A
cut out　〈口〉停止,放弃　2A
cute /kjuːt/ a. 漂亮的;有吸引力的　4A

D

data /ˈdeɪtə/ n. 数据;资料　9A
dawn /dɔːn/ vi. 破晓;开始;被理解　1B
deal /diːl/ n. 〈口〉交易,买卖　1A
decade /ˈdekeɪd/ n. 十年　9B
decorate /ˈdekəreɪt/ vt. 装饰,装潢　5A
deep-seated /ˌdiːpˈsiːtɪd/ a. 根深蒂固的　10A
defend /dɪˈfend/ vt. 为……辩护　3B
degree /dɪˈɡriː/ n. 程度　7A
demand /dɪˈmɑːnd/ n. 需要;需求　7A
democracy /dɪˈmɒkrəsi/ n. 民主　10A
demographic /ˌdeməˈɡræfɪk/ a. 人口的　4A
densely /ˈdensli/ ad. 密集地,稠密地　3A
depart /dɪˈpɑːt/ vi. 离开,出发　6B
deposit /dɪˈpɒzɪt/ n. 存款　1A
　　　　　　　　　vt. 使沉积　10A
depressed /dɪˈprest/ a. 沮丧的;忧愁的　9B
deserve /dɪˈzɜːv/ vt. 应受,值得　3B
design /dɪˈzaɪn/ vt. 设计;构思　1A
desire /dɪˈzaɪə/ n. 愿望,欲望　10A
　　　　　　　　vt. 想望,渴望　3A
desperate /ˈdespərət/ a. 拼命的,不顾一切的　3A

destination /ˌdestɪˈneɪʃn/ *n.* 目的地,终点 3A
destiny /ˈdestɪni/ *n.* 命运 1A
detail /ˈdiːteɪl/ *n.* 细节,详情 5B
determine /dɪˈtɜːmɪn/ *vt.* 决定;确定 9B
digital /ˈdɪdʒɪtl/ *a.* 数字的 8A
dimensional /dɪˈmenʃənl/ *a.* ……维的 4A
dioxide /daɪˈɒksaɪd/ *n.* 二氧化物 2A
diploma /dɪˈpləʊmə/ *n.* 文凭 7A
diplomat /ˈdɪpləmæt/ *n.* 外交官;外交家 2A
discomfort /dɪsˈkʌmfət/ *n.* 不适 9A
display /dɪsˈpleɪ/ *vt.* 展示;陈列 4A
distinctive /dɪˈstɪŋktɪv/ *a.* 区别性的,有特色的 5A
distress /dɪsˈtres/ *n.* 痛苦;危难,不幸 3B
do without 没有……也行 8A
dorm /dɔːm/ *n.* 〈美口〉宿舍(dormitory 的缩略) 1A
dot /dɒt/ *n.* 点;微小的东西 1A
double /ˈdʌbl/ *vi.* 加倍 4A
dozens of 许多 4A
dragon /ˈdrægən/ *n.* 龙 6A
dream of 梦想 10A
dressing room 化妆室;(运动场等的)更衣室;梳妆室 6A
drive away 赶走 9A
driveway /ˈdraɪvweɪ/ *n.* 私人车道 8A
drop out 退出;退学 1A
drop-in /ˈdrɒpɪn/ *n.* 〈美俚〉旁听生 1A
due to 由于,因为 10B
dull /dʌl/ *a.* 枯燥无味的;单调的 2A

E

echo /ˈekəʊ/ *n.* 回声;反响 3A
effective /ɪˈfektɪv/ *a.* 有力的;给人深刻印象的 3B
efficient /ɪˈfɪʃənt/ *a.* 有效的,效率高的 5A
eliminate /ɪˈlɪmɪneɪt/ *vt.* 消灭,消除 10A
embarrass /ɪmˈbærəs/ *vt.* 使困窘,使局促不安
embody /ɪmˈbɒdi/ *vt.* 体现 10A
emerge /ɪˈmɜːdʒ/ *vi.* 出现;浮现 5A
emergency /ɪˈmɜːdʒənsi/ *n.* 紧急情况,突然事件,非常时刻 8B
emission /ɪˈmɪʃn/ *n.* (光、热、气等的)散发;散发之物 2A
emit /ɪˈmɪt/ *vt.* 散发,发出 2A

employee /ˌɪmˈplɔɪiː/ n. 雇员,职员,员工 1B
enable /ɪˈneɪbl/ vt. 使……能够;使……成为可能 7A
engage in 从事,参加 6A
enormous /ɪˈnɔːməs/ a. 巨大的 4B
enterprise /ˈentəpraɪz/ n. 企业,公司 5A
entrepreneur /ˌɒntrəprəˈnɜː/ n. 企业家 4A
environment /ɪnˈvaɪərənmənt/ n. 环境,四周 3A
era /ˈɪərə/ n. 时代,纪元 3A
errand /ˈerənd/ n. 差事 3A
establish /ɪsˈtæblɪʃ/ vt. 设立;建立 7A
estimate /ˈestɪmət, ˈestɪmeɪt/ vt. 估计 4A
ethic /ˈeθɪk/ n. 道德观;道德准则 3A
evaluation /ɪˌvæljuˈeɪʃn/ n. 评估;评价 9A
eventually /ɪˈventʃuəli/ ad. 终于,最后 3B
every so often 〈口〉有时,不时 3A
evil /ˈiːvl/ a. 邪恶的 9A
excessive /ɪkˈsesɪv/ a. 过多的;过分的 6A
exchange /ɪksˈtʃeɪndʒ/ vt. 交换;互换 4A
exclude /ɪksˈkluːd/ vt. 把……排除在外,拒绝 4B
exercise /ˈeksəsaɪz/ vt. 训练;锻炼 9A
expense /ɪkˈspens/ n. 价钱,花费,费 8A
expression /ɪksˈpreʃn/ n. 表达,陈述 5A
expressive /ɪksˈpresɪv/ a. 表现的;表达的 9A
extended family (数代同堂等的)大家庭 3A

F

facility /fəˈsɪləti/ n. 设施,设备;场所 7A
faint /feɪnt/ a. 模糊的;微弱的 8A
fall in love with 爱上 1B
fan /fæn/ n. 迷;(……的)热情崇拜者或拥护者 2A
fantasy /ˈfæntəsi/ n. 幻想,白日梦 10A
fascinating /ˈfæsɪneɪtɪŋ/ a. 迷人的;有极大吸引力的 1A
feature /ˈfiːtʃə/ n. 特征,特点 3A
female /ˈfiːmeɪl/ a. 女性的;妇女的 6A
fetus /ˈfiːtəs/ n. 胎儿 9A
fight back 还击,抵抗 5A
figure out 想出,推断出 1A
find out 找出,发现;查明(真相) 1A
fire /ˈfaɪə/ vt. 开除,辞退 1B

firm /fɜːm/ *a.* 坚定的　9A
fit into　合身，合适　6B
fixed /fɪkst/ *a.* 固定的；确定了的　5B
flexibility /ˌfleksəˈbɪləti/ *n.* 机动性；灵活性　7A
focus /ˈfəʊkəs/ *n.* 焦点；(注意、活动、兴趣等的)中心　1B
fodder /ˈfɒdə/ *n.* 素材　3A
folk /fəʊk/ *n.* 人，人们　3A
folk art　民间艺术　6A
follow /ˈfɒləʊ/ *vt.* 按照……去做；听从；采用；关注；注视　2A；4A
follow somebody's example　仿效某人；学习某人　5B
font /fɒnt/ =fount *n.* 〈印〉(同样大小和式样的)一副铅字　1A
fortune /ˈfɔːtʃuːn/ *n.* 财富，命运　5A
fossil /ˈfɒsl/ *n.* 化石　2A
fragment /ˈfræɡmənt/ *n.* 片断；碎片　3A
frequently /ˈfriːkwəntli/ *ad.* 时常；经常地　7A
fresh /freʃ/ *a.* 新的；新近的　9B
frontier /ˈfrʌntɪə, frʌnˈtɪə/ *n.* 边远地区　10A
fuel /ˈfjuːəl/ *n.* 燃料　2A
fulfill /fʊlˈfɪl/ *vt.* 实现；满足　10A
function /ˈfʌŋkʃn/ *vi.* 运行，起作用　8B
funeral /ˈfjuːnərəl/ *n.* 葬礼　3A

G

gallon /ˈɡælən/ *n.* 加仑　10A
garden /ˈɡɑːdn/ *vi.* 从事园艺　8A
generate /ˈdʒenəreɪt/ *vt.* 发生；产生　2A
genuinely /ˈdʒenjuɪnli/ *ad.* 真诚地　3A
get mad about　〈口〉对……大为恼火　8A
get rid of　摆脱，除去，处理掉　6A
gifter /ˈɡɪftə/ *n.* 〈俚〉送礼人　4A
go on holiday　去度假　2A
go under　倒闭，垮掉　5A
grant /ɡrɑːnt/ *vt.* 同意，准予，授予　10A
graphical /ˈɡræfɪkl/ *a.* 图的；用图表示的　4A
gridlock /ˈɡrɪdlɒk/ *n.* 交通全面大堵塞　10A
guideline /ˈɡaɪdlaɪn/ *n.* 指导方针；准则　2A
guilty /ˈɡɪlti/ *a.* 自觉有罪的，内疚的　2A
gut /ɡʌt/ *n.* [~s]〈口〉勇气，胆量　1A

H

hand in hand 密切关联地；手拉手 4A
hand out 分派 3B
hand over 交出，移交 5B
harbor /ˈhɑːbə/ vt. 包含；怀有 3A
have an effect on 对……产生影响 8B
headline /ˈhedlaɪn/ n. （报刊的）大字标题；[pl.] 新闻提要 3A
healing /ˈhiːlɪŋ/ a. （可）使愈合的；有疗效的 9A
hence /hens/ ad. 因此；由此 5A
hesitate /ˈhezɪteɪt/ vi. 犹豫，踌躇；不情愿 8A
hide-and-seek /ˌhaɪdənˈsiːk/ n. 捉迷藏 3A
hire /ˈhaɪə/ vt. 雇用；租用 1B
honor /ˈɒnə/ vt. 〈美〉=honour 给……以荣誉；使增光 1A
hook /hʊk/ vt. 钩住；连接 8B
hormone /ˈhɔːməʊn/ n. 〈生化〉荷尔蒙 9A
hornet /ˈhɔːnɪt/ n. 大黄蜂 8A
hostess /ˈhəʊstɪs/ n. 女主人 3A
houseware /ˈhaʊsweə/ n. 家用器皿 6A
hypothesis /haɪˈpɒθɪsɪs/ n. 假设 9A

I

icon /ˈaɪkɒn/ n. 画像；图像 4A
identical /aɪˈdentɪkl/ a. 相同的 9B
identify /aɪˈdentɪfaɪ/ vt. 认出，识别 4B
idle /ˈaɪdl/ vi. 懒散 8A
ignorance /ˈɪgnərəns/ n. 无知，愚昧 2A
ignore /ɪgˈnɔː/ vt. 忽视；不理睬 2B
illustrate /ˈɪləstreɪt/ vi. 举例说明 3A
image /ˈɪmɪdʒ/ n. 像；图像；形象 4A
imaginative /ɪˈmædʒɪnətɪv/ a. 想象的；虚构的 9A
imitate /ˈɪmɪteɪt/ vt. 模仿，仿效 5A
imitation /ˌɪmɪˈteɪʃn/ n. 模仿，模拟 5A
immense /ɪˈmens/ a. 巨大的；广大的 7A
immigrant /ˈɪmɪgrənt/ n. 移民 6A
impress /ɪmˈpres/ vi. 给人印象，引人入胜 3B
improper /ɪmˈprɒpə/ a. 不适当的，不合适的 8A
in (full) bloom （盛）开着花 8A
in a word 总之，简言之 6A

in action 在活动中；在运转中 5A
in addition to 除……之外 10B
in advance 预先，事先 10B
in check 受抑制的(地)，有控制的(地) 9A
in demand 有需要；销路好 7A
in itself 本质上；就其本身而言 9A
in response to 作为(对……的)回答 5A
in return 作为(对……的)交换；(作为对……的)报答或回报 4A
in search of 寻找；寻求 8A
interest /ˈɪntrɪst/ n. 利息 8B
in terms of 根据；按照 9A
in the face of 面对，在……面前 3A
in utero /ɪnˈjuːtərəʊ/ ad. & a. 〈拉〉在子宫内(的)；尚未出生(的) 9A
inanimate /ɪnˈænɪmət/ a. 无生命的 4A
in-box /ˈɪnbɒks/ n. 收件箱 8A
income /ˈɪnkʌm/ n. 收入；收益 6A
inconvenient /ˌɪnkənˈviːniənt/ a. 不方便的 8A
indefinitely /ɪnˈdefɪnətli/ ad. 无限期地 7A
India /ˈɪndiə/ n. 印度(亚洲国家) 2A
individual /ˌɪndɪˈvɪdʒuəl/ n. 个人 6A
individualism /ˌɪndɪˈvɪdʒuəlɪzəm/ n. 个人主义(行为)；个性 10A
inevitable /ɪnˈevɪtəbl/ a. 不可避免的，必然(发生)的 8A
infinite /ˈɪnfɪnɪt/ a. 无限的，极大的 10B
initial /ɪˈnɪʃl/ a. 最初的，开始的 8A
inject /ɪnˈdʒekt/ vt. 注入 3B
insight /ˈɪnsaɪt/ n. 洞察力；见识 2B
insignificant /ˌɪnsɪɡˈnɪfɪkənt/ a. 不重要的；无价值的 2A
inspire /ɪnˈspaɪə/ vt. 给……以灵感；鼓舞，激起 5B
install /ɪnˈstɔːl/ vt. 安装，安置 8A
instantly /ˈɪnstəntli/ ad. 立即，即刻 5A
instead of 作为……的替换 4A
instruction /ɪnˈstrʌkʃn/ n. 教育；教学 1A
insulate /ˈɪnsjuleɪt/ vt. 使……隔离或绝缘(尤指对热量、电流或声音) 2A
insurance /ɪnˈʃʊərəns/ n. 保险 7A
integral /ˈɪntɪɡrəl/ a. 构成整体所必需的；组成的 10A
integrate /ˈɪntɪɡreɪt/ vt. 使结合，使成为一体 10B
intellectual /ˌɪntəˈlektʃuəl/ n. 知识分子 6A
intend to 想要，打算，计划 8A
intense /ɪnˈtens/ a. 强烈的，剧烈的 10A

interrupt /ˌɪntəˈrʌpt/ *vt.* 打断,打扰;中止,阻碍　8B
interstate /ˌɪntəˈsteɪt/ *a.* 州与州之间的　10A
interview /ˈɪntəvjuː/ *n.* 采访,访谈;接见　3B
intuition /ˌɪntjuˈɪʃn/ *n.* 直觉　1A
investment /ɪnˈvestmənt/ *n.* 投资;投资的对象　7A
investment-driven /ɪnˈvestməntˈdrɪvn/ *a.* 投资驱动的　5A
involve /ɪnˈvɒlv/ *vt.* 需要;包含;使卷入,连累　5A;9A
isolate /ˈaɪsəleɪt/ *vt.* 使隔离,使孤立　8A
It is one thing … ; it is (quite) another thing …　……是一回事;……是另一回事　10A
item /ˈaɪtəm/ *n.* 条,项;注意或关心的对象　6A

J

jet /dʒet/ (jetted; jetting) *vi.* 搭乘喷气式飞机　3A
journal /ˈdʒɜːnl/ *n.* 期刊,杂志;日报　9A
justify /ˈdʒʌstɪfaɪ/ *vt.* 证明……正当(或有理);为……辩护　8A

K

kale /keɪl/ *n.* 无头甘蓝类,甘蓝类蔬菜　8A
karma /ˈkɑːmə/ *n.* 命运;因果报应　1A
keep off　(使)不接近　10A
knight /naɪt/ *n.* (欧洲中世纪的)骑士,武士　6A
knock-off /ˈnɒkɒf/ *n.* (时装样本等的)翻印本;名牌的仿冒品　5A
know of　知道……情况　6B

L

label /ˈleɪbl/ *n.* 标签,标记　1A
lament /ləˈment/ *vi.* 悲叹　10A
lane /leɪn/ *n.* (乡间)小路(巷)　8A
laptop /ˈlæptɒp/ *n.* 便携式电脑,笔记本电脑　8A
last /lɑːst/ *vi.* 持久;持续　2A
later on　以后,后来　1A
launch /lɔːntʃ/ *vt.* 发射;发动　7A
lawn chair　〈美〉草坪躺椅　3A
lead to　导致,通向　5B
leading /ˈliːdɪŋ/ *a.* 首位的,最主要的　9A
leafy /ˈliːfi/ *a.* 叶子覆盖着的　8A
lease /liːs/ *n.* 租约,租契　8A
legacy /ˈlegəsi/ *n.* 遗产　3A
length /leŋθ/ *n.* 长度　7A

let down 使失望 1A
level /ˈlevl/ vt. 把……拉平;使相等,使平等 10A
level /ˈlevl/ n. 级别;层次 7A
license /ˈlaɪsəns/ vt. 发许可证给 7A
　　　　　　　　　　n. 许可证 7A
licensure /ˈlaɪsenʃə/ n. 许可证的颁发 7A
lift /lɪft/ vt. 撤销(命令) 6A
light up 点燃;照亮 2B
lightweight /ˈlaɪtweɪt/ a. 无足轻重的 4A
lime /laɪm/ n. 酸橙树;酸橙 6A
limited /ˈlɪmɪtɪd/ a. 有限的 8A
lingerie /ˈlænʒəri/ n. 女内衣 4A
lo /ləʊ/ int. 看哪,瞧(表示惊讶或用以唤起注意) 5A
load /ləʊd/ n. 工作量 7A
local /ˈləʊkl/ a. 地方(性)的;当地的 6A
lock /lɒk/ vt. 锁,锁上 5A
logical /ˈlɒdʒɪkl/ a. 逻辑的;符合逻辑的 9A
logo /ˈləʊgəʊ/ n. (公司等的)专用标识;标识图案 5A
longevity /lɒnˈdʒevɪti/ n. 长寿 9A
look back 回顾,回忆 1A
love affair 强烈爱好 10A
lower /ˈləʊə/ vt. 使……降低;减少 9A
luxury /ˈlʌkʃəri/ n. 奢侈,奢侈品;华贵 5A

M

mail delivery 邮递 8A
maintain /meɪnˈteɪn/ vt. 保持,维持 4B
Majesty /ˈmædʒɪsti/ n. 陛下(对帝王、王后等的尊称) 9A
majority /məˈdʒɒrəti/ n. 大多数;大半;大多 2A
make a deal with 与……达成一笔交易 2A
make a difference / make all the difference 状况有(极大)改善;起作用 1A
make an effort 作出努力 5A
make fun of 开玩笑 6B
make one's move 有所动作,采取行动 3A
make one's way 前进,行进 8A
make sense of 理解;弄懂 7B
make the most of 从……处获取尽可能多的好处 2A
mall /mɔːl/ n. 大型购物中心 3A
mango /ˈmæŋgəʊ/ n. 芒果 2A

manufacturer /ˌmænjuˈfæktʃərə/ *n.* 制造商，工厂主 5A
manure /məˈnjuə/ *n.* 粪肥 10A
market /ˈmɑːkɪt/ *vt.* 经营；销售 5A
marvelous /ˈmɑːvələs/ *a.* 惊人的，了不起的 10B
masculine /ˈmæskjəlɪn/ *a.* 男性的；男子气概的 10A
massive /ˈmæsɪv/ *a.* 可观的；巨大的 7A
match /mætʃ/ *vt.* 和……相配；和……相称 6A
material /məˈtɪərɪəl/ *a.* 物质的，实体的 6A
mature /məˈtʃuə/ *vi.* 成熟；长成 10A
MBA abbr. =Master of Business Administration 工商管理学硕士 5A
measure /ˈmeʒə/ *n.* [常 *pl.*] 措施，办法 9B
meditation /ˌmedɪˈteɪʃn/ *n.* 沉思，冥想 9A
melody /ˈmelədi/ *n.* 曲子；曲调 9A
menswear /ˈmenzweə/ *n.* 男装 5A
mention /ˈmenʃn/ *vt.* 提及，说起 6B
metaphor /ˈmetəfə/ *n* 比喻的说法 10A
minimum /ˈmɪnɪməm/ *a.* 最低的，最小的 7B
minor /ˈmaɪnə/ *a.* 较少的；较次要的 6A
mobility /məʊˈbɪləti/ *n.* 流动（性） 10A
moderate /ˈmɒdərɪt/ *a.* 适度的；中等的 2B
modest /ˈmɒdɪst/ *a.* 适中的；适度的 6A
monitor /ˈmɒnɪtə/ *vt.* 监督；监视 9A
monthly /ˈmʌnθli/ *a.* 每月的，每月一次的 8B
mood /muːd/ *n.* 心境；情绪 2A
moreover /mɔːˈəʊvə/ *ad.* 再者，此外 8A
mortgage /ˈmɔːgɪdʒ/ *n.* 抵押贷款，按揭 10A
mud /mʌd/ *n.* 泥；烂泥 2A
muddy /ˈmʌdi/ *a.* 灰暗的，暗淡的 5A
mysterious /mɪˈstɪərɪəs/ *a.* 神秘的 3A
mythology /mɪˈθɒlədʒi/ *n.* 神话 10A

N

naively /naɪˈiːvli/ *ad.* 天真地；幼稚地 1A
neglect /nɪˈglekt/ *vt.* 忽视，忽略 10B
nerve /nɜːv/ *n.* 〈解〉神经 9A
nonetheless /ˌnʌnðəˈles/ *ad.* 尽管如此；然而 4A
note /nəʊt/ *vt.* 特别提到，指出 3A
nothing but 只有，只不过 10A
novel /ˈnɒvl/ *a.* 新奇的；新颖的 4A

novel /ˈnɒvl/ n. 小说　2A
now that　既然，由于　8A

O

obtain /əbˈteɪn/ vt. 获得；达到　7A
occasion /əˈkeɪʒn/ n. 时候，场合　2A
occasional /əˈkeɪʒənl/ a. 偶尔的，间或发生的　8A
occasionally /əˈkeɪʒnəli/ ad. 偶然地　2A
occur to　被想到　3A
odd /ɒd/ a. 奇特的　7B
of course　当然　1A
offer /ˈɒfə/ vt. 提供，给予　1A
on the track　在正道上；未离目标；正确　2A
online /ˈɒnlaɪn/ a. 联机的，在线的　8A
opportunity /ˌɒpəˈtjuːnəti/ n. 机会　3A
option /ˈɒpʃn/ n. 自由选择　10A
or so　……左右；……上下　1A
orchestral /ɔːˈkestrəl/ a. 管弦乐队的　9A
order /ˈɔːdə/ vt. 订购，订货　7B
organic /ɔːˈɡænɪk/ a. 有机(体)的，有机物的　8A
otherwise /ˈʌðəwaɪz/ ad. 否则，不然　5B
out of date　过时的　3A
out of the ordinary　不寻常的　8A
outlet /ˈaʊtlet/ n. 经销店　6A
overall /ˈəʊvərɔːl/ a. 包括一切的；全部的　2A
overflow /ˌəʊvəˈfləʊ/ vt. 多得使……无法容纳；从……中溢出　6A
overweight /ˈəʊvəweɪt/ a. 超重的　2B
oxygen /ˈɒksɪdʒən/ n. 氧；氧气　2A

P

pace /peɪs/ vi. 踱步　10A
pad /pæd/ n. 衬垫　7A
pajamas /pəˈdʒɑːməz/ [pl.] n. =pyjamas 睡衣裤　4A
palatial /pəˈleɪʃl/ a. 富丽堂皇的　3A
pants /pænts/ n. [pl.] 长裤　8A
paradise /ˈpærədaɪs/ n. 天堂，乐园　8A
parking lot　〈美〉停车场　8A
parrot /ˈpærət/ n. 鹦鹉　3A
participate in　参与，参加　3A

partner /ˈpɑːtnə/ *n.* 合伙人;伙伴　4A
pass down　传递,传下来　6A
pass on　传递　9A
passenger /ˈpæsɪndʒə/ *n.* 乘客,旅客　8A
pathfinder /ˈpɑːθfaɪndə/ *n.* 探路者,探索者　10A
peculiar /pɪˈkjuːliə/ *a.* 奇怪的;特有的,独具的,独特的　8A
perform /pəˈfɔːm/ *vt.* 做;执行,履行　7B
permanent /ˈpɜːmənənt/ *a.* 永久(性)的,固定的　8B
persuade /pəˈsweɪd/ *vt.* 劝;说服　7B
phenomenon /fɪˈnɒmɪnən/ *n.* [*pl.*] phenomena　现象　10A
physical /ˈfɪzɪkl/ *a.* 身体的;有形的;实物的　2B　4A
pick up　(偶然地、无意地)获得(知识、消息等)　3A
piety /ˈpaɪəti/ *n.* 虔诚的行为　3A
pitch /pɪtʃ/ *n.* 音高　9A
pixel /ˈpɪksl/ *n.* 〈电子〉像素　4A
place much/little value on　认为……很重要/不重要　4A
plaid /plæd/ *n.* 方格花纹　5A
play a role　扮演角色;起作用　9B
plus /plʌs/ *n.* 有利的事情;好处　7A
point out　指出　3B
policy /ˈpɒləsi/ *n.* 政策;方针　7A
Polish /ˈpəʊlɪʃ/ *n.* 波兰语　3A
politician /ˌpɒlɪˈtɪʃn/ *n.* 积极从事政治活动的人;政客　2A
pool /puːl/ *n.* 集中使用的物资、服务等　7A
pop /pɒp/ (popped; popping) *vi.* 冷不防地出现(或发生)　1A
porch /pɔːtʃ/ *n.* 门廊;入口处　3A
pose a threat to　对……构成威胁　2B
positive /ˈpɒzətɪv/ *a.* 积极的;正面的,肯定的　2B
post /pəʊst/ *vt.* 邮寄;贴出　8B
poster /ˈpəʊstə/ *n.* 招贴(画);海报;布告　1A
potential /pəˈtenʃl/ *a.* 潜在的;可能的　6A
poverty /ˈpɒvəti/ *n.* 贫困,贫穷　9B
practice /ˈpræktɪs/ *vi.* (医生、律师等)开业,从事职业　7A
practitioner /prækˈtɪʃənə/ *n.* 从事者,实践者;开业医生　9A
predict /prɪˈdɪkt/ *vt.* 预言,预测,预告　8B
prefer /prɪˈfɜː/ *vt.* 更喜欢,宁愿　8A
preppy /ˈprepi/ *n.* 预备学校学生;(尤指在衣着、举止等方面)像预备学校学生的人
　　　　a. 预备学校学生的;(衣着式样)刻板规矩的　5A
presence /ˈprezəns/ *n.* 存在;在场　4A

prevail /prɪˈveɪl/ *vi.* 获胜;占优势(over, against) 3B
previous /ˈpriːviəs/ *a.* 以前的 1B
priceless /ˈpraɪslɪs/ *a.* 无价的;无法估价的 1A
prize /praɪz/ *vt.* 珍视,重视 10A
productive /prəˈdʌktɪv/ *a.* 富有成效的 9B
profile /ˈprəʊfaɪl/ *n.* 人物或事物之简介,概况 4A
program /ˈprəʊɡræm/ *n.* 课程;教学大纲 7A
prolific /prəˈlɪfɪk/ *a.* 丰富的;大量的 4A
promising /ˈprɒmɪsɪŋ/ *a.* 有希望的,有前途的 8A
promote /prəˈməʊt/ *vt.* 宣传;推销(商品等) 5A
proportionally /prəˈpɔːʃənəli/ *ad.* 成比例地 1A
prospective /prəsˈpektɪv/ *a.* 将来的;预期的 7A
provider /prəˈvaɪdə/ *n.* 供给者 7A
pry /praɪ/ *vt.* 撬开;使劲分开 10A
psyche /ˈsaɪki/ *n.* 灵魂 10A
psychological /ˌsaɪkəˈlɒdʒɪkl/ *a.* 心理的;心理学的 9A
pull into 把(车、船等)驶入 8A
punctuality /ˌpʌŋktʃuˈæləti/ *n.* 守时,准时 10B
put on 放录音 9A
put up 提出 (问题、建议等) 1A

Q

qualify as 具备合格条件;把……归做 6A
quest /kwest/ *n.* (长时间的)寻找;追求 6A
quit /kwɪt/ (quit 或 quitted; quitting) *vi.* 离开;放弃 1A
quota /ˈkwəʊtə/ *n.* 定额;限额;配额 2A

R

race track (赛马、赛车等的)跑道 2A
rack /ræk/ *n.* 货架 6A
radiation /ˌreɪdiˈeɪʃn/ *n.* 放射物;辐射 8B
raft /rɑːft/ *n.* 木筏 10A
range /reɪndʒ/ *n.* 范围;行列 7A
    vi. (在一定范围内)变动,变化 3A
range between ... and (在一定幅度或范围内)变动 9A
range from ... to (在一定范围内)变动,变化 3A
rarely /ˈreəli/ *ad.* 很少;难得 7A
rather than 不是……(而是);与其……(不如) 7B
reach /riːtʃ/ *vt.* 传到;达到;提升到 8A

recall /rɪˈkɔːl/ vt.　回想起；回忆起　2B
recognizable /ˈrekəgnaɪzəbl/ a.　可认出的，可辨认的　5A
recognize /ˈrekəgnaɪz/ vt.　（正式）承认；认识到　7A
recreation /ˌrekrɪˈeɪʃn/ n.　娱乐，消遣　10A
reflect /rɪˈflekt/ vt.　反映　2B
refresh /rɪˈfreʃ/ vt.　使更新；使振作精神，使恢复活力　5B
register /ˈredʒɪstə/ vt.　登记，注册　10A
registered /ˈredʒɪstəd/ a.　注册的；登记过的　7A
reject /rɪˈdʒekt/ vt.　拒绝；驳回；抵制　1B
relatively /ˈrelətɪvli/ ad.　相对地；比较而言　6A
relax /rɪˈlæks/ vi.　放松；休息　2A
relaxation /ˌriːlækˈseɪʃn/ n.　松弛，放松；缓和　9A
release /rɪˈliːs/ vt.　释放；放开　1B
relent /rɪˈlent/ vi.　变温和；变宽容　1A
relevant /ˈreləvənt/ a.　有关的，有重大关系的　5B
relieve /rɪˈliːv/ vt.　使减轻，使解除（痛苦、忧愁等）　2A
remark upon　评说，谈论　3A
remarkable /rɪˈmɑːkəbl/ a.　不同寻常的，值得注意的　1B
remind /rɪˈmaɪnd/ vt.　提醒；使想起　3B
remnant /ˈremnənt/ n.　残余物　3A
remove /rɪˈmuːv/ vt.　清除；消除　9B
rent /rent/ vt.　租借，租用　8A
replace /rɪˈpleɪs/ vt.　替换，取代　1B
replace with　用……替代；用……取代　2B
represent /ˌreprɪˈzent/ vt.　代表　10A
rescue /ˈreskjuː/ n.　援救；解救　2A
resemble /rɪˈzembl/ vt.　像，类似　5A
reserve /rɪˈzɜːv/ vt.　预定　10B
resist /rɪˈzɪst/ vt.　抵制，抗拒　6B
resolve /rɪˈzɒlv/ vt.　解决　2B
resonate /ˈrezəneɪt/ vi.　共鸣；回响　4A
resource /rɪˈsɔːs/ n.　[常作~s]资源　7A
respond /rɪˈspɒnd/ vt.　回答，答复　3A
retain /rɪˈteɪn/ vt.　保持，保留　10A
retaliate /rɪˈtælieɪt/ vi.　回报　4A
return /rɪˈtɜːn/ n.　收益　7A
revenue /ˈrevənjuː/ n.　收入　4A
review /rɪˈvjuː/ vt.　复审；再检查　7A
revision /rɪˈvɪʒn/ n.　修订；修改　6A

rhythm /ˈrɪðəm/ n. 节奏;旋律 9A
ridiculous /rɪˈdɪkjələs/ a. 可笑的,荒谬的 5B
risk /rɪsk/ n. 风险,危险 9A
rock-band /ˈrɒkbænd/ n. 摇滚乐队 2A
romantic /rəʊˈmæntɪk/ a. 浪漫的 1A
routine /ruːˈtiːn/ a. 常规的 9A
　　　　　n. 例行公事;日常工作 3A
run /rʌn/ vt. 经营,管理 1B
rural /ˈrʊərəl/ a. 农村的,乡村的;田园的 3A
rush hour 高峰时间;(上下班时的)交通拥挤时间 10A

S

sans serif /sænˈserɪf/ n. =sanserif 〈印〉无衬线字体 1A
save /seɪv/ vi. 储蓄;积攒;节省 2A
save up 储存;储蓄 2A
savings account 储蓄存款户头 8B
scan /skæn/ vt. 浏览;扫描 7B
scarf /skɑːf/ n. 围巾,披巾 5A
scary /ˈskeəri/ a. 惊恐的 1A
scavenger /ˈskævɪndʒə/ n. 拾荒者 4A
schedule /ˈʃedʒuːl/ n. 日程安排(表);议事日程 3A
　　　　　vt. 排定;安排 7B
scope /skəʊp/ n. 范围 7A
score /skɔː/ n. 〈音〉总谱 9A
scurry /ˈskʌri/ vi. 急赶 3A
sector /ˈsektə/ n. 部门 7A
security /sɪˈkjʊərəti/ n. 安全;保证 7A
seductive /sɪˈdʌktɪv/ a. 诱惑的 10A
separate /ˈsepəreɪt/ vt. 分开;隔开 9B
serif /ˈserɪf/ n. 〈印〉衬线(例如字母 H 的上下四根短而细的横线) 1A
set /set/ vt. 制定(规则等);决定 7A
settle /ˈsetl/ vi. 安顿下来 6A
shame /ʃeɪm/ n. 羞耻,羞愧 7B
shocking /ˈʃɒkɪŋ/ a. 令人震惊的 3A
shortage /ˈʃɔːtɪdʒ/ n. 缺乏;不足 7A
show off 炫耀,卖弄 5A
sign /saɪn/ n. 标记,符号 5A
　　　　　vt. 签(名) 1A
sign up for 登记注册,登记报名 8B

signal /ˈsɪgnəl/ *n.* 信号；标志　8A
significant /sɪgˈnɪfɪkənt/ *a.* 相当数量的；重要的　3A
similarly /ˈsɪmɪləli/ *ad.* 相似地，类似地　6A
sisterhood /ˈsɪstəˌhʊd/ *n.* 姐妹关系；姐妹情谊　6A
so much so that 到这样的程度以至　4A
soar /sɔː/ *vi.* （物价、失业人数等）猛增，剧增　10A
sociologist /ˌsəʊsɪˈɒlədʒɪst/ *n.* 社会学家　6A
soothing /ˈsuːðɪŋ/ *a.* 安慰的；抚慰的　9A
somewhat /ˈsʌmhwɒt/ *ad.* 稍微，有点　8B
Spain /speɪn/ *n.* 西班牙（欧洲国家）　2A
specific /spɪˈsɪfɪk/ *a.* 具体的；明确的　3A
spirit /ˈspɪrɪt/ *n.* 神灵，幽灵，鬼怪　9A
splash out 随意花钱　2A
spread out （人群等）散开；伸展，延伸　6B
stable /ˈsteɪbl/ *a.* 稳定的　9A
staff /stɑːf/ *n.* 全体员工　7A
state /steɪt/ *vt.* 陈述　6A
stealthily /ˈstelθɪli/ *ad.* 隐秘地，暗中地　8A
steeplechase /ˈstiːpltʃeɪs/ *n.* 障碍赛跑（的场地）　3A
stimulate /ˈstɪmjuleɪt/ *vt.* 刺激；激励　9A
sting /stɪŋ/ (stung) *vt.* 刺，蜇，叮　8A
stock /stɒk/ *n.* 备料，库存　7B
stoop /stuːp/ *n.* 俯身，弯腰　3A
stress /stres/ *n.* 压力，重压　2A
　　　　vt. 加压力于　2B
stuff /stʌf/ *n.* 东西；物质　9A
stumble /ˈstʌmbl/ *vt.* 使绊倒；走入歧途　1A
substitute /ˈsʌbstɪtjuːt/ *n.* 代替者；代用品　4A
subtle /ˈsʌtl/ *a.* 细微的　1A
suite /swiːt/ *n.* 〈音〉组曲　9A
suppress /səˈpres/ *vt.* 压制；抑制　9A
surface /ˈsɜːfɪs/ *n.* 表面；面　8A
surgery /ˈsɜːdʒəri/ *n.* 外科手术　7B
suspect /səˈspekt/ *vt.* 推测；怀疑　6B
suspicious /səˈspɪʃəs/ *a.* 猜疑的；可疑的；(of)表示怀疑的　8A
sympathetic /ˌsɪmpəˈθetɪk/ *a.* 〈解〉交感神经的　9A
symptom /ˈsɪmptəm/ *n.* 症状，征候　2B
syndrome /ˈsɪndrəʊm/ *n.* 〈医〉综合征；症候群　9A

T

tag /tæg/ *n.* 标签　5A
take advantage of 对……加以利用　3A
take off 开始；开始流行　5A
take office 就职　8A
take part in 参加　4A
take place 发生　9A
talented /ˈtæləntɪd/ *a.* 有天才的，有才干的　1B
tangible /ˈtændʒəbl/ *a.* 可触知的；有形的　4A
tap /tæp/ *vt.* 开发；着手利用　9A
target /ˈtɑːɡɪt/ *n.* 目标　2A
taste /teɪst/ *n.* 爱好，兴趣　6A
temple /ˈtempl/ *n.* 神庙　1A
tend to 趋向；往往会　9A
term /tɜːm/ *n.* 词语；名称　6A
territory /ˈterɪtəri/ *n.* 领土，版图　10B
textile mill 纺织厂　8A
Thailand /ˈtaɪlænd/ *n.* 泰国（亚洲国家）　2A
the minute (that) 一……就　1A
theme /θiːm/ *n.* 主题　4A
thereby /ˌðeəˈbaɪ/ *ad.* 因此；从而　9A
think of 想起　7A
threaten /ˈθretn/ *vt.* 恐吓，威胁　2A
thrilled /θrɪld/ *a.* 兴奋的　3A
to somebody's surprise 令某人惊讶的是　6B
to some degree 有点，稍微　6A
toad /təʊd/ *n.* 蟾蜍，癞蛤蟆　3A
token /ˈtəʊkən/ *n.* 纪念品；表示　4A
tool /tuːl/ *n.* 工具　9A
touch on 谈到，论及　6A
track /træk/ *vt.* 跟踪；追踪　7A
train /treɪn/ *vt.* 训练；培养　7A
tranquility /trænˈkwɪləti/ *n.* 宁静　9A
transaction /trænˈzækʃn/ *n.* （一笔）交易；业务　4A
transfer /trænsˈfɜː/ (transferred; transferring) *vt.* 转移；迁移　10A
transform /trænsˈfɔːm/ *vt.* 改变，转变　10A
transport /trænsˈpɔːt/ *vt.* 运送，运输　2A
treasure /ˈtreʒə/ *n.* 财富，珍宝　6A

treat /tri:t/ vt. 治疗 7A
trend /trend/ n. 倾向,趋势 5A
trigger /ˈtrɪɡə/ vt. 触发,引起 9A
trinket /ˈtrɪŋkɪt/ n. 廉价的小装饰物、首饰等 4A
tuition /tjuːˈɪʃn/ n. 学费 1A
turn out 结果是,(最后)证明是 1A
turn to 求助于 9A
typeface /ˈtaɪpfeɪs/ n. 字体 1A
typography /taɪˈpɒɡrəfi/ n. （书籍等的）排印；印刷版面式样 1A

U

ultimate /ˈʌltɪmɪt/ a. 终极的,最后的；根本的 9A
unbelievable /ˌʌnbɪˈliːvəbl/ a. 难以置信的 9A
unconscious /ʌnˈkɒnʃəs/ a. 无意识的 9A
undergo /ˌʌndəˈɡəʊ/ (underwent, undergone) vt. 经历,经受 5A
unique /juːˈniːk/ a. 唯一的；独特的 5A
unwed /ˌʌnˈwed/ a. 没有结婚的,未婚的 1A
update /ʌpˈdeɪt/ vt. 更新,使现代化 5B
urge /ɜːdʒ/ vt. 力劝；鼓励 6B
urine /ˈjʊərɪn/ n. 尿 10A

V

valuable /ˈvæljuəbl/ a. 有价值的,宝贵的 7A
value /ˈvæljuː/ n. 价值 1A
vary /ˈveəri/ vt. 使……变化；使……有不同 1A
vehicle /ˈviːɪkl/ n. 车辆；(用来表达思想、情感的)工具,手段 10A
vendor /ˈvendə/ n. 小贩,摊贩 5A
via /ˈvaɪə/ prep. 经由,经过,通过 8B
view /vjuː/ n. 景色,风景 8A
virtual /ˈvɜːtʃuəl/ a. 虚拟的 4A
vocational /vəʊˈkeɪʃənl/ a. 职业的 7A

W

waiting list 等候者名单 1A
walk /wɔːk/ n. 走道 8A
waterfront /ˈwɔːtəfrʌnt/ n. 滨水区 3A
wealth /welθ/ n. 财富 3A
wear and tear 磨损 6A
weight gain 体重增加 6A

what is more 而且　9A

when it comes to 涉及，至于　4A

wholesale /ˈhəʊlˌseɪl/ *a.* 批发的　6A

widget /ˈwɪdʒɪt/ *n.* 小装置；小玩意儿　4A

Wi-Fi /ˈwaɪfaɪ/ *abbr.* =Wireless Local Area Network 无线局域网　8A

willing /ˈwɪlɪŋ/ *a.* 情愿的，乐意的　5A

willingness /ˈwɪlɪŋnɪs/ *n.* 情愿，乐意，自愿　6A

wisdom /ˈwɪzdəm/ *n.* 智慧，才智　3A

with the exception of 除……之外　6A

withdrawal /wɪðˈdrɔːəl/ *n.* 退缩；逃避现实　8A

womb /wuːm/ *n.* 子宫　9A

wooded /ˈwʊdɪd/ *a.* 长满树木的　8A

work /wɜːk/ *vi.* 奏效　5B

work out 产生结果；成功　1A

worthwhile /ˌwɜːθˈhwaɪl/ *a.* 值得（做）的　10B

Y

yoga /ˈjəʊɡə/ *n.* 瑜伽　9A